EMPLOYEE BENEFITS

David A. De Cenzo

Towson State University

Stephen J. Holoviak

Shippensburg University

Prentice Hall, Englewood Cliffs, New Jersey 07632

DeCenzo, David A.
    Employee benefits / by David A. De Cenzo, Stephen J. Holoviak.
        p.   cm.
    Includes bibliographical references.
    ISBN 0-13-273699-3
    1. Compensation management--United States. 2. Employee fringe
benefits--United States. I. Holoviak, Stephen J. II. Title
HF5549.5.C67D43 1989
658.3'25--dc20   89-16232
                                                      CIP

Editorial/production supervision and
  interior design: **Carolyn Kart**
Cover design: **Ray Lundgren**
Manufacturing buyer: **Ed O'Dougherty**

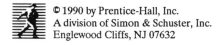 © 1990 by Prentice-Hall, Inc.
A division of Simon & Schuster, Inc.
Englewood Cliffs, NJ 07632

Printed in the United States of America

10 9 8 7 6 5 4 3 2 1

ISBN 0-13-273699-3

Prentice-Hall International (UK) Limited, *London*
Prentice-Hall of Australia Pty. Limited, *Sydney*
Prentice-Hall Canada Inc., *Toronto*
Prentice-Hall Hispanoamericana, S.A., *Mexico*
Prentice-Hall of India Private Limited, *New Delhi*
Prentice-Hall of Japan, Inc., *Tokyo*
Prentice-Hall of Southeast Asia Pte.Ltd., *Singapore*
Editora Prentice-Hall do Brasil, Ltda., *Rio de Janeiro*

To our families
who gave up many benefits so we could write about
those others receive

CONTENTS

PREFACE

COVERAGE

The field of human resource management has become more widely accepted as an integral part of operating a business enterprise. As more emphasis has been placed on the human asset of the organization, there has become a need to further explore this growing concern. While many textbooks exist on the topic of personnel/human resource management, most provide only a cursory overview of the benefits offered to employees.

As time has witnessed a significant change in attitudes toward employees, so too has this change been reflected in appropriate employee benefit levels. Years ago benefit administration was not that complicated a process — certain benefits were mandated by law, other benefits were based on top management philosophy. Changing environments, changing demo-graphics, and changing organizational philosophies have all had the affect of causing organizations to rethink and reshape their benefit packages. The purpose of this text is to explore benefit administration in light of these changing times. This transformation reflects offering benefits that meet the needs of the workers. We have balanced the realities of market pressure to offer benefits, the managerial desire to utilize benefits as a motivator, and the right of an employee to be treated with dignity. The carrot and stick is not the approach of this book. Rather, it is designed to focus on meeting worker requirements.

Employee Benefits was written to fill a void in the personnel/human resource management market. As such, this text is being written as a supplemental text, one that can be used to augment current topic coverage of benefits within a personnel/human resource management class, to stand alone as a text in a one–semester "Special Topics" course for human resource management majors, or as introductory reading for someone beginning a career in benefit administration. Accordingly, this text was written for individuals who have had some human resource management exposure, either in practice or in the classroom. For those who desire to use the text as a supplement to a current human resource management text, by the time benefits are covered, the students should have the necessary understanding of personnel/human resource management to comprehend the material.

This book contains twelve chapters. These chapters were selected based on experience in teaching the subject, and our research, which included interviews with the International Foundation of Employee Benefit Plans on topic coverage. The layout of the text is one that follows a relatively accepted process of benefits administration. That is, we start with an overview, narrow our focus into more specific areas of benefits administration, then go back to a wide perspective to finish the text. Each chapter begins with "Learning Objectives," identifying specifically what the reader should learn after reading the chapter. The chapter is presented using ample first, second, and tertiary headings. The chapter material concludes with a summary section, indicating the learning experience that should have taken place. There is also a "Key Terms" section at the end of each chapter, highlighting key concepts contained in the reading material. Questions for review and discussion follow the text material to reinforce learning and to facilitate thought-provoking discussions. We have also included an "Additional Readings" section for individuals who wish to pursue a specific topic in more detail. Finally, in an effort to produce a text that is highly readable, we have used many examples to clarify concepts. Pedagogical experience indicates that readers will remember and understand concepts best when they are illustrated through examples. We have therefore attempted to provide a richness of examples to facilitate understanding.

ACKNOWLEDGMENTS

We would like to deviate from talking about the text and acknowledge some of the people who have made major contributions to its development. Authors rely heavily on the comments and suggestions of their reviewers. Ours provided us information that was an asset to the text. We want to express our sincere appreciation to Robert G. Ballassari, CPA, Brown; Oakes, Wannall & Nobrega, P.C.; Jerry T. Edge, San Diego University; Robert Figler, The University of Akron; Marilyn Duff, Maryland Blue Cross/Blue Shield; Stanley J. Phillips, Tennessee Technological University; and Anthony F. Campagna, The Ohio State University. Any errors or omissions, however, remain our responsibility.

We would also like to thank the individuals at Prentice-Hall for their extensive assistance in bringing this text to fruition. While there have been many at P-H who have assisted us, a few deserve special recognition. We want to thank Alison Reeves, our acquisition editor, for signing this project, Carolyn

Kart, our Production Editor, Jenny Kletzin, our Supplements Editor, and Brenda Melissaratos, our Copy Editor.

A project of this nature often reflects the indirect work of other special individuals. Specifically we would like to acknowledge the assistance of Penny Cosby, Washington D.C./Baltimore Area Regional Director of the International Foundation of Employee Benefits Plans for her ideas, support, and encouragement in the creation of the text. Also Dee Birschel who was instrumental in providing us with an extensive annotated bibliography on benefits. We would like to thank Dr. Sam Barone, Dean, and Dr. Tom Basuray, Chair, Department of Management, Towson State University, and Dr. Joseph W. Hunt, Dean, and Dr. Charles Hollon, Chair, Department of Management and Marketing, Shippensburg University, for support and teaching schedules to facilitate a rather hectic year of research and writing. And finally, but certainly not least, we want to thank Mary Doughney, Towson State University, for her manuscript preparation. Mary's work has not gone unnoticed, although during the deadline hours we often appeared to act that way.

Finally, there are some personal acknowledgments we want to make. Our families have been extremely supportive of this project. Their support and encouragement created an environment that made the writing months appear as hours. To them, who add much more than thirty-nine percent to our lives, we dedicate this book.

David A. De Cenzo
Towson, Maryland

Stephen J. Holoviak
Chambersburg, Pennsylvania

CHAPTER ONE

EMPLOYEE BENEFITS: AN OVERVIEW

LEARNING OBJECTIVES

After reading this chapter you will be able to:

* *Discuss why employers offer benefits to their employees.*
* *Discuss benefits and their impact on motivation.*
* *Discuss the costs of benefits.*
* *Discuss the impact of demographic trends on benefits offered.*
* *Discuss Social Security as an employee benefit.*
* *Discuss unemployment compensation benefits.*
* *Discuss workers' compensation benefits.*
* *Identify the major voluntary benefits offered by organizations.*
* *Identify the costs of the major voluntary benefits offered by organizations.*
* *Discuss the importance of costing benefits.*

INTRODUCTION

When an organization is designing its overall compensation program, one of the critical areas of concern is the benefits package. Today's workers expect more than just an hourly wage or a salary from their employer. They want additional payments in kind that will improve and enrich their lives. These in-kind payments in an employment setting are called employee benefits, and they are the subject of our book.

Employee benefits have grown in importance and variety over the past few decades. Once perceived as something nice to do for your employees, they have been transformed into a well thought out, well-planned package. Employers today realize that the benefits provided have an impact on whether applicants accept their employment offers or, once employed, whether workers will continue their association with the organization. Benefits, therefore, are necessary components of an effectively functioning compensation program. The irony that this creates, however, is that benefits must be offered to attract and retain good workers, yet as a whole, benefits do not affect a worker's performance. This book is designed to reinforce that benefits are a means neither to exploit employees nor to artificially tie them to an organization. Rather, benefits are a tool at the disposal of trained experts to balance the working environment of the employee. The information received in the course of this book will prepare you to use benefits in a professional manner and retain the balance of worker dignity. The carrot and stick use of benefits is not appropriate for a well-educated work force.

Benefits are offered to employees regardless of their performance levels. They are what is called membership based—that is, they are provided to all employees to some degree without regard to productivity. While this does not appear to be a logical business practice, there is evidence that the absence of adequate benefits and services for employees can contribute to employee dissatisfaction, and increased absenteeism and turnover.[1] Accordingly, because of the negative impact that can arise from failing to provide adequate benefits, billions of dollars are spent each year to ensure that something of value is available for each worker.

Over the decades, this something of value has changed drastically. The benefits offered in the early 1900s were clearly different from those of the 1980s. In the early 1900s, much emphasis was placed on time off from work. As the first personnel departments arrived on the scene, their main emphasis was to ensure that workers were "happy and healthy" by administering, such benefits as scheduled vacations, planning company picnics and other social activities, and sometime later, processing a 3 x 7 sign-up form for some type of health insurance. Those days of simplicity are long gone. Today's benefit offerings are more widespread, more creative, and clearly more abundant. As indicated in Table 1–1, the benefits offered in the 1980s are clearly designed to "ensure something of value for each worker."

---

[1] Frederick Herzberg, *Work and the Nature of Man* (New York: World, 1966).

TABLE 1–1   MAJOR EMPLOYEE BENEFITS OFFERED (Percentage of Employees Participating in) 1986

Paid:		*Retirement & Savings Plans:*	
Vacations	100	Defined Benefits Pension	76
Holidays	99	Non-Contributory	71
Jury Duty Leave	93	Defined Contribution	60
Funeral Leave	88	Employee Stock Ownership	30
Rest Time	72	Profit Sharing	22
Military Leave	66		
Sick Leave	70	*Additional Benefits:*	
Personal Leave	25		
Lunch Time	10	Parking	86
		Educational Assistance	76
Insurance Plans:		Employee Discounts	57
		In-House Infirmary	46
Health	95	Severance Pay	45
Non-Contributory	54	Recreational Facilities	33
Dental	67	Non-Productive Cash Bonus	20
Vision	38		
Life	96		
Non-Contributory	87		
Long-Term Disability	48	*Mean Number of Paid Holidays:*	10.0
Non-Contributory	38		

Source: U.S. Bureau of the Census, *Statistical Abstract of the United States: 1989* (Washington, D.C.: GPO, 1989) p. 410.

Who's Footing the Bill?

Most of us are aware of inflation and the impact that it has had on the wages and salaries of every American. It seems incredible that only fifty years ago, a worker earning $100 a week was ranked among the top 10 percent of the wage earners in the United States. Although hourly wages and monthly salaries have consistently increased in recent years, we often overlook the more rapid growth in benefits offered employees. Since the cost of employing any worker includes both direct wage or salary and those benefits and services the organization provides the employee, the growth in both benefits and services has resulted in dramatic increases in labor costs to organizations. What do those dramatic cost increases mean for employers? In the 1980s the costs of employee benefits were just over 9 percent of corporate revenues generated.[2] In fact, from 1979 to 1987 the cost of providing "something of value to each

---

[2] *Employee Benefits Journal* 12, no. 2 (June 1987): p. 38.

employee" increased from $5,560 per year to $10,708 per year.[3] That's an increase of almost 93 percent in eight short years (see Table 1-2).

TABLE 1-2   EMPLOYEE BENEFITS AS AVERAGE PERCENT OF PAYROLL
                 AND AVERAGE PAYMENT PER YEAR PER EMPLOYEE
                 1979–1986

YEAR	AVERAGE PAYMENT AS A PERCENTAGE OF PAYROLL	AVERAGE PAYMENT PER YEAR PER EMPLOYEE
1979	36.6	$5,560
1980	37.1	6,084
1981	37.3	6,627
1982	36.7	7,187
1983	36.6	7,582
1984	36.6	7,842
1985	37.2	8,166
1986	39.3	10,283
1987	39.0	10,708

Sources: U.S. Chamber of Commerce, *Employee Benefits*, (Washington, D.C., 1985), p. 5; Commerce Clearing House, Human Resource Management: Ideas and Trends, no. 162, February 8, 1988, p. 17, and no. 188 February 8, 1989, p. 18.

In 1929 benefits offered to employees averaged 3 percent of total wages and salaries. By 1950 the rate was up to 16 percent. Currently benefits range from a low of 18 percent to over 60 percent[4] of total wages and salaries paid, with the current average approximately 39 percent of direct compensation.[5]

Organizations are paying 39 cents for every dollar in direct wage, so there must be a good reason. Generally, as mentioned above, offering good benefits serves as a tool to attract and retain good employees. While simply offering benefits is no guarantee that employees will stay with the organization, the lack of benefits will surely cause some people to leave. Offering many benefits is often based on a total compensation philosophy. If an organization expects to get the "best," then it must pay for the "best." In return, organization

---

[3] Ibid.; Commerce Clearing House, *Human Resource Management*: Ideas and Trends, no. 162, February 8, 1988, p. 17.

[4] Note: Variations in the percentage of benefits can be explained in terms of the ratio of the cost of benefits per employee to total wage or salary. Using the figure noted above ($10,283), a $25,000 a year employee has a benefit package totaling 41 percent of direct compensation, while a $100,000 a year employee has a benefit package totaling 10 percent of direct compensation. Additional benefits or perks for higher-level managers may not be included in these calculations. Also see Anita Bruzzese, "Benefits Cost 39.3% of Payroll," a report of the U.S. Chamber of Commerce, *Employee Benefits News* 3, no. 3, (March 1988):1.

[5] *Employee Benefits Journal*, p. 38, and Commerce Clearing House, *Human Resource Management*, p. 17.

performance should improve. Competition for employees can also cause an organization to rethink its benefits package: If a worker has a choice of joining an organization with good benefits or one without, the decision is easy to make. Organizations survey other companies to determine not only their wage structure but also their benefits packages. Deciding what to offer will often depend more on the "going" job market benefits offered than on any other factor.

Employers have also found that benefits present attractive areas of negotiation when large wage and salary increases are not feasible. Both the employers and the employees realize, too, that benefits are not altruistically motivated. For example, if employees were to purchase life insurance on their own, they would have to pay for it with net dollars, that is, with what they have left after paying taxes. If the organization pays for it, the benefit is nontaxable (up to $50,000)[6] for each employee, who therefore considers it more attractive.

The Movement Today

So far we have shown that there has been a dramatic increase in the number and types of benefits offered, and a tremendous increase in their costs. The fact that companies need to offer benefits to their employees does not justify these drastic changes. What is it then that has triggered the sweeping changes in benefit offerings from the early 1900s to the 1980s, and is expected to cause further changes in the 1990s? The answer lies in the demographic composition of the work force.

Benefits offered to employees reflect many of the trends existing in our labor force. As the decades have witnessed drastic changes in the composition of the work force—changes in educational levels, family status, and employee expectations, benefits have had to be adjusted to meet the needs of the workers.[7] What specifically have we seen the past few decades with respect to demographic changes? The next section will explore what has been happening in the work force in an effort to show why the benefits offered today are different from those of twenty years ago.

DEMOGRAPHICS: THE TIMES ARE CHANGING

Taking a look at yesteryear reveals that our society, as many aspects of our lives, has been changing. Fifty years ago some certainty existed. That is, the

---

[6] This assumes that the insurance policy is part of a group term plan. Should it be a single policy, other than term insurance, or if the plan discriminates in favor of the more highly paid employees, then the entire benefit would be taxable.

[7] As we will discuss in Chapter 2, management practice, government regulations, and labor unions have also had a major impact on the increases in employee benefits.

work force was comprised of a relatively homogeneous group — predominantly males. From the benefits point of view this stability translated into the male being the sole breadwinner. Workers shared various characteristics; many were married with children, and had a spouse that stayed home. This typical worker had typical benefit needs—a retirement plan, sick leave, vacation time, and health insurance. Providing these to the workers was customary and, for the most part, uncomplicated.

Needless to say, this typical worker is a rarity in today's work force. The days of a single wage earner in the family are almost over. The trends in the composition of the work force today reveal that it is becoming increasingly difficult to determine what is "typical." As such, benefits offered are being forced to take on different focuses.

The Work Force Composition

The greatest change experienced in our work force has been the tremendous influx of women. The mother who stays at home to raise her children is becoming as atypical as the slide rule for mathematical calculations (see Table 1–3).

TABLE 1–3   LABOR FORCE PARTICIPATION FOR WOMEN, HUSBANDS PRESENT, BY AGE OF OWN YOUNGEST CHILD, (Percent) 1975–1986

YEAR	TOTAL	NO CHILDREN	CHILDREN UNDER 18
1975	44.5	44.0	44.9
1980	50.2	46.0	48.2
1985	54.3	48.2	61.0
1988	56.7	49.1	65.2

Source: U.S. Bureau of the Census, *Statistical Abstract of the United States: 1989*, (Washington, D.C.: GPO, 1989), p. 386.

Women now comprise almost half of the labor force. Labor force participation rates for women have been growing significantly over the past few decades. In the late 1980s, more than 50 percent of all women aged 30-45 were in the labor force; for those in the 20-29 age bracket, the rate is over 70 percent.[8] In addition, roughly 20 percent of all U.S. households are those with single parents.[9] As more and more women enter the work force—whether single, married with a gainfully employed spouse, or a single parent—the benefits offered must be tailored to their specific needs.

---

[8] *Employee Benefit Journal*, p. 38.

[9] Ibid.

Male versus Female Participation Rates

With this steady influx of women in the work force, the labor force participation rates of men continue to decline. As shown in Table 1–4, for all age groups, a decreased percentage of males, from 1960-1988 both married and single, is present in the work force. For women, the opposite is true, especially for married women.

We also see that this trend is expected to continue. If college enrollments are any indication of future labor force participation, the female labor force participation rate should increase. During the past ten years there has been greater than a 65 percent increase in college enrollment for females as opposed to a little over 13 percent for males.[10]

TABLE 1–4   Labor Force Participation Rates by Marital Status, Sex, and Age 1960–1988 (Percentage)

		Males				
YEAR	MARITAL STATUS	20–24	25–34	35–44	45–64	OVER 65
1960	M	97.5	98.6	98.4	93.0	37.1
	S	76.6	85.3	85.3	74.:	24.3
1970	M	95.0	98.2	98.1	96.6	30.2
	S	69.0	86.2	82.3	66.6	21.0
1980	M	98.6	97.5	97.0	84.4	20.4
	S	79.6	87.3	79.9	65.2	20.0
1986	M	95.8	97.3	96.3	81.8	17.3
	S	80.7	88.3	84.5	61.4	17.8
1988	M	95.7	97.0	96.7	82.4	17.5
	S	80.1	88.4	82.4	65.9	20.7
		Females				
1960	M	30.0	27.7	36.2	35.2	5.9
	S	73.4	79.9	79.7	75.1	21.6
1970	M	47.4	39.3	47.2	44.1	7.9
	S	71.1	80.7	73.3	67.8	17.6
1980	M	60.5	59.3	62.5	46.9	7.2
	S	72.2	84.2	78.6	62.8	12.0
1986	M	63.1	66.4	69.0	50.4	7.0
	S	75.0	81.1	79.6	69.3	8.0
1988	M	65.9	68.6	72.7	52.7	7.4
	S	74.8	81.8	81.5	65.2	10.9

Source: U.S. Bureau of the Census, *Statistical Abstract of the United States: 1989,* (Washington, D.C.: GPO 1989), p. 385

---

[10] Ibid.

What Does It Mean?

Our labor force has experienced drastic changes. More women have entered the working world, and more men are leaving it. Additionally, males are leaving the work force at a much earlier age. Waiting until age 65 to retire is becoming ancient history for both men and women, who want to enjoy their retirement years more. Early retirement options, self-funded annuities, and a desire to improve one's quality of life are all working to require new retirement benefit programs.

In Review

Every demographic change that occurs over time is ultimately felt in benefit offerings. From two wage earners, to single parents, to early retirements, benefits must be tailored to meet these special needs. No longer will a noncontributory retirement plan suffice. Mobility of our work force, brought on in some cases by dual-career couples, makes the traditional retirement plan somewhat outdated. Two working spouses also create more benefit chaos when they duplicate benefits. And with the increased number of working parents, the need for child care as a benefit becomes paramount.

As corporations put together their benefit packages, they must be aware of the composition of the labor force. Demographics of our society and ultimately our work force create specific needs that must be met in order to achieve the goal of "something of value" for each worker.

WHERE TO BEGIN

In putting together a benefits package, there are two issues to be considered: (1) what benefits must be offered by law and (2) what should be offered to make a company attractive to applicants and current workers. This section will explore these areas—legally required benefits and those offered on a voluntary basis.

Legally Required Benefits

Certain employee benefits must be supplied by the organization regardless of whether it wants to or not. With a few exceptions, the hiring of any employee will require the organization to pay Social Security premiums,[11] unemployment compensation, and workers' compensation. The payment of these premiums is borne solely by the organization in an effort to provide each employee with some basic level of financial protection at retirement,

---

[11] Social Security here refers to FICA taxes, for Old Age, Survivors, and Disability Insurance (OASDI).

termination, or as a result of an injury. These benefits also provide for a death benefit for dependents in case of a worker's death.

Let's take a closer look at these legally required benefits.

Social Security.   A major source of income for American retirees has been the benefits provided by Social Security insurance. In 1985, these benefits exceeded $91 billion a year.[12] By 1987, 174 million workers were covered by Social Security.[13]

Social Security insurance is financed by contributions made by the employee and matched by the employer, computed as a percentage of the employee's earnings. Table 1–5 shows the tax rate as approved by Congress.

TABLE 1–5   **Social Security Contribution Rates / Employer Contributions 1970 1990 (Percentage)**

YEAR	CONTRIBUTION RATES
1970	4.80
1975	5.85
1980	6.13
1985	6.70
1986	7.15
1987	7.51
1989	7.51
1990	7.65

Source: Adapted from U.S. Bureau of the Census, *Statistical Abstract of the United States: 1989*, (Washington, D.C.: GPO, 1989), p. 353.

In 1989, for instance, the rate was 7.51 percent (levied on both the employee and the employer) of the worker's earnings up to $48,000 a year, or a maximum levy of $3,604.80. This cost has risen rapidly for both employers and employees. As recently as 1965, the maximum was only $174 a year. Prior to 1983, employees became eligible for full benefits at age 65. With the revisions placed into law since then, anyone born after 1938 will have to wait up to two additional years before receiving full benefits. Survivor benefits are also administered through this program if an employee dies. Should the employee become too disabled to engage in gainful employment, the Social Security program will also provide benefits.

---

[12] U.S. Chamber of Commerce, Employee Benefits, (Washington, D.C., 1985) p. 32.

[13] U.S. Bureau of the Census, *Statistical Abstract of the U.S.: 1989* (Washington, D.C.: GPO, 1989) p. 352.

Social Security is undoubtedly an important part of America's attempt to protect and care for the aged and ensure a minimum living standard for them. However, because of serious financial problems, the Social Security law was revised in 1983. The law aimed at increasing the time period before younger workers are eligible to receive full benefits. It also increased the contributions that all employees and employers will be making over the next ten years. These changes should ensure the viability of the system through the twenty-first century.

Social Security has traditionally been referred to as an insurance program. This is a misnomer. Under a straight insurance program, the insured pays premiums and in return receives a promise to pay, from the insurer, a certain sum to the insured's heirs if he dies, or to the insured himself if he lives long enough to retire. The amount of premiums paid will determine the policy payoff.   But Social Security pays off depending on need—those with dependents collect more. Furthermore, there is a minimum level of benefits available to everyone, but unlike pension benefits, Social Security benefits vary based on the year, one's additional earnings, and the age of the recipient.[14]

In reality, Social Security is a transfer program of funds from one generation to another.   Today's workers pay taxes to support yesterday's workers who are disabled or retired. Our children and grandchildren will, in theory, provide our benefits from payroll taxes they will pay when they join the work force. This is necessary because the trust fund that has accumulated, from which future benefits will be paid, would be totally consumed in a little over a year if current payroll tax inputs were to stop. So, more correctly, Social Security is a pay-as-you-go program rather than an insurance program. It is largely a tax-financed welfare program that is an essential part of our total social programs.

What are the implications of Social Security's financial problems for managers and their organizations? Further changes are being made that will increase both the tax rate and the maximum income. This provides greater resources for Social Security but also raises the cost of both the employee's and the employer's contributions. If, for example, the rate for employers increased to 12 percent, and the maximum wage base increased to $60,000, the maximum cost to the employer would jump from $3,003 to $7,200 a year. Although a considerable part of this jump would reflect inflation, it would also represent a significant increase in the smorgasbord of benefits that politicians have deemed desirable to provide through Social Security. While this appears to be a large increase, such a rate will arise out of necessity if political forces seek to

---

[14] For 19889, individuals between the ages of 65 and 70 may earn up to $8,800 without losing benefits, up from $8,480 in 1988. Those between 62 and 64 may earn $6,480 in 1989, up $360 from 1988. Individuals age 70 or older have no reduction of benefits regardless of income.

continue expansion of Social Security benefits and if these costs, or a large part of them, cannot be absorbed through general tax revenues.

Unemployment Compensation.   Unemployment compensation laws provide benefits to people who are without a job, who have worked a minimum number of weeks, who submit an application for unemployment compensation to their state employment agency, who register for available work, and who are willing to accept any suitable employment offered them through their state unemployment compensation commission. The premise behind unemployment compensation is to provide an income to individuals who have lost a job through no fault of their own (e.g., layoffs, plant closings).

The funds for paying unemployment compensation are derived from a combined federal and state tax imposed on the taxable wage base of the employer. At the federal level, the unemployment tax rate is 6 percent, with a credit for certain taxes paid to the state. State unemployment compensation tax is often a function of a company's unemployment experience. That is, the more an organization lays off employees, the higher its rate. Table 1-6 reveals the average employer contributions for unemployment compensation.

TABLE 1–6   **Average Employer Contribution Rate as a Percentage of Taxable Wages, 1985**

U.S total	2.5
High	5.9
Low	1.2

Source: U.S. Bureau of the Census, *Statistical Abstract of the United States: 1987*, (Washington, D.C.: GPO, 1986), p. 361, and *Statistical Abstract of the United States: 1989*, (Washington, D.C.: GPO, 1989), p.358.

Eligible unemployed workers receive an amount that varies from state to state but is determined by the worker's previous wage rate and the length of previous employment. Benefits commonly range from $50 to $75 a week but may run to $150 a week or higher.[15] This compensation is provided for only a limited period—typically, the base is twenty-six weeks but may be extended by the state another twenty-six weeks in unusual situations. This extension was employed in the recession of the early 1980s, especially for auto workers and steel workers, who constituted a large percentage of the unemployed.

---

[15] For 1987, unemployment compensation averaged $140 per week for all states, with the highest average being $174 in Maine, and the lowest being $98 in Tennessee. {U.S. Bureau of the Census, *Statistical Abstract of the United States: 1989*, (Washington, D.C.: GPO, 1989), p. 358.

Unemployment compensation and parallel programs for railroad, federal government, and military employees cover more than 75 percent of all members in the work force. Major groups that are excluded include self-employed workers, employees who work for organizations that employ fewer than four individuals, household domestics, farm employees, and state and local government employees.

As recent recessions have demonstrated, unemployment compensation provides stable spending power throughout the nation. In contrast to the early 1930s, when millions of workers lost their jobs and had no compensatory income, unemployment compensation provides a floor that allows individuals to continue looking for work while receiving assistance in between jobs.

Workers' Compensation.   Every state currently has some type of workers' compensation to compensate employees or their families for death or permanent or total disability resulting from job-related endeavors. (Federal employees and others not working within the states are covered by separate legislation.)

The rationale for workers' compensation protection is to protect employees and to attribute the cost for occupational accidents to the employing organization. This accountability factor considers workers' compensation costs as part of the labor expenses incurred in meeting the organization's objectives.

Workers' compensation benefits are based on fixed schedules of minimum and maximum payments. For example, the loss of an index finger may be calculated at $500, or the loss of an entire foot at $5,000. When comprehensive disability payments are required, the amount of compensation is computed by considering the employee's current earnings, future earnings, and financial responsibilities.

The entire cost of workers' compensation is borne by the organization. Its rates are set based on the likelihood of an accident plus the actual history of company accidents. The organization, then, protects itself by covering its risks through public, private-external, or private-internal insurance programs. Some states provide an insurance system for the handling of workers' compensation. These may be voluntary or required. Some organizations cover their workers' compensation risks by purchasing insurance from private insurance companies. Finally, some states allow employers to be self-insurers. Self-insuring, while usually limited to large organizations, requires the employer to maintain a fund from which benefits can be paid.

Most of the workers' compensation laws stipulate that the injured employee will be compensated either by a monetary allocation or by the payment of medical expenses, or a combination of the two. Almost all workers' compensation insurance programs, whether publicly or privately controlled, provide incentives for employers to maintain good safety records. Insurance rates are computed based on the organization's accident experience. Hence employers are motivated to keep accident rates low.

Conclusion. The preceding discussion focused on the costs associated with providing the legally required benefits. What has occured in the legally required area has been equally matched and surpassed when one considers the cost of providing voluntary benefits.

The next section will take an introductory look at the major voluntary benefits offered by employers.

Voluntary Benefits

The menu of benefits voluntarily offered to employees can be astounding. As Table 1–1 revealed, there are many different benefits offered—all of which carry significant costs. Space precludes us at this time from going into great depth for each of these major, and costly, benefits offered by organizations. We can, however, identify them and reveal their costs. Table 1–7, represents the dollar amount and the percentage of these benefits as they comprised part of the $8,166 in benefit costs incurred in 1985. As we proceed through the text, we will examine most of these voluntary benefits in greater detail.

TABLE 1–7   Major Voluntary Benefits Offered by Cost and Percentage of Total Outlay, 1985

BENEFIT	COST OUTLAY	PERCENTAGE
Retirement	$2,695	33
Health	1,552	19
Paid Vacations	1,049	13
Paid Rest Periods, Lunch Periods, Wash-up time	752	9
Holiday Pay	611	7
Sick Leave	286	4

Source: U.S. Chamber of Commerce, *Employee Benefits 1985* (Washington, D.C., 1985), p. 13.

In Review

Rather than covering all of the benefits offered by companies, what we have tried to show is how expensive these benefits are. They are offered in many cases to "sweeten the pot," but, simultaneously, workers have become accustomed to them and find it difficult to accept less or pay more for what they have.

Companies are still offering the benefits described, but skyrocketing costs are causing them to rethink the process. While benefits serve a valuable purpose for both the employer and the employee, continual escalation of their costs may lead to major problems in the future.

Realization of this is a driving force for writing this text. Benefits must still be offered, but done so such that laws are complied with, and something of value is offered to employees—and in a cost-effective manner. New strategies and approaches must be explored in offering employee benefits. It is with this in mind that we constructed this book. The following section will review the specific topic areas contained in the remaining chapters.

FLOW OF THE TEXT

The construct and contents of this text is the outcome of our teaching and research interests, as well as discussions with practitioners in the field. In discussing employee benefits, certain topics appear to arise over and over. As such, we have taken these topical areas and arranged them in what we believe to be a practical and logical order for discussing benefits.

Part I: Overview of Benefits

The first three chapters of this text are intended to provide the reader with some background information regarding benefit administration. Chapter 2 focuses on the history of benefits in the United States. Many of the benefits offered, at times, reflect changing legislation. As such, the laws affecting benefits offered will also be explored. Benefits in general do not exist in isolation. They are part of a comprehensive compensation package offered by the organization. The functioning of compensation and the role of benefits in the overall plan are the topic of Chapter 3. In Chapter 4, we discuss how benefits, while membership rewards, can be tied to productivity.

Part II: Components of Benefits Packages

Part II covers the lion's share of this text. The major voluntary benefits offered are explored. Chapter 5 explores the arena of health benefits. The various types of health coverage are explored—such as traditional coverage, health maintenance organizations, and preferred provider benefits organizations. What goes into health coverage decisions will be discussed as well as new methods of containing health care costs. The complex situations of employee disability and death benefits are the focus of Chapter 6 —"Disability and Survivor Benefits." How these are packaged, what they do, and how they are administered will be explored. The topic of retirement is the subject of Chapter 7. Retirement plans, annuity calculations, legal issues, and various methods of retirement options will be discussed. Chapter 8 looks at executive benefits, outplacement, relocation, and incentive programs. Special emphasis is given to those benefits offered to a company's higher-paid employees.

Part III: Affording the Benefits Package

Chapters 9 and 10 focus on the cost factors in offering benefits. How one "costs-out" benefits offerings as part of the total compensation package is discussed in Chapter 9. Chapter 10 looks at cost-management measures that can be implemented in order to lower the percentage of the total wage bill going for benefits.

Part IV: Integrative Issues in Employee Benefits

The last section in tnis text explores some of the newer issues in benefit administration. Chapter 11 focuses on flexible benefits. As more concern arises over cost-management measures, coupled with tailoring benefits to our changing society, these "cafeteria-style" benefit offerings are once again gaining popularity. The "state-of-the-art" issues in flexible benefits will be explored. Lastly, where are benefits heading? The realization that employee benefits are dynamic and exist in an ever-changing society indicates that we must prepare ourselves today for providing tomorrow's benefits. The last chapter, Chapter 12, looks at these future trends in employee benefits.

SUMMARY

After reading this chapter you will know that:

* *Employers offer benefits to attract and retain their employees. Benefits are expected by all employees, and as such, those offered must meet some need of each employee.*
* *Benefits are membership based; that is, they are not tied to productivity. Their impact on motivation is slight. However, their absence can lead to worker dissatisfaction.*
* *Benefits offered are not cost free. Benefits now cost about 39 cents for every wage dollar spent. In 1987 benefits averaged $10,708 per employee per year.*
* *As society changes, so too do the needs of workers. More females, more dual career couples, and more single parents are entering the work force and the impact of these changes has resulted in the reshaping of benefits offered.*
* *Social Security is a transfer program, funded by today's workers and employers to support workers who are disabled or retired. About 174 million workers are covered by Social Security.*

* *Both unemployment compensation and workers' compensation are legally required benefits. Unemployment compensation provides benefits to employees who are without a job. Workers' compensation is designed to compensate employees or their families for death or permanent or total disabilities resulting from job-related activities.*
* *Health insurance coverage is offered to employees to help reduce an employee's financial risk due to medical needs. Health benefits account for almost 21 percent of the total benefit costs. Health insurance coverage today can be offered as traditional coverage, or through one of many alternatives, such as health maintenance organizations.*
* *Pension programs are designed to assist employees in providing an income for their retirement years. In most organizations, funding pension plans is the most expensive benefit offered. Variations of pension plans include contributory and noncontributory programs.*
* *The major voluntary benefits offered, in addition to pension programs and health insurance, are vacations, holiday pay, paid rest periods, and sick leave.*
* *Benefits are not costfree to organizations; as such, they must be managed. The composition of the benefits package must be analyzed for affordability. Costing out the benefits provides the measure of whether one can afford a benefit. Additionally, concerns over benefit cost containment indicate a need for determining the cost of offering each benefit.*

KEY TERMS

Benefits	Legally required benefits
Compensation program	Membership-based rewards
Cost containment	Old Age, Survivors, and Disability
Costing benefits	Insurance (OASDI)
Cost of benefits	Pay roll based stock ownership
Demographics	plans (PAYSOP)
Direct wage bill	Preferred provider
Employee stock ownership	organizations (PPOs)
plans (ESOP)	Social Security
FICA	Sick leave
Health insurance	Unemployment compensation
Health maintenance	Vacation benefits
organizations	Voluntary benefits
Holiday pay	Workers' compensation
Labor force	

QUESTIONS FOR REVIEW AND DISCUSSION

1. Why are benefits described as being membership based?
2. Why might employees choose to have their employer purchase benefits for them rather than receive cash and make the purchase themselves?
3. Discuss the rise in benefit costs over the past few decades.
4. How have changes in demographic trends affected benefit offerings?
5. What benefits are provided by Social Security and how are they financed?
6. What benefits accrue to an organization that offers a liberal sick-leave policy and liberal vacation and holiday schedules?
7. What are the two most expensive benefits offered to employees? Approximately what do they cost on average?
8. "An organization could not attract and retain competent employees today without a good benefits package." Do you agree or disagree with this statement? Why?
9. What is the purpose of offering benefits to employees?
10. What benefits should be offered to employees such that their needs/expectations can be met while simultaneously containing costs for the employer?

ADDITIONAL READINGS

BOND, ROBERT L., and LARRY I. STEIN.   "KSOPs: A Marriage of Convenience." *Employee Benefits Journal* 12, no. 4 (December 1987.)

CURRAN, PETER F.   "Flexible Benefits: Key to Cost Control." *Cashflow Magazine* 8 (July 1987.)

"Great Moments in Workstyle: Company Gyms, Employee Education, Profit Sharing—It Was All Happening a Hundred Years Ago." *Inc.* 8, no. 1 (January 1986.)

KITTRELL, ALISON.   "Workers Pay More Health Costs: Survey." *Business Insurance* 21 (July 20, 1987.)

SLATER, KAREN.   "Pension Plans May Offer More under Tax Bill." *Wall Street Journal*, May 12, 1986, p. 27

CHAPTER TWO

BENEFITS: AN HISTORICAL REVIEW

LEARNING OBJECTIVES

After reading this chapter you will be able to:

* *Discuss the impact of management practices on the evolution of benefits.*
* *Discuss the impact of labor unions on the evolution of employee benefits.*
* *Identify mandatory bargaining issues.*
* *Discuss the impact of the Wagner Act on employee benefits.*
* *Discuss how concession bargaining has affected benefit offerings for unionized employees.*
* *Discuss the importance of the 1949 Supreme Court decision regarding pension programs as a mandatory bargaining issue.*
* *Discuss the impact of the Fair Labor Standards Act on benefits administration.*
* *Discuss the impact of the Employee Retirement Income Security Act on benefits administration.*
* *Describe 401(k) program offerings as a pension benefit.*
* *Discuss the impact of the Health Maintenance Act on benefits administration.*
* *Discuss the impact of the Consolidated Omnibus Budget Reconciliation Act on benefit administration.*
* *Discuss the impact of the Civil Rights Act and other similar legislation on benefits administration.*

INTRODUCTION

Tracing the history of employee benefits in the United States is a major feat. It is difficult to pinpoint just when benefits were first offered. There are references in the Bible to imply that benefits were around at that time. In prehistoric days, some cavemen were treated differently from others. While this treatment is not intended to reveal a concerted effort on someone's part to provide benefits, it does reveal that benefits have been with us for as long as one person has worked for another. Even Rip Van Winkle was the recipient of a benefit, when he awoke after twenty years of sleep a free citizen of the United States. How, then, do we begin a discussion of employee benefits in modern times?

Benefits, in the form as we know them today, probably got their start in the post–Civil War years.[1] Table 2–1 reveals some of the specific benefit offerings from the post–Civil War era to the present. As we trace through the years, one aspect becomes apparent: The benefits offered to employees do appear to closely follow the changing attitudes of management, the push for greater benefit offerings by the unionized workers in the United States, and federal legislation that had been enacted into law. As such, it is almost impossible to separate the historical implications of benefits without simultaneously discussing the management practice and the unionized and legal frameworks from which they came. The remainder of this chapter will look at the practices and laws that affect employee benefits, and present them in a manner that represents their historical place in benefit administration.

TABLE 2–1   History of Benefits (Selected Events)

1866	The Crane Company introduced a medical department for employees.
1875	First private pension plan adopted; provided benefits for employees age 60 or over who had 20 years with the company.
1885	Proctor & Gamble granted a Saturday Afternoon half-holiday for all workers.
1886	Westinghouse Corporation granted paid vacations.
1887	Proctor & Gamble established a profit-sharing program.
1894	National Wallpaper Company and the Wallpaper Craftsmen negotiated a guaranteed annual wage.
1902	First state's workmen's compensation law enacted in Maryland; declared unconstitutional in 1904.
1911	First group life insurance plan for employees inaugurated by the Pantasote Leather Company.
1912	First major group insurance plan introduced at Montgomery Ward.

---

[1] Robert M. McCaffrey, *Managing the Employee Benefits Program* (New York: American Management Association, 1972), p. 7.

TABLE 2–1   History of Benefits (Selected Events) *Cont.*

1916   Dennison Manufacturing Company announced plan for payment of unemployment benefits.

1926   Sun Oil Company established an employee savings plan with company contributions.

1929   Blue Cross concept of prepaid medical costs initiated at Baylor University Hospital.

1935   Social Security Act provided basis for federal retirement system and state-administered unemployment insurance programs.

1937   Railroad Retirement Act federalized a private industry's pension program.

1940   National Labor Relations Board ruled that vacations, holidays, and bonuses were proper subjects for collective bargaining.

1949   Supreme Court upheld ruling on Inland Steel and United Steelworkers of America negotiations that pensions were bargainable.

1955   Ford Motor Company and United Auto Workers negotiated supplemental unemployment benefits.

1962   United Steelworkers of America gained extended vacation plan in negotiations with American Can Company and Continental Can Company.

1966   Medicare, developed to provide medical care for the aged, became operative.

1968   Treasury Department adopted new rules with limiting integration of private pension plans with Social Security retirement benefits.

1970   Tax Reform Act of 1969 changed tax treatment of employee moving expenses and profit-sharing and stock-option plans.

1971   Occupational Safety and Health Act of 1970 established a national commission on State Workmen's Compensation Laws.

1973   Health Maintenance Organization Act establishes rights to offer alternative health care coverage.

1974   Employee Retirement and Income Security Act becomes law to correct past mishandling of pension programs.

1978   Civil Service Reform Act.

1978   Pregnancy Discrimination Act passes which requires employers to treat pregnancy as a short term disability under their current health program.

1981   Tax Reform Act permits individuals to save money for their retirement on a pre-tax basis.

1983   Social Security Reform Act.

1984   Retirement Equity Act redefined rules of ERISA affecting women, and lowered vesting ages.

1986   Tax Reform Act limits the number of individuals eligible for individual retirement accounts.

1986   Amendment to the Age ·Discrimination Act removes the cap for mandatory retirement age.

1986   Consolidated Omnibus Budget Reconciliation Act (COBRA) provides for continuation of health care coverage for most employees separated from their organizations.

MANAGEMENT PRACTICE

The field of management has evolved tremendously over the past one hundred years. Workers throughout history have been perceived in the range from necessary evils that must be reckoned with to valuable assets. As we look at the changes in management practices over the years, there has been a greater push in the past few decades to focus on the needs of employees, and to develop techniques to motivate them. The behavioral school of management, which began this focus in the 1940s, has long held that if we treat our employees in such a way that creates a positive work environment, then greater worker satisfaction and, ultimately, greater productivity will result. This environment has been of particular interest, especially when considering the dire need to make organizations more effective and efficient in competing on a global level. But what role have benefits played in creating that environment?

It was not that long ago when the six-day, twelve-hour work day was common. Workers in those times had very little say in how they were treated, or what management was to offer them. There were no laws that protected the workers from unsafe working conditions, from abusive management, from pay inequities, and the like. Employees were clearly at the mercy of management. Yet as social attitudes began to change (or rebel if one focuses on the union movement in the United States) workers desired more. There was a demand to be treated as assets to the company. Many workers realized that management had a greater concern for some of its equipment than it did for the workers who ran the machinery. As the concern became more vocal, and the field of management became more formal, many organizations recognized the value of creating the positive working environment to increase their profits. In many respects, this spillover reflects the impetus for many of the changes management has made.

Management has the responsibility and legal right to manage and operate the business in accordance with some set goal. In many cases, this goal is survival, which can be translated into profit-maximizing behavior. In order to make profits, organizations have realized that one of the critical ingredients for success is people, for the definition of management itself views management as "a process of efficiently getting activities completed with and through other people."[2] Translating this concern into benefits has not been too difficult.

---

[2] Stephen P. Robbins, *Management*, 2nd ed. (Englewood Cliffs, N.J.: Prentice Hall, 1988), p. 6.

First of all, as mentioned in Chapter 1, workers' needs have changed. As society has changed, it has created a greater need for certain benefits. Yet business must view these needs in conjunction with its overall corporate goals. For instance, time off from work reflects management's commitment to provide employees time to "recharge their batteries." Vacation periods are costly, yet there is a body of research that supports why workers should be given time off. The day-to-day strain from working takes its toll on workers, and it becomes necessary to remove them from that pressure periodically. Employers have therefore required employees to use their vacation time, not to store it up, or to sell it back. In modern organizations, it is not only vacation time that is of concern. Many of the newer benefits offered under the umbrella of employee assistance programs (EAPs) reflect management's attitude of helping a troubled employee. While initially directed at aiding the alcoholic employee, these programs are geared toward returning an employee to work as early as possible because it is more cost effective. The traditional treatment of a troubled employee usually resulted in the employee's termination. That termination proved to be costly for both parties—the employee who then had a job loss to add to his problem, and the organization that had to search for a replacement. Even when replacements were easily found, there was a time lag before the new employee was fully trained. Over time, companies realized it was more cost effective to provide the assistance to troubled employees, and have them return to productive work, than to hire new workers. Other benefits offered by organizations can be explained in similar fashion. Benefits are a means of attracting and retaining productive workers, assisting troubled employees, and assisting the organization in remaining competitive in a highly competitive environment.

LABOR UNIONS

Similar to management practices, labor unions have had an impact on benefit offerings. While the discussion of the impact of unions focuses specifically on those gains made in collective-bargaining situations, one must realize the effect these gains have had on the general work force. With only about 17 percent of our work force unionized (the lowest percentage for decades since its all-time high of about 37 percent), one may not expect to see much of an impact. There is, however, a spillover effect. Spillover effects relate to situations in which the gains made in the unionized sector are often passed on to the nonunion counterparts. Why? For many reasons. But, for many organizations, it revolves around remaining nonunion. While our context in this book is not centered on labor relations/collective bargaining, an understanding of what occurs in this arena is important for the benefits administrator.

The historical plight of unions in our society is well documented. With their beginnings in the mid 1800s, unions have constantly sought to find ways to protect their members and to fight for bread-and-butter issues,[3] which translated into wage and benefit concerns. For example, the unions' early plight was not an easy one, for big business and the courts looked at unions as entities that were disruptive to American industries. While some union success was achieved (e.g., shorter work weeks, time off from work), their gains were limited. It was not until 1935 that labor unions effected major changes.

In 1935 the most progressive and favorable piece of labor legislation was passed. The National Labor Relations Act, also called the Wagner Act, provided full freedom for unions to exist. Among its regulations were what we call mandatory bargaining issues—wages, hours, and terms and conditions of employment. Nestled in these mandatory bargaining issues are benefits, and unions wasted no time in bargaining for more. This was especially true in periods of wage freezes, such as that during World War II.

It would be beyond the scope of this book to attempt to describe each of the benefits unions fought for. It is reasonable to say that employee benefits existing today are similar in both the unionized and nonunionized work forces. Unions believe that anything affecting their wages, hours, and terms and conditions of employment, must by law be put on the bargaining table by management. As such, especially in recent years, there has been much greater emphasis placed on benefits negotiations.

When many organizations experienced the effects of the economic downturn in the mid- to late-1970s, wage increases were reduced. The days of negotiating a 30 percent increase in wages over the life of a contract were over. Companies could no longer afford to pay these higher wages, for to remain competitive they had to tighten their expenditures on direct labor costs. In lieu of greater wage increases, companies began to offer more benefits. While providing benefits is not cost free, it was a lesser expense, all things being considered, for the companies. The benefits agreed to in those collective-bargaining contracts varied in their offerings and scope. For example, during this period unions fought for and achieved such benefits as supplemental unemployment benefits, longer vacations, more holidays, and a four-day work week.[4] The benefits obtained during these periods were constrained only by the creativity and limitations brought to the negotiating table by both parties.

Attempts to expand the bread-and-butter issues, especially benefits, resulted in some gains for union members. This trend however, did not

---

[3] For detailed background information on the history of early unionization, see William H. Holley and Kenneth M. Jennings, *The Labor Relations Process*, 2d ed. (Chicago: Dryden Press, 1984).

[4] Fred K. Foulkes, "Benefit Objectives and Issues," in *Employee Benefits Handbook*, ed. Fred K. Foulkes (Boston: Warren, Gorham & Lamont, 1982), pp. 1-6.

continue in all cases. Economic downturn led to more financial losses for some companies. To survive, they had to request concessions from their union members. These concession bargaining sessions, or negotiating over wage and benefit give-backs, became dominant in the early 1980s. Faced with their bleak future, companies sought relief from their unions in terms of the direct wage bill and specific work rules. The most widely cited case of concession bargaining during this time was the Chrysler–United Auto Workers negotiations.

In an effort to save the ailing car manufacturer, the UAW members agreed to take a cut in their pay and benefits. In return, their jobs would be saved. From a labor perspective, the jury is still out on the appropriateness of this action. The history of unionization in the United States rarely focused on unions "giving something back" to organizations after they were "won" in hard-fought negotiations. From the corporate perspective, however, the give-backs had to be given—the direct wage bill had to be significantly cut. Much of the underlying motive in concession bargaining was that when times got better, the give-backs would be returned. This is not happening, as many companies do not desire to return to those high costs associated with elevated levels of wages and benefits. Call it business savvy, effective benefit administration, or constrained labor relations, but most companies appear prepared to avoid repeating their mistakes and use benefits as a "payoff" for a lack of, or limited, pay increases.

One other benefit deserves special attention here—the union retirement fund. As cited in Table 2–1, the 1949 Supreme Court ruling that union pensions are a bargaining issue has had a tremendous effect on corporate America. Unions were given the right to be directly involved in how their retirement programs are established, how they are funded, and more importantly, how they are managed. The billions of dollars contained in union pension funds result in a major investment impact. Unions realize the subtle power of this money, and as such they have demanded that their investments be administered in a way that supports the "union cause." In effect, unions now want to know where their money is being invested, and if they don't like where the money is being lent, they demand divestiture. This adds a new element for benefits administrators. They must recognize that investing union pension funds, which ultimately are lent to companies that are "anti-union," is greatly frowned on by the union hierarchy; that is, the benefits administrator must be more aware of how the union members' money is being used.

Earlier we stated that unions, as well as management practices, have had an impact on current employee benefits. Even though these effects are recognizable, clearly the greatest impact on benefits comes from federal legislation. The next section will explore the major laws that affect benefits administration.

BENEFIT LEGISLATION

The most critical element guiding benefit offerings and administration has been the federal legislation enacted over the years. Whereas the Wagner Act gave unions the right to negotiate over mandatory bargaining issues, many pieces of legislation have been directed solely toward employee benefits. This section looks at the most important laws and describes how they affect benefits administration.

The Legally Required Benefits

In Chapter 1 we discussed Social Security, unemployment compensation, and workers' compensation as legally required benefits. We do need to recognize, however, their importance to the benefits administrator. In dealing with certain requirements, specific costs and constraints are imposed. For the benefits administrator, these legally required benefits must be included in any benefits package provided by the organization, and must be administered according to government guidelines. (In Chapter 9, we'll take a closer look at the costs of these legally required benefits as they impact an organization. At that time, if only for cost considerations, we can obtain some insight they have on the organization.)

Fair Labor Standards Act (FLSA)

The Fair Labor Standards Act (FLSA) is a law that indirectly affects benefits administration. The law, as passed in 1938, focused on the number of hours each week an employer could "work" his employees without paying premium wages. It clarified two categories of workers—exempt and nonexempt. Traditionally these two terms mean whether one's employment falls under the guidelines of the FLSA (nonexempt) or is exempt from it. While it is not in itself an accurate description of the difference between the two categories, exempt employees are usually professional level and above in an organization, and are paid according to a salary structure. Nonexempt employees, on the other hand, are traditionally the lower-level jobs in the organization and are paid an hourly wage.[5]

One of the greater impacts this law has created for benefits administrators is in the area of overtime pay. Under the FLSA guidelines, certain conditions exist in which nonexempt employees are credited with overtime pay usually at the rate of one and one-half times their hourly wage rate. These conditions vary according to the worker's regularly scheduled

---

[5] The confusion over what is a managerial, professional, or technical worker is expected to heighten in future years. The shift in emphasis toward technical manager/automated work environments has clouded the once-clear FLSA guidelines. Future guidelines to diminish this confusion are anticipated.

workweek. For instance, an individual working a shortened workweek, four ten-hour days as opposed to five eight-hour days, is customarily not eligible for overtime pay for the two extra hours worked each day. Generally accepted, however, is that any work over forty hours per week is paid at the premium wage rate.

When overtime rates are included in wages, typically those benefits that are contingent on that pay base increase. Costs for Social Security, for example, will increase proportionally to the increase in pay due to overtime pay received.

Employee Retirement Income Security Act

The Employee Retirement Income Security Act (ERISA) has had one of the greatest impacts on benefit administration. Passed in 1974, its purpose was to deal with the largest problems imposed by private pension plans—people were not getting their benefits. This was chiefly due to the design of private pension plans, which almost always required a minimum tenure with the organization before individuals were guaranteed a right to pension benefits, regardless of whether they stayed with the organization. These permanent benefits, called vesting rights, were typically withheld until employees served ten to fifteen years with the company. In some cases, no vesting privileges were identified. This meant, for example, that a 60-year-old employee with twenty-five years of service who left the company for whatever reason would have no right to a pension benefit. ERISA was enacted to prevent such abuses.

ERISA requires employers who decide to provide a pension plan to design a retirement program under specific rules. Typically each plan must convey to employees "new eligibility requirements for coverage, breaks in service, restoration of service following a break, plan payment methods, and new vesting requirements."[6] Currently, vesting in companies comes after five years of service, and pension programs must also be available to all employees over the age of 21.[7]

ERISA has also created guidelines for the termination of a pension program. Should an employer voluntarily terminate a pension program, the Pension Benefit Guaranty Corporation (PBGC) must be notified. Similarly, the act permits the PBGC under certain conditions (such as inadequate pension funding) to lay claim on corporate assets—up to 30 percent of net worth—to pay benefits that had been promised to employees.

---

[6] Rodney N. Mara, "Communication of Benefits," in *Employee Benefits Handbook*, ed. Fred K. Foulkes (Boston: Warren, Gorham & Lamont, 1982), p. 6-2.

[7] The Tax Reform Act of 1986 requires full vesting after five years, partial vesting after three years, and seven-year full vesting with plan years beginning after December 1, 1988. Those companies with a retirement plan year prior to that date were not required to go to the new lower vesting rules until December 1, 1989.

Tax Reform Act

With the reform of tax laws in 1982 came two important programs for employees. The first of these is called an individual retirement account (IRA). The purpose of an IRA is to make the individual partly responsible for his or her retirement income. The law permitted each worker to defer paying taxes on up to $2,000 of earned income per year ($2,225 for employee and spouse where spouse did not work) with interest on these accounts also accumulating on a tax-deferred basis.

IRAs appeared to be very popular for the few years they received favorable backing from the Internal Revenue Service. However, with the new tax code established in 1986, this tax reform bill significantly limited IRAs for many workers. To be eligible for deferring income to an IRA, workers now must meet specific conditions, revolving around whether one is a participant in a recognized pension program at work, and also the amount of one's adjusted annual income. The purpose here is to focus IRAs to the lower-income workers who may not have a pension program at their place of work, or for those who deserve to augment the one they have. IRAs to a large extent were not directly affecting the work of a benefits administrator. To a large extent, IRAs were administered by each individual worker and resulted in little work for the benefits specialist. One program that was also part of the 1982 tax reform did, however, create much work for those handling benefits—the establishment of capital accumulation programs, more commonly known as 401(k)s.

A 401(k) program is named after the IRS tax code section that established its existence. These programs permit workers to set aside a certain amount of their income on a tax-deferred basis. In many cases, what differentiates the 401(k) from the IRA is the amount permitted to be set aside and the fact that many companies contribute an amount to the 401(k) on the employee's behalf.[8] Because of this matching feature, many companies call their 401(k) a matching contribution plan, meaning that both the employer and the employee are working jointly to create a retirement program. These matching contribution programs are usually offered in addition to the employers noncontributory retirement plan (discussed in Chapter 7).

The 401(k) programs have been popular with employees since their inception. Accordingly, the administration of the plan, in meeting the IRS rules and regulations, and the paperwork involved have meant significantly more work for the benefits administrator in offering retirement programs.

---

[8] Most companies offering matching contribution features to their 401(k) programs limit the amount of their contribution. Typically, their matching amount is set as one half of the amount the employee contributes, with a 3 percent maximum. Thus an employee setting aside 4 percent of salary will have a 2 percent match, with up to 3 percent for a 6 percent deduction.

Health Maintenance Act

The Health Maintenance Act, enacted in 1973, required all employers offering health insurance programs to their employees to also offer alternative health care options. These alternatives, or health maintenance organizations (HMOs), are designed to provide health care coverage at a fixed cost to both the employer and the employee.

Offering various alternatives of health care can be cumbersome. For the benefits administrator, enrollment procedures can be a lengthy and time-consuming process. The benefits administrator must be aware of all of the coverage that the company offers, and be able to communicate this information to all employees. While brochures can assist in communicating the necessary information, the forms processing is still tedious (benefits communication is a topic of Chapter 4). The Health Maintenance Act, while giving more freedom of choice to employees, has in many cases, created an administrative nightmare for some benefits administrators.

Consolidated Omnibus Budget Reconciliation Act

One of the main features established by the Consolidated Omnibus Budget Reconciliation Act (COBRA) was the continuation of employee benefits for a period up to three years after the employee leaves the company.[9] Because of the high unemployment rates in the early 1980s, supplemented by the downsizing of corporate America, a large number of individuals were out of work and, more importantly, no longer had medical insurance. To combat this problem, COBRA was enacted in 1984.

When employees resign or are laid off through no fault of their own, they are eligible for a continuation of their health insurance. The costs of this coverage are generally borne by the severed employee, but COBRA provides that these benefits be offered through the company's current group health insurance plan. This way, while it may be more of an expense for the employee, it is still cheaper than purchasing a similar policy on an individual basis.

Civil Rights Act

In any discussion of legislation affecting human resources, and more specifically benefits, one would be remiss not to spend a few pages regarding the impact of the 1964 Civil Rights Act. This act, especially Title VII, stipulates that it is illegal to discriminate in selection, promotion, or termination on the basis of race, color, sex, race, or national origin. Subsequent amendments, as well as other similar legislation, have added other

---

[9] For employees that have been terminated or have had their hours reduced, their coverage is for a period of eighteen months. For most other situations, the coverage is extended up to thirty-six months. See Commerce Clearing House, *Topical Law Reports*, 69 (August 1987): 2615-11.

protected groups, such as the handicapped, Vietnam War veterans, and the aged. In some states, marital status is included in the list of those protected. To the benefits specialist, this means that the benefits offered must be administered in such a manner that is not discriminatory.

Age Discrimination. It is illegal to discriminate against an individual on the basis of age. As passed in 1967, individuals between the ages of 40 and 65 were protected; amended to age 70 in 1978, and uncapped in 1986.[10] Most organizations, therefore, cannot force employees to retire at any age. While a worker may be unable to remain in his or her current job, for the most part the worker cannot be forced out of the organization.[11] This clearly has an impact on an organization's retirement program. For those individuals who work past the traditional retirement age, however, special rules may apply.

Sex Discrimination. As outlined in the wording of the Civil Rights Act, it is illegal to discriminate on the basis of sex when administering benefits:

> It is illegal for an employer to provide dependents' benefits to employees who are the principal wage earner or the head of the household, or to limit coverage to dependents of male employees or to provide benefits only to wives of male employees but not to [spouses of] female employees.[12]

The courts have interpreted this to mean that the employee portion of the costs of these programs offered must be the same for both the male and female employee. Benefit costs cannot be adjusted for sex differences—such that females tend to live longer.

In addition to the sex discrimination provisions, the Pregnancy Disability Act of 1978 (supplemented by state laws prohibiting discrimination based on pregnancy)clarified maternity benefits. The twist to this amendment was one of participation. If a company does not offer health-related benefits to the employees, the company is exempt from providing pregnancy benefits. But any health benefit offered, in whatever capacity, binds the organization to recognize pregnancy as a short-term disability. Therefore, companies must cover the costs of maternity in the same manner they cover the costs of other short-term disabilities. For example, if a health insurance package contains a

---

[10] The upper limit was not removed for college professors and certain government agencies, like the CIA or FBI.

[11] For instance, a recent Supreme Court decision ruled that it is permissible for airlines to refuse pilots to captain an airline past the age of 60. Yet the Court said that does not mean the aged employee must be retired. The employee should be permitted to move into another position, for instance, a flight navigator.

[12] Michael W. Sculnick, "Federal Labor and Employment Laws," in *Employee Benefits Handbook*, ed. Fred K. Foulkes (Boston: Warren, Gorham & Lamont, 1982), p. 16-36.

provision that it pays 90 percent of the costs for short-term disability, then that same percentage must be applied to maternity cases. Additionally, the female employee's employment must be protected while she is out on maternity leave. That is, after the specified time period allotted for pregnancy leave expires,[13] the female employee is guaranteed a position in the company. While the job may not be the exact position she left, it must be one that is comparable.

Conclusion

We have tried to discuss the major legislation benefits administrators must deal with in packaging their benefits. We by no means claim to say that our discussion will create legislative experts. To make such a claim would be preposterous. Our goal is to look at what is present, and to make the benefits specialist aware that the laws greatly affect how one administers company benefits.

SUMMARY

After reading this chapter you will know that:

* *Management practices have influenced benefit offerings in many ways. Current management thought is to offer a benefit that assists in the attracting and retaining of good employees. In the past decade, more concern has been given to providing benefits that meet an employee's specific needs. In some cases, this has translated into benefits such as employee assistance programs.*
* *Labor unions have created an environment in which their gains not only affect their members, but also the general work force. As such, this has created a spillover effect. Unions traditionally bargain over the bread-and-butter issues. Recently, unions have been negotiating for more benefits because large-scale pay increases were not available.*
* *The mandatory bargaining issues for labor and management are wages, hours, and terms and conditions of employment.*
* *The Wagner Act created an environment that was very positive toward unions. This act gave unions certain freedoms and required management to recognize unions as the workers' representative. The Wagner Act also established the mandatory bargaining issues, which means that management had to negotiate over such items as benefits.*

---

[13] Pregnancy leaves can vary according to company policy. However, as a general guideline, normal deliveries are afforded six weeks to recuperate, cesarean sections, ten weeks.

* *Concession bargaining is the process of negotiating wage and benefit give-backs. Faced with financial problems, companies seek relief from their unions by negotiating for lesser wages and benefits.*

* *The 1949 Supreme Court decision regarding pension programs recognized a union's retirement program as a negotiable item. Accordingly, unions have a voice in the retirement plan's design, its implementation, and investment procedures.*

* *The Fair Labor Standards Act provided for premium pay for workers who work over a specified number of hours. When overtime rates are applied to one's gross pay for the pay period, those benefits that are contingent on the gross amount, such as Social Security, increase in cost.*

* *The Employee Retirement Income Security Act has had one of the greatest impacts on benefits administration. ERISA requires that pension programs be funded appropriately, that the provisions of the program be communicated to employees, and ensures that employees' retirement is protected from abuse. ERISA created a requirement that after a specified period of time (now five years) employees have a permanent claim to their pension funds (called vesting rights).*

* *A 401(k) program is a retirement program named after the IRS tax code from which it was established. These programs are usually set up such that employees may contribute a portion of their yearly income to a retirement account on a tax deferred basis. Many companies that offer 401(k) programs provide an additional incentive to participate by offering matching contribution features.*

* *The Health Maintenance Act requires employers who offer health insurance to their employees to also offer alternative health care options. HMOs are a means of obtaining health care coverage with a fixed out-of-pocket expense.*

* *The Consolidated Omnibus Budget Reconciliation Act provides for the continuation of health benefits for a period of time, usually six months, after an employee severs employment with the organization.*

* *The Civil Rights Act, and other similar legislation, has had a great impact on benefits administration. The benefits specialist must ensure that the benefits offered are being administered without adversely affecting any particular group. The most notable issues arising for the benefits administrator are in the areas of age and sex discrimination.*

KEY TERMS

Age discrimination	Mandatory bargaining issues
Bread and butter issues	Matching contribution plans
Capital accumulation plans	Nonexempt Jobs
Civil Rights Act of 1964	Overtime pay
Consolidated Omnibus Budget	Pension Benefit Guarantee
Reconciliation Act of 1984	Corporation (PBGC)
Employee Retirement Income	Pregnancy Disability Act of 1978
Security Act of 1974 (ERISA)	Sex discrimination
Exempt jobs	Shortened work week
Fair Labor Standards Act of 1938	Title VII
401(k)	Vesting rights
Health Maintenance	Wage-hour Act
Organization Act of 1973	
Individual retirement accounts	

QUESTIONS FOR REVIEW AND DISCUSSION

1. How have changes in management practices over the past two decades affected the benefits offered to employees?

2. Describe benefits offered to employees that are a direct spillover from gains made by the unionized sector of the work force.

3. "Unions are using the 1949 Supreme Court ruling to the detriment of management. Based on the decision, unions have a greater voice in where their retirement funds are invested and, as such, are creating an atmosphere of dictating management investment options." Do you agree or disagree with the statement? Explain.

4. "When a company negotiates for wage and benefit give-backs during financially troubled times, it has a responsibility to return the give-backs to the workers when the financial outlook improves." Do you agree or disagree with the statement? Explain.

5. How does overtime pay affect benefits?

6. Describe the rationale behind the enactment of ERISA? Has it been working?

7. How do 401(k) programs operate? What can an employer do to ensure participation?

8. What is the significance of the Consolidated Omnibus Budget Reconciliation Act? Why was it established?

9. How has the Pregnancy Disability Act of 1978 affected benefits administration? Under what conditions is an employer bound by the act?

10. "Sex differences should be considered when benefits are offered. If one group lives longer, or displays other characteristics that affect the cost of a benefit, this should be factored into the cost calculations." Do you agree or disagree with the statement? Explain.

ADDITIONAL READINGS

CLARK, JEFFREY, and STEPHEN BOGART.   "Employer Fringe Benefits Can't Discriminate against Pregnancy" *Business Journal* 3, no. 23 (March 24, 1986): 24.

Commerce Clearing House. "Human Resource Management, Ideas and Trends: Benefits Survey." no. 162, February 1988.

MINER, W. J.   "Ask a Benefits Actuary: Discriminating Tests Require Actuarial Help" *Business Insurance* 21 (June 1987): 52.

SCHULTZ, PAUL T., and FRANCES G. SIELLER.   "Retirement Equity Act of 1984" *Employee Relations Law Journal* 10 (Winter 1984): 546-50.

SLATER, KAREN.   "Pension Plans Offer More under Tax Bill" *Wall Street Journal*, May 12, 1986, p. 27.

CHAPTER THREE

COMPENSATION AND HUMAN RESOURCE MANAGEMENT

LEARNING OBJECTIVES

After reading this chapter you will be able to:

* *Describe the goals of compensation administration.*
* *Describe the human resource planning process.*
* *Describe the strategic planning process and how it relates to human resource planning.*
* *Describe the job analysis process.*
* *Describe the three outcomes of job analysis.*
* *Describe how retrenchment affects human resource planning.*
* *Describe the goals of recruitment.*
* *Describe the goals of selection.*
* *Describe socialization, training, and development.*
* *Describe the performance evaluation process.*
* *Describe the job evaluation process.*
* *Describe how wage surveys, wage curves, and wage structures are related.*
* *Describe how benefits fit into the total human resource framework.*

INTRODUCTION

An organization does not establish its benefits package in isolation. The benefits offered to employees oftentimes closely align with the compensation philosophy of the organization. For instance, if the organization's intention is to attract and retain the "best" employees, then its compensation and benefits system will exhibit those characteristics. If, however, the organization is interested only in filling vacancies with "warm bodies," then a different picture is painted.

As part of the focus of this book, in conjunction with the management practice of recognizing the value of employees, we would like to spend some time talking about the role of compensation in benefits. The pay levels set in an organization reflect the worth the organization places on the value of the job. To determine this worth, employers must proceed through a process known as job analysis. But the chore does not stop there. Why are various jobs needed in the organization? How are individuals selected for employment? Why does the organization evaluate performance of its employees? Answers to questions such as these will be answered in this chapter as we look at the overall human resource management function in relation to the benefits package.

ROLE OF COMPENSATION ADMINISTRATION

Employees who work for organizations do so in exchange for rewards. Probably the most important reward, and certainly the most obvious, is money. But just how much money should be paid? The search for an answer throws us directly into the topic of compensation administration.

The goals of compensation administration are to design the lowest cost-pay structure that will attract, motivate, and retain competent employees. This structure, while low in cost, must, however, be perceived as fair by the employees. Fairness is a term that frequently arises in the administration of an organization's compensation program. Organizations generally seek to pay the least they can in order to minimize costs. So fairness means a wage or salary that is adequate for the demands and requirements of the job. But, of course, fairness is a two-way street. Employees also want fair compensation. If they perceive that their work effort does not lead to a satisfactory reward (wage/salary level), employees will attempt to correct this problem in many ways, most of which are negative in nature. Accordingly, both the employer and the employee search for wages that are fair.

How do employers know if they have a fair compensation plan? How do they know if it is actually effective in motivating employees? The answers lie in hard work. Employers must conduct surveys of pay scales in similar jobs in their competitive area, and then translate that information into a salary structure of their own.

Organizations must recognize that while they pay employees, compensation systems are predominantly designed around jobs. That is, the skills, knowledge, and abilities, in association with the job incumbent's responsibilities, determine a pay range. The actual performance of the incumbents determines where they are placed within a pay range. We must also keep in mind that government policies have an impact on wages. In designing the wage structure, the human resource specialist must be aware of the requirements of such laws as the Fair Labor Standards Act, the Equal Pay Act, the Civil Rights Act, and laws that directly affect benefits administration (Chapter 2). The point of mentioning these laws is to make you aware that government constraints may reduce management's discretion on compensation decision, and set guidelines for determining what is fair compensation.

Before we get into the specifics of determining the wage structure, let us first review necessary prerequisites of compensation administration.

THE TOTAL FRAMEWORK

Human Resource Planning

Whenever an organization is in the process of determining its human resource needs, we say that it is actively engaged in human resource planning. Human resource planning is one of the more important elements in a successful human resource management program. Specifically, human resource planning is the process by which an organization ensures that it has the right number and kinds of people at the right places, at the right time, capable of effectively and efficiently completing those tasks that will help the organization achieve its overall objectives. Human resource planning, then, translates the organization's objectives and plans into the number of workers needed to meet those objectives. Without clear-cut planning, estimation of an organization's human resource need is reduced to mere guesswork.

In many organizations, few employees outside of upper management know the short- and long-range objectives. It is not surprising, therefore, that management may find itself without the necessary human resources to fill unexpected vacancies, make replacements created by natural attrition, or meet opportunities created by the growth or development of new products or services. To ensure that these people are available, to provide smooth development of an organization, companies engage in human resource planning. Its purpose is to assess where the organization is, where it is going, and what implications these assessments have on future supplies of, and demand for, human resources. Attempts must then be made to match supplies and demands, making them compatible with the achievement of the organization's future needs.

Strategic Planning. Decades ago most organizations did very little strategic planning. The efforts made were often more an exercise in guessing than in determining the strategies of the organization. Today that has changed. With more emphasis on global competition, and the need to find one's niche to be competitive, the strategic planning process has taken on greater importance. While our intention is not to go into the detail of strategic planning that a management text would do[1] it is important for the human resource specialist to understand what is going on. More importantly, in today's organizations the human resource director is playing a more vital role in the strategic planning of the organization.

The process of strategic planning is a long and tedious one. Our intent in this section is not to advocate that it is a simple technique, but rather to provide a general overview of the process. The first step in strategic planning is to determine the organization's mission, which is designed to answer the questions; Who are we, and what business are we in? The necessity to define clearly one's line of business is paramount, for business survival today is often contingent on an organization's niche in the marketplace. Once the organization has determined what business it is in (typically after months of extensive investigation), the executives set the company direction for the next several years — generally one year, five years, and twenty years. These plans are referred to as the strategic plans which provide the guidelines for the organization to follow. More importantly, these plans identify the goals of the organization for the short and long terms. Once these directions have been established, the organization must provide specific details as to how the strategic plans are to be met. This information is translated into operational, or short-term plans, which lay out the necessary day-to-day activities to meet the corporation's goal synergistically. In order to make these operational plans "operational," various aspects of the organization must be assessed. Changes that are to be made should be made at that time; in support of the strategic plans established. That is, the structure of the organization, and its people needs, may require some fine tuning. Figure 3–1 is a composite of the strategic planning process. Notice that strategies need to be established first. Given a set of strategic plans, the organization must consider its structure. In this context, structure refers not only to the reporting relationships in the organization, but also to the specific jobs required. Once the structure has been set, it is then time for the people. During the structure assessment, when organizations determine what jobs are needed, they must identify the number, and the skills, knowledge, and abilities required of the incumbent to be a successful performer. That determination of job requirements is attained through a process called job analysis. One interesting aspect of this process is that each job in the organization is ultimately tied to its strategic plan. In a day and age when effectiveness and efficiency are so important to assist in the global competitive environment of business, there is reason to understand why human resource management is becoming more valuable to the organization.

---

[1] For a comprehensive review of strategic planning, see James Brian Quinn, Henry Mintzberg, and Robert M. James, *The Strategic Process* (Englewood Cliffs,N.J.: Prentice Hall, 1988).

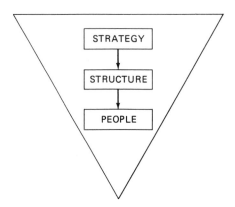

FIGURE 3-1   Strategic Planning Process

Job Analysis.   To ensure that each job in the organization is required, and to understand how that job fits into the overall scheme of things, a systematic exploration of the activities within a job, or job analysis, must be conducted.   It is a basic technical procedure, one that is used to define the duties, responsibilities, and accountabilities of a job.   This analysis "involves compiling a detailed description of tasks, determining the relationship of the job to technology and to other jobs, and examining the knowledge, qualifications, employment standards, accountabilities and other incumbent requirements."[2]

In sum, a job analysis indicates what activities and accountabilities the job entails.   There is no mystery to a job analysis; it is an accurate recording of the activities involved.   A bit of caution, however, about the job analysis is in order.   One of the biggest misconceptions about it is that it is a tangible product.   It is not.   The job analysis is the conceptual, analytical process or action from which we develop our tangible outcomes: job descriptions, job specifications, and job evaluations.

A job description is a written statement of what the jobholder does, how it is done, and why it is done.   This information should accurately portray job content, environment, and conditions of employment.   A common format for a job description includes the job title, the duties to be performed, the distinguishing characteristics of the job, and the authority and responsibilities of the jobholder.   The importance of an accurate job description cannot be overstated.   As mentioned above, it is critical to the overall attainment of an

---

[2] Richard I. Henderson, *Compensation Management*, 4th ed. (Reston,Va.: Reston Publishing Co., 1985), p. 154.

organization's strategic objectives. It is also necessary for recruiting and selection matters, for performance appraisal purposes, and for compensation administration. In fact, almost all human resource management activities, including compliance with antidiscrimination laws, revolve around sound job descriptions.

The second by-product of job analysis is the job specification,which states the minimum acceptable qualifications that the incumbent must possess to perform the job successfully. Based on the information acquired through job analysis, the specification identifies the knowledge, skills, and abilities needed to do the job effectively. Individuals possessing the personal characteristics identified in the job specification should perform the job more effectively than individuals lacking them. The job specification, therefore, is an important tool in the recruitment and selection process, for it keeps the selector's attention on the list of qualifications necessary for an incumbent to perform the job, and assists in determining whether candidates are qualified.

In addition to providing data for job descriptions and specifications, the job analysis is also valuable in providing the information that makes comparison of jobs possible. If an organization is to have an equitable compensation program, jobs that have similar demands in terms of skills, education, and other personal characteristics should be placed in common compensation groups. Job evaluation contributes toward that end by specifying the relative value of each job in the organization. It, therefore, is an important part of compensation administration.

Putting It Together.   We have a lot of pieces floating in the air at this point. Let's put them together with respect to human resource planning as shown in Figure 3–2. If we consider the need to plan strategically, then the first concern is to ensure that the goals of the organization have been set. This not only tells us where the organization is going, but also alludes to the demand for human resources. Realizing that a specific mix of human resources is required when this is established, we must assess what human resources currently exist in the organization (called a human resource inventory[3]). If any discrepancies are identified, that is, if there are specific needs and no one in-house to fill those needs, then they must be filled from outside of the organization. In other words, the supply and demand of labor are being matched for the organization. If supply exceeds demand, there are more employees than needed, and some must be removed from the organization.

---

[3] A human resource inventory is a report compiled on the current human resources of an organization. Typically it includes a list of the names of the employees, their education levels, training, prior employment, current position, performance ratings, salary levels, languages spoken, capabilities, and specialized skills. The advent of computerized systems for human resources has helped to facilitate this process.

This process of removing people is often called downsizing, or retrenchment.[4] If, however, demand exceeds supply, a recruiting drive is necessary. It is important to note that both outcomes may occur simultaneously. After linking specific jobs to the strategic plan, some job openings may occur in areas of the organization. At the same time, however, some jobs may have become obsolete, or are no longer viable parts of the objectives of the company.

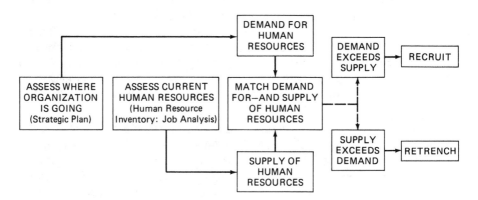

FIGURE 3-2   Human Resource Planning Process

When the human resource planning efforts are completed, and if job openings exist, applicants must then be recruited and selected.

Recruitment and Selection

The Recruiting Effort.   Successful human resource planning should have identified the human resource needs. The next step, then, is to get people to apply to the organization. Recruiting is the discovering of potential candidates for actual or anticipated organizational vacancies, that is, the bringing together of those with jobs to fill and those seeking employment.

The goals of the ideal recruitment effort are twofold. The first emphasis is to attract a large number of qualified applicants who will take the job if offered. Second, the recruiting effort should provide information so that the unqualified applicants can self-select themselves out of job candidacy. In essence, a good recruiting program is one that will attract the qualified and not attract the unqualified. This dual objective is designed to maximize the recruiting budget expenditures.

---

[4] For more information on retrenchment in an organization, see David A. De Cenzo and Stephen P. Robbins, *Personnel/Human Resource Management*, 3d ed (Englewood Cliffs;N.J.: Prentice Hall, 1988), pp. 87-91.

Although all organizations will at one time or another engage in recruiting, some do so to a much larger extent. Obviously, size of the organization is a factor. However, certain other variables will also influence the extent of recruiting. These variables can be seen as employment market conditions, the image of the organization, the job itself, and the effectiveness of past recruiting efforts. Working conditions and salary and benefits packages offered to employees will also impact the acquisition and retention of new employees. This aspect is critical to the recruiting process and directly linked to compensation administration. Once again, the compensation philosophy plays a vital role in determining whether the goals of recruiting are met.

The Selection Process. After the pool of qualified applicants is recruited, the organization must begin the process of thinning this set. That is one of the major objectives of selection. The organization needs to assess the applicants against the criteria established in the job analysis in order to predict which job applicants will be successful if hired. Doing so involves various steps, called the selection process.

All selection activities, from an initial screening to a possible physical examination, exist for the purpose of making effective selection decisions. Each activity in the process forms a predictive exercise—managerial decision-makers seek to predict which applicants will be successful if hired. Successful, in this context, refers to performing well on the criteria that the organization uses to evaluate its employees.

In a selection decision, four outcomes are possible. As shown in Figure 3–3, two of these outcomes would indicate correct decisions; two would indicate errors. Correct decisions are those where the applicant was predicted to be successful and later did prove to be successful on the job, or where the applicant was predicted to be unsuccessful and would have performed accordingly. In the former case, we have successfully accepted; in the later case, we have successfully rejected. The purpose of selection activities is to develop outcomes shown as "correct decisions" in Figure 3–3.

Problems occur when errors are made: rejecting candidates who later perform successfully on the job (reject errors) or accepting those individuals who subsequently perform poorly on the job (accept errors). These problems are, unfortunately, far from insignificant. Reject errors historically meant that the costs in performing selection activities would be increases. Today, selection techniques that result in reject errors may open the employer to charges of violating Title VII of the Civil Rights Act, especially if certain categories of applicants (such as women and minorities) are disproportionately rejected.[5] Accept errors, on the other hand, have very obvious costs to the

---

[5] A June 1989 Supreme Court decision has changed the interpretation of disproportionate selection. The burden is now on the individual to prove the allegation.

		ACCEPT	REJECT
LATER JOB PERFORMANCE	SUCCESSFUL	CORRECT DECISION	REJECT ERROR (Potential Adverse Impact)
	UNSUCCESFUL	ACCEPT ERROR (Bad Business Decision)	CORRECT DECISION

FIGURE 3-3   Selection Decision Outcomes

organization, including the cost of training, the costs generated (or profits forgone) due to the employee's incompetence, the cost of severance, and the subsequent costs of further recruiting and selection screening.[6] The major thrust of any selection activity, therefore, is to reduce the probability of making reject or accept errors while increasing the probability of making correct decisions.

Of lesser importance, but still an objective of the selection process, is informing and selling the candidate on the job and the organization. This secondary objective receives less attention probably because it is so closely intertwined with recruitment, but it shows itself throughout the selection process. In actuality, the selection process represents an effort to balance the objectives of evaluating and attracting. The interview is an obvious example of an activity that must serve both objectives. While the interviewer is attempting to acquire information about the candidate to make an intelligent selection decision, he or she is informing the applicant about the job and the organization. Topics discussed often include the pros and cons of working for the organization, and from a personal standpoint, growth potential, how performance is evaluated, company benefits, and salary ranges.[7] This latter activity is critical if the organization is to be successful in "selling" itself to the candidate. If the organization fails to do this, there is little likelihood that the

---

[6] For a review of the costs of turnover, see Thomas F. Cawsey and William C. Wedley, "Labor Turnover Costs: Measurements and Control," *Personnel Journal*, February 1979, pp. 90-95.

[7] This information given is often referred to as a realistic job preview (RJP). For more information on RJPs, see John P. Wanous, "Effects of a Realistic Job Preview on Job Acceptance, Job Attitudes, and Job Survival," *Journal of Applied Psychology*, June 1973, pp. 327-32; and D. R. Ilgen and W. Seely, "Realistic Expectations as an Aid in Reducing Voluntary Resignations," *Journal of Applied Psychology*, August 1974, pp. 452-55.

applicant would accept the job even if offered. Additionally, this trading of information between applicant and interviewer can be valuable in allowing individuals with low chances of being chosen to self-select out of the process. This saves both the organization and the applicant from "losing face" due to a rejection decision.

In summary, selection has two objectives: (1) to predict which job applicants would be successful if hired and (2) to inform and sell the candidate on the job and the organization. Unfortunately, these two objectives are not always compatible. Putting a candidate through hours of filling out forms, taking tests, and completing interviews rarely endears the organization to the candidate. These are tiresome and often stressful activities. Yet if selection activities place too great an emphasis on public relations, obtaining the information needed to make successful selection decisions may be hindered. Accordingly, a manager's dilemma in selection is how to balance the desire to attract people with the desire to gather relevant selection data.

Socialization, Training, and Development

Socialization. Socialization is an important aspect in assisting a new employee to adapt to the environment of the newly joined organization—a different work activity, a new boss, different groups of co-workers and probably a different set of standards for what constitutes good performance.

The benefits of socialization flow to the organization and to the new employee. "Organizational results are not simply the consequences of the work accomplished by people brought in to the organization; rather, they are the consequences of the work these people accomplish after the organization itself has completed its work on them."[8] The organization gets higher productivity, greater employee commitment, and lower turnover rates. Employees achieve reduced anxiety, increased awareness of what is expected on the job, and an increased feeling of being accepted by their peers and bosses. When socialization works, employees receive the confidence and satisfaction that comes from feeling that they are members in good standing in the organization.

Training and Development. Training is a learning experience that seeks a relatively permanent change in individuals to improve their ability to perform on the job. We typically say training can involve the changing of skills, knowledge, attitudes, or work behaviors. It may mean changing what employees know, how they work, their attitudes toward their work, or their interactions with their co-workers or their supervisors.

---

[8] John Van Maanen, and Edgar H. Schein, "Toward a Theory of Organizational Socialization," in *Research in Organizational Behavior*, ed. Barry M. Staw (Greenwich, Conn.: JAI Press, 1979), p. 255.

In our definition, training reflects those activities that are designed to assist the operative employees in doing their jobs better. Its emphasis is in the present time frame, facilitating better understanding of the job skills, knowledge, and abilities needed to perform more effectively and efficiently on one's current job. Development, on the other hand, carries with it a futuristic orientation in that it focuses on jobs an employee may hold in the future. As such, development is more concerned with education—or assisting a worker to become a better performer. Education in this context refers to development activities that attempt to instill sound reasoning processes in an effort to enhance one's ability to understand and interpret knowledge. Thus development focuses more on the employee's personal growth.

Performance Evaluations

One of the last areas to be discussed in this total human resource framework is the manner in which an employee's performance is appraised. Because organizations exist to achieve goals, the degree of success that employees have in reaching their individual goals is important in determining organization effectiveness. The evaluation of this success, therefore, becomes a critical part of human resource management and translates into pay for performance, which also affects compensation administration.

But what does performance really mean? Employees are performing well when they are productive. But how is productivity measured? It is most desirable to have objective measures of productivity. These objective measures refer to hard data on one's effectiveness—such data as units produced, dollar volume of sales, percentage of crimes solved, and so on. Unfortunately for some jobs, these hard measures are lacking. Does that mean those positions are not evaluated? No, it does not. What it does reveal, however, is that in those cases where quantifiable measures are not easily obtained, substitute measures must be used. Those measures can be almost anything, from attitude about the job to enthusiasm and appearance.

In addition to productivity, performance also includes personal data such as measures of accidents, turnover, absences, and tardiness. That is, a good employee is one who not only performs well in terms of productivity but also minimizes problems for the organization by getting to work on time, by not missing days, and by minimizing the number of work related accidents.

To evaluate a worker's performance, the work being done must be compared to some standard. There are generally three types of standards that exist. The first is the absolute standard. That is, the employee is measured against corporate standards set for his or her job. In this case, each employee is evaluated independently of any other employee's work behavior. In a relative standard, each employee is rated against all other employees, producing a ranking of the best to the worst. The third approach makes use of objectives. Employees are evaluated by how well they accomplished a specific set of mutually acceptable objectives that have been determined to be critical in the successful completion of their jobs. This approach is often called management by objectives.[9] (It would be beyond our scope to go into specific detail about the various types of performance appraisal techniques, or the problems associated with each. Our goal however, is to emphasize the role of the performance evaluation in compensation administration. As such, broad-based coverage of performance evaluations will not be provided.[10]

In many organizations pay increases are tied to a performance evaluation. After a period of time, usually one year, employees are evaluated using the existing performance appraisal system of the organization. Typically, if one achieves a rating other than unsatisfactory, a pay increase is awarded. In instances such as these, the performance evaluation has a direct link to compensation adminstration. Once again, the compensation philosophy plays a major role. As employees are evaluated, are there company policies that govern the number of employees that can be appraised as outstanding? Given the highest percentage increase? Or are there constraints placed on the review because an employee has "maxed out" in his or her salary range, and a pay increase can only be given if the range limits are moved? Answers to questions such as these are contingent on the process established in the compensation program. We would like to think that there is a direct link of pay increases to performance level, and that it should be awarded according to the effort put forth. But that may not be probable in all cases. A performance evaluation will affect the compensation of an employee, but it does so only to the extent the compensation program allows. There is no chicken and egg syndrome here. Compensation administration dictates what will be done.

Job Evaluation and Pay

Job Evaluation Defined. Earlier we stated that the job analysis is the process of determining the duties of a job, authority relationships, skills required, working conditions, and additional relevant information. One of the outcomes of the job analysis is the job evaluation. Job evaluation uses the information in the job analysis to determine systematically the value of each job in relation to all jobs within the organization, that is, to rank all the jobs in the organization and place them in a hierarchy that will reflect the relative worth of each. Most important, however, is that this ranking is that of jobs, not people. Job evaluations assume average performance by the job incumbent. In

---

[9] For a comprehensive review of management by objectives, see H. John Bernardin and Richard W. Beatty, *Performance Appraisal: Addressing Human Behavior at Work* (Boston: Kent Publishing, 1984), chaps. 4, 6.

[10] For a more thorough coverage of performance appraisals, see David A. De Cenzo and Stephen P. Robbins, *Personnel/Human Resource Management* (Englewood Cliffs, N.J.: Prentice Hall, 1988), chap. 14.

effect, this process ignores individual abilities or the performance of the worker.

The ranking that results from a job evaluation is the means to an end, not an end itself. It should be used to determine the organization's pay structure. There are, however, external factors that may negate the job evaluation process. Factors such as a collective bargaining agreement or labor market shortages may require deviations from the "standard" analysis of job evaluation.

The heart of job evaluation is determining what criteria will be used to rank jobs. It is easy to say that jobs are valued and ranked by their relative worth, but there is far more ambiguity when attempting to state what makes one job higher than another in the job-structure hierarchy. Most job evaluation techniques use some combination of skill, effort, responsibility, and working conditions as major criteria. Each of these, however, can be broken down into smaller parts. "Skill, for example, is often measured by education and experience, mental effort is often differentiated from physical effort, and responsibility of various kinds may be delineated."[11] Nonetheless, however the criteria are defined, four methods of job evaluation can be used: the ranking method (ranking jobs from highest to lowest); the classification method (establishing job grades); the factor comparison method (assigning a dollar value based on various job factors, like mental requirements, skill requirements, and so on); and the point method (allocating point values for the degree a criterion is present in a job). Once the job evaluation is complete, its data become the nucleus for developing the organization's pay structure.[12] This means establishing pay rates or ranges that are compatible with the ranks, classifications, or points arrived at through job evaluation.

Any of the four job evaluation methods can provide the necessary input for developing the organization's overall pay structure. Each has its strengths and weaknesses, but because of its focus on relevant job criteria, the point method has become the preferred choice. In using the point method, point totals are combined with wage survey data to form wage curves.

Wage Surveys.   Most organizations use surveys to gather information on pay practices within specific communities and among firms in their industry. This information is used for comparison purposes. It can tell management if the organization's wages are in line with those of other employers and, in cases where there is a short supply of individuals to fill certain positions, may be used to set wage levels.

---

[11] David W. Belcher, *Compensation Administration* (Englewood Cliffs,N.J.: Prentice Hall, 1974), p. 90.

[12] For a thorough mathematical discussion of various methods of determining the pay structure, see Henderson, *Compensation Management*, pp. 379-425.

Wage survey data are available from the Department of Labor, through the Bureau of Labor Statistics. These data are broken down by geographic area, industry, and occupation. Many industry and employee associations also collect their own information and make their results known. Some organizations, especially the larger ones, conduct their own surveys.

Wage Curves.   When management arrives at point totals from job evaluation and obtains survey data on what comparable organizations are paying for similar jobs, a wage curve can be constructed to tell management the average relationship between points of established pay grades and wage base rates. In addition, it can identify jobs whose pay is out of the trend line.

Wage Structure.   It is only a short step from plotting a wage curve to developing the organization's wage structure. Jobs that are similar in terms of class, grades, or points are grouped together. The more important jobs are paid more; and as individuals assume jobs of greater importance, they rise within the wage hierarchy. Pay grades generally have a range, and successive ranges overlap with the preceding one. This is done to reflect differences in seniority, as well as performance. Also, while most organizations create a degree of overlap between grades, employees who reach the top of their grade can only increase their pay by moving to a higher grade, or as stated in "Performance Evaluations," by having the maximum of the range increased.

Conclusion

Compensation administration is part of every organization. These systems must be tailored to meet the objectives and needs of the company. While exact techniques can be offered for developing salary ranges, compensation systems in practice differ in scope. Regardless of the system used, the bottom line is that people work for money. Money is used to attract, motivate, and retain the best employees; the importance of compensation administration, therefore,cannot be overstated.

In this chapter we have tried to provide a basis for human resource management and show its relationship to compensation. There is no doubt about the complexities and intricacies involved. The awareness, however, that it is all linked does reveal the need for the benefits specialist to understand all of the ramifications that human resource policies have on benefits administration. If benefits are a function of one's salary and level in the organization (e.g., more vacation time, life insurance benefits, and so on), then anything that affects compensation will ultimately spill over to the benefits arena.

SUMMARY

After reading this chapter you will know that:

* The goals of compensation administration are to design the lowest cost-pay structure that will attract, motivate, and retain competent employees. The program must also be perceived as fair by employees.

* Human resource planning is a process of ensuring the right number and kinds of employees, at the right places, at the right time, capable of effectively and efficiently completing those tasks that will help the organization achieve its goals.

* The strategic planning process of an organization sets the direction for the organization to follow. After establishing its mission, goals and objectives are set. In order to achieve these goals, structural issues must be addressed, including the skills, knowledge, and abilities an incumbent needs to be a successful performer. Once the structure is in place, and the jobs identified that are needed to achieve the organization's goals, human resource planning attempts to match the demand for human resources with its supply.

* Job analysis is the process of systematically analyzing the activities with each job. It is designed to define the duties, responsibilities, and accountabilities of the job.

* The three outcomes of job analysis are the job description (a description of what the jobholder does), the job specification (those personal characteristics a jobholder must possess to be successful on the job), and job evaluation (determining the relative worth of each job).

* Retrenchment is a special case of human resource planning. When the supply of human resources is greater than the demand, an organization must find ways to downsize. This downsizing is called retrenchment.

* The goals of recruiting are twofold. The first focuses on attracting a large number of qualified applicants, who, if offered the job, would accept it. The second focus is on providing enough information to prospective applicants so that the unqualified self-select out.

* The goals of selection are to predict which applicants would be successful if hired, and to inform and sell the candidate on the job and the organization.

* The performance evaluation process involves assessing an employee's performance against various criteria. This process can use absolute standards, relative standards, or objectives.

* Job evaluation is a process that ranks all the jobs in the organization in accordance to their relative worth. Using various criteria, jobs are rated based on their contribution to the overall organization's goal attainment.

* Wage surveys are used to gather information from an organization's surrounding community, or industry, regarding pay levels for similar jobs. This information is analyzed, resulting in a wage curve. This curve shows

the relationship between points of an established pay grade and wage rates. The wage structure uses the above information in forming pay ranges.

* Benefits are a function of one's salary and level in the organization. The effects of changes in a compensation system ultimately affect benefits administration. Compensation and benefits share a closely linked relationship.

KEY TERMS

Accept errors	Productivity
Classification method	Operational plans
Compensation administration	Ranking method
Development	Recruiting
Downsizing	Reject errors
Factor comparison method	Retrenchment
Human resource planning	Selection
Job analysis	Socialization
Job description	Strategic planning
Job evaluation	Strategic plans
Job specification	Training
Management by objective	Wage curve
Mission	Wage structure
Performance	Wage survey
Point method	

QUESTIONS FOR REVIEW AND DISCUSSION

1. What is compensation administration? What does it entail?
2. Define human resource planning. Outline the steps involved in the human resource planning process.
3. "The activities of each worker must be linked to the strategic plan of the organization." Describe how this can be accomplished through a human resource planning effort.
4. "A retrenchment effort is short term. The company must buckle down, sweat through it until it can resume normal operations." Do you agree or disagree with the statement? Discuss.
5. What is the relationship between job analysis, job description, job specification, and job evaluation?

6. What is the "dual objective" of recruiting? Of selection?

7. Contrast reject errors and accept errors. Which one is more likely to open an employer to charges of discrimination? Why?

8. Discuss what you believe to be an optimum performance appraisal system. Describe its content and how it would operate.

9. Differentiate between wage surveys, wage curves, and wage structures.

10. Discuss how subjectivity can be successfully removed from compensation.

ADDITIONAL READINGS

"Behind-the-Scenes Look at Hiring Practices." *Policy and Practice Series: Personnel Management* 33, no. 24 (May 19, 1986): 1-3.

Bureau of National Affairs. "Performance Appraisals: Making Them Work" *Bulletin to Management* 37 no. 9 (February 27, 1986): 67-71.

"Here's Help in Planning a Move or Adding New Locations." *Alert* 36, no. 1 (January 1, 1986): 3-4.

Quinn, Gene. "Surviving Layoff." *EAP Digest* 7, no. 3 (March-April 1987): 31-34.

Selter, Marvin R. "On the Plus Side of Employee Leasing." *Personnel Journal* 65, no. 4 (April 1986): 87-88

CHAPTER FOUR

BENEFITS
AND PRODUCTIVITY

LEARNING OBJECTIVES

After reading this chapter you will be able to:

* *Describe the impact of the numerous variables on productivity.*
* *Identify the relationship between quality and productivity.*
* *Describe which aspect of employee stock ownership plans help promote productivity improvements.*
* *Describe the type of recognition programs having a reverse effect on productivity.*
* *Describe what points to emphasize with respect to employee assistance programs to have them effect productivity improvements.*
* *Describe the relationship between benefits, productivity, job descriptions, and performance evaluation systems.*
* *Describe how pensions can be proactive to induce workers to stay extra years versus retiring early.*
* *Describe how unions deal with the connection between benefits programs and productivity.*
* *Describe the effect of new technologies on a company's ability to communicate benefits to its members.*

INTRODUCTION

Only among dictionaries is there any apparent consistency in the definition of productivity. The top producing foreign countries measure productivity through quality improvements and teamwork efforts. They appear to shy away from the U.S. tradition of crowing superstars, believing this causes too much general discord and lack of attention to product quality. In the United States the definition of productivity falls into two main categories. The first group measures productivity as short-term earnings per share and other bottom-line measures. The second measure comes from straight numeric output. Both of these definitions can produce a false sense of security. To focus on short-term bottom-line data can result in such major long-term difficulties as lowered product quality, shifts of employment to lower-paying Third World countries, divestiture of company assets, and neglect of individual employee benefits.

To limit our measure of productivity to straight numeric terms allows for the "head-in-the-sand" routine. For example, a Labor Department publication, reported virtually across-the-board increases in productivity. However, the increases were not the result of strong growth in output. In many cases, this positive productivity gain resulted from employee layoffs—reducing labor hours faster than the output fell.[1] Obviously we would not as a nation like to continue this sort of "increase" in productivity. This straight numeric process could theoretically have us increasing productivity until the point of bankruptcy.

The productivity perspective examined in this chapter will deviate from both methods mentioned above. Specifically, we want to look at the effect of productivity improvements as they relate to benefits. Certainly numeric figures and earnings per share will be part of the discussion, as they should be, but the quality issues will also be integrated. Productivity enhancement becomes a "state of being," approached from many points of view.

MOTIVATION REVIEWED

When attempting to cure productivity woes, we frequently look to the concept of motivation. The average worker perceives motivation as being synonymous with inspiration. This involves either the spiritual-like inspiration that comes from the depths of the worker to produce high quality or high output, or that delivered by management to generate the same results. With this shallow level of understanding, motivation becomes both a whipping tool and a rationalization. If workers are not performing up to expected levels they are often classified as not motivated. This inspirational mode, however, is not the definition of motivation we promote in this chapter. Rather, we would like to view motivation as a function of management to create a positive work environment, one that is conducive for employees to put forth the effort necessary to achieve productivity goals.

---

[1] U.S. Department of Labor, Bureau of Labor Statistics, *Productivity Measures for Selected Industries and Government Services*, Bulletin no. 2296 (Washington, D.C.: GPO, 1982), p.2.

This frame of reference means that when an employee is apparently "not motivated," management does not immediately assume it is a worker problem. Rather, before any claim is made that the employee is not working up to potential, a number of items must first be examined. These components include:

- When was the worker's job description last updated? Is the employee doing the job according to the outdated job description, but not the way you envision the job operating now?
- When was the job last analyzed? Has the nature of the work changed? How is this change communicated to the employee?
- Is the performance evaluation system linked to the job description? Are you measuring the appropriate criteria?
- Do you pay for performance or reward other factors? Are compensation and benefits plans linked to job performance?
- Is management ensuring that it provides the best tools, information, job design, equipment, and layout to employees so that a job well done can be achieved?

If there are aspects lacking from this list, they should be addressed before labeling someone unmotivated. Finally, do employee skills, knowledge, and ability match the jobs? There are many actions that can be taken before labeling employees unproductive and then mentally writing them off. Most of these options lay in management's court as points of professional management.

INFLUENCES ON PRODUCTIVITY

Jerome Rosow, president of the Work in America Institute, details four broad factors that will influence productivity in the future. These areas include the availability of capital, the rate of interest on capital, the introduction of new technology, and the productive quality of the work force.[2] The relative importance of each, however, is somewhat tempered by inflation.

This grouping of four is balanced by the more traditional list of productivity factors, such as research and development, government regulations, energy prices, changes in the work ethic, and the influx of women and minorities into the work force. The Council of Economic Advisers has indicated that while many factors affect productivity, none can be singled out as a reason for productivity declines. In fact, the hope for improved productivity is often questionable.[3]

---

[2] Jerome Rosow, "Productivity and People," in *Productivity: Prospects for Growth*, ed. Jerome Rosow, (New York: D. Van Nostrand Company, 1981), p. 243.

[3] Ibid., p. 245.

For the purposes of our discussion, the Rosow study highlights the complexity and interconnection of the variables affecting productivity. For example, if energy prices rise, cost reductions are in order. And typically the first place where funding is cut is in research and development. If capital spending does not occur, the likelihood of sufficient money for new technology is reduced. If management style is based on philosophies not in tune with those of the younger and more educated workers, the motivation to achieve a productive and quality-conscious work force will be in question.

Quality and Productivity

In the seventh annual productivity survey of industrial engineers conducted by the Institute of Industrial Engineers, approximately 64 percent had quality improvement programs implemented in their organizations. Of them, about 45 percent reported the programs were effective. Within this group, about 60 percent believe recognition, and specifically not money, was the path to increase productivity levels.[4] Other points of interest from the survey included:

- The major obstacle to productivity was management's failure to dedicate sufficient manpower for productivity changes.
- Fifty-nine percent believe loyalty of workers had declined, with 30 percent believing people do not work as hard now as eighteen years ago.[5]

The group was also asked to rank items having the greatest impact on improving the quality of goods and services produced. From a high to low ranking, these included: worker training, corporate culture, quality circles, quality control procedures, vendor/user relationships, and more capital expenditure.[6]

There is some similarity between the various measures that affect productivity and quality. Many experts agree there is a delicate balance between the two items. Increasing output at the expense of quality is a blueprint for disaster. To understand this we only have to look to the U.S. auto and steel industries. On the reverse side, in seeking to increase quality, there is a frequent increase in both output and quality, except when high output is specifically sacrificed for high quality. The production of the Volvo is an example of knowingly accepting a trade-off between high quality and lower output levels.

---

[4] "Surveys Reveal Quality Trends," *Association for Quality and Participation (AQP) Report*, July/August 1988, p. R-1.

[5] Ibid.

[6] Ibid.

In the search for clues for a link between benefits and productivity, few good examples exist. It appears our original intent was to enhance the quality of life for workers, not to tie it to output measures. Today, however, with global competition, the need to make the connection between the two is paramount. Yet most successful examples are isolated cases and are more along the lines of compensation/incentive plans. There are, however, ways to help make this connection stronger.

Employee Stock Ownership Plans and Productivity

There have been a group of studies recently that show employee stock ownership plans (ESOPs)[7] encourage company productivity.[8] These reporting organizations range from the ESOP Association to the International Foundation of Employee Benefit Plans (IFEBP) to a host of academic researchers. There has been a slight edge in favor of the ESOP organizations in terms of productivity and employee motivation.[9] However, there is some reasonable doubt as to the cause. The ESOP Association revealed that the idea of company ownership provided the impetus. Other research, however, tends to support the notion that productivity increased because the fears of retirement and financial security were eased.

Various research articles tend to support the fact that fears regarding retirement can have an impact on high output. If ESOPs reduce these fears, and the company can manage all of the reporting requirements of such programs, then ESOPs should be a viable option. However, it can just as well indicate that some modification to an existing retirement plan may have the same net effect. For that matter, if tension and stress could be the issue for the workers' decline in productivity, maybe an employee assistance plan (EAP)is a better option.

Employee Assistance Programs: Positive Programs for Productivity

Employee assistance programs may provide many services to employees—such as health, financial, legal, or marital counseling. The viewpoint expressed here, however, is its potential use as a motivator for productivity. A caution worth noting about the following studies is the overall lack of hard numerical data (input/output analysis) that lead to "quantified" opinions. This does not mean that the professional opinions of managers and consultants are not valid; it just implies that there is not a 100 percent backing of opinion with output ratios.

---

[7] In an employee stock ownership plan, money is borrowed with company stock pledged as security. As the loan is repaid, the stock is given to the employees.

[8] "ESOPs Key to Performance," *Employee Benefit News* 1, no. 5 (July/August 1987): 16.

[9] "Study: Include ESOPs as a Benefit," *Employee Benefit News* 2, no. 4 (April 1988): 15.

The Coopers and Lybrand benefits consulting firm surveyed organizations about their EAPs. In broad terms, their research supported the belief that organizations believed them to be an excellent return on investment and worth the time and effort. The major findings cited in the report were:

- Morale increased by 40 percent.
- Absenteeism decreased 28 percent.
- Disciplinary actions decreased 25 percent.
- Accidents decreased 18 percent.
- Productivity increased 25 percent.[10]

Additionally, two large EAP consulting firms offer the following points to increase probability of EAPs being a success at helping productivity to grow:

- Find a way to ensure confidentiality. If necessary, have outsiders run the program. Average fees are $10 to $30 per employee per year depending on which services are used.
- Combine EAP services with corporate wellness and related medical benefits to increase utilization.[11]

The difficulty for benefits specialists, or those entrusted with this task, is justifying the cost. Health-care and pension costs are rising quickly and appear somewhat out of control. How do you walk into the boss' office and suggest some additional benefits spending? If dollars saved are what is needed in an argument, Control Data Corporation estimates it saves $2 for every $1 invested in their EAP. In addition, Control Data estimates that its EAP saved $1,600 per serious disability case because the program returned the worker to a productive state that much sooner.[12]

GETTING WORKERS TO WORK

The Hay Group in Chicago conducted broad range employee compensation and benefits research across nearly five hundred organizations. The results present challenges but offer insights to at least begin recovery. What startled the researchers was that 39 percent of the respondents believe that their employee performance planning and review programs were completely

---

[10] Lynn Densford, "Bringing Employees Back to Health. Work," *Employee Benefit News* 2, no. 2 (February 1988): 19.

[11] Ibid.

[12] Ibid, p. 20.

inadequate. The same number felt their compensation system had no measurable effect on behavior—meaning it is a useless tool to increase productivity. Even the bonuses, awards ceremonies, trips, and so on, were only good for the short-term. Other points of interest in the survey include:

- Fifty-seven percent of the respondents believe productivity increases were the top agenda item for the near planning term at their organizations.
- Fifty percent set productivity goals of 210 percent increases, and 30 percent set 5 to 10 percent increases for the short run.
- Fifty-eight percent felt that their current productivity improvement programs have high visibility.
- The most effective programs used were goal setting and quality circles.
- The least effective programs used are special incentive systems, differential pricing, and entrepreneurial incentives.[13]

The results of this unpleasant situation is a "patchwork" of programs usually following the latest management fad. Instead, there needs to be a comprehensive system that ties together all of the elements. Such elements include job descriptions, job analysis, performance evaluations, compensation systems, and benefits programs. Unless we work toward making the pieces work together, we will be asked to accept a process that is more reactionary than proactive. How can benefits assist in this matter? Let us look at making benefits fit the puzzle.

CHANGING BENEFITS FROM NEUTRAL TO PROACTIVE

Can benefits actually be more than "neutral if present, and negative if not," as Frederick Herzberg's Two Factor Motivation Model tell us?[14] It is our premise that, properly tied to performance criteria and wages and flexible enough to be built around individual needs, benefits can be proactive.

Retirement Programs and Inducement to Work

Organizational contributions to pensions are typically viewed as a neutral point when trying to induce high-quality, high-output employee performance.

---

[13] "Motivation and Recognition—Paying for Performance," *Employee Benefit News* 1, no. 7 (October 1987): 31.

[14] See for example F. Herzberg, B. Mausner, and B. B. Snyderman, *The Motivation to Work* (New York: John Wiley & sons, 1959).

Most experts agree that the average increment plan cannot support anyone in the retirement years. To make matters worse, the law allows certain levels of deductions for Social Security payments. The workers know this, and they know about the Social Security deductions and figure it is all a "carrot." After all, if companies really want pensions to be a proactive force to get people to increase output, they would not try to sidestep their responsibility by low payout and deducting Social Security in the first place.

The most dramatic evidence of pensions having a proactive effect is to permit people to retire at an earlier age. The company sweetens the offers to make leaving the organization the smart move instead of staying and working harder. From a psychological point of view, this can have some negative reaction on those who remain with the organization.

In addition, demographic studies forecast business is going to need every person possible in the work force because there will not be enough workers, even taking into account the declines in output. Pensions will need to be proactive to induce workers to stay with the company and on the job longer.

Pensions and Job Mobility

Despite all its inherent problems, defined pension benefit plans have at least one major plus. They reduce job mobility and labor turnover. If communicated properly, they can be a reason to continue employment with the company. Unfortunately it is also a reason for continued employment of less desirable workers. This, of course, is not the fault of the pension system but attributable to the performance evaluation mechanism.

As long as wages increase over time, the use of final or average earnings in the final years in the retirement formula may hurt those who elect to leave. Will earlier vesting stop this? The belief is no because the same calculation is used in either event.[15]

To illustrate, consider a worker who earns $20,000 after twenty years and $40,000 after forty years. Her company plan pays an annual retirement benefit of 1.5 percent of final earnings for each year of service. If she remains with the company for her career, the pension benefit will be $24,000 (.015 X 40 X $40,000). Now, if she leaves after twenty years and moves to another company (assuming constant salary levels), retirement calculations can be shown as follows. The pension received from both employers is $18,000. Retirement from company number one is $6,000 (.015 X 20 X $20,000); from employer number two, $12,000 (.015 X 20 X $40,000). If workers are aware of this potential loss of benefit, the probability of moving may be reduced. Accordingly, vesting brings in the idea of capital loss. That is, if a worker

---

[15] Steven Allen, Robert Clark, and Ann McDerned, "Why Do Pensions Reduce Mobility?," *Industrial Relations Research Association Series: Proceedings of the Fortieth Annual Meeting* (Chicago, 1987), p. 205.

leaves work before legally being entitled to the benefits, that worker normally forfeits some level of benefit payment.[16]

Pensions As an Inducement to Work More Years

The question now turns to deciding if pensions are a possible tool for the organization to use to induce workers to remain on the job additional years. In the not-too-distant future, this will be the new "game" in benefits management, not early retirement. Labor shortages are already beginning to appear in fast-food and similar low-wage service-type jobs. The problem is being addressed by hiring nontraditional workers for these industries (i.e., older retired workers, the handicapped, and so on). However, as the shortages extend to higher-wage jobs, competition for these workers will increase and the shortages magnified.

What is the gain that can be expected from each year's continued employment? From a model offered by David Elwood, the suggestion is that the incremental gain in pension benefits for each year is an important incentive.[17] Pensions rotate the wage profile most when wage inflation is present. When there is both real wage growth and inflation during one's career, pensions cause the real wages of young workers to rise only slightly; the most dramatic effect is in the latter years for older workers.[18] This offers us some good points to prepare arguments to keep workers from early retirement, especially in light of added longevity of people today.

THE ROLE OF UNIONS IN BENEFITS AND PRODUCTIVITY

We frequently hear from our business contemporaries that the need for unions is gone; things are different now from what they were in the 1940s. Although that may be many peoples' view, many of the fears that led to unionization in the 1940s still continue today. For our purposes, we will focus on one of the major fears—job security, which is a major platform item in the union movement. Anything that threatens or is perceived to threaten job security is held in suspicion. Change must be explained, and explained again, especially where it may impact job security.

---

[16] We show these calculations for example purposes. The assumptions that pension plans are similar, or that salaries will be no different when one moves to another organization may not hold. Additionally, workers move to other organizations for reasons other than pensions, such as personality problems with bosses, lack of career mobility, greater salaries, and so on.

[17] David T. Elwood, "Pension and the Labor Market," in *Pensions, Labor, and Individual Choice*, ed. David Wise (Chicago: University of Chicago Press, 1985), p. 36.

[18] Ibid., p. 37.

Further complicating the issue are talks of productivity improvement, job evaluation, compensation systems, and a host of other items involved in establishing work performance standards. To be handled properly, any of these systems involve well-researched and well-designed standards. Unions get very nervous about standards that are enforced by the company. They perceive such tactics as ways to increase output without increasing wages. For managers, increases in productivity are an accomplishment. To workers, increased output may result in additional inventories. If these inventories are not sold, the result is layoff, or that the needed quantities can now be produced with fewer workers.

Because of oversights, lack of knowledge, or lack of desire, management is frequently at fault for failing to communicate to the union the essential aspects of any changes it wants to make. To have a chance at success, management must include unions at every step of the process. It will take more time in the planning state, but the results are usually more positive. Unions have the right to protect workers. Recent history has shown that when they understand and support a program, they are more inclined to cooperate and encourage members' participation.[19]

One reason noted earlier why unions are willing to act so cooperatively is to help ensure their own survival. Being part of productivity plans, quality circles, and the like, raises the esteem of the union in the eyes of the employees. This elevated esteem helps sign up new members in the technical service and professional ranks. There are many unions that have made quality awareness and productivity part of their bargaining agendas, beating management to the punch on these two issues.

USING BENEFITS IN A PROACTIVE MANNER

You have heard this phrase before: Enhancing the awareness of workers about benefits is difficult. To say a word on behalf of organizations, there are many legitimate attempts being made to communicate information regarding benefits to employees. The problem is not in the lack of effort. A recent Mercer-Merdinger Survey of benefits managers who installed major plans found that 39 percent indicated that if they would do it again, communication would be the key point. A Hewitt survey revealed the primary focus of benefit activity for the next two years will be better employee benefit communications. The survey indicated that internal communications is second only to health-

---

[19] Richard I. Henderson, *Compensation Management* 4th ed. (Virginia: Reston Publishing Company, 1983), p. 135.

care cost containment in importance.[20] But just saying that more communication is needed is not enough. There are barriers that must be overcome.

Benefit Communication Barriers

Before jumping into any proposed solutions, it is important to resolve the communications problem surrounding benefits. The questions listed below should be answered before proceeding with benefits communication.

- Are employees reading their benefits brochures?
- Are benefits presentations effective in conveying the information?
- Is the benefits material written in such a manner that the employees understand what is being stated?
- Are workers prepared to think clearly about their benefit needs.[21]

Without having the certainty that the benefits communication program will meet its targeted goal, there is little sense in proceeding. Benefits managers must ensure that these programs will produce the results they want.

Options Available to Implement Benefit Communications

The history of benefits communications is somewhat enjoyable to review. In the pre–1950s era the insurance company issued a legal document to the worker. In the 1960s this changed, as company brochures and manuals were added. The 1970s brought in the use of slide shows, accompanied by color brochures. Videos emerged in the 1980s. For the 1990s, the focus is on the continued use of interactive video disks. This method of communicating is not cheap. The cost of the system is about $12,000 for noncustomized hardware. Software support ranges from $2,000 to $100,000.[22] The micro and personal computers may also be used without the video disks, providing employees with answers to their benefits inquiries. Companies like AT&T and Metropolitan Life have begun marketing electronic benefits communication systems.[23] These companies boast employee participation in the voluntary programs, like EAP, which will help the company from running into trouble with

---

[20] Deborah Watters, "New Technologies for Benefit Communications," *Personnel Administrator* 31, no. 11 (November 1986): 110.

[21] Adopted from Ibid. p. 112.

[22] Ibid., p. 114.

[23] Richard Stolz, "Electronic Benefits System Communicates to Employees," *Employee Benefit News* 2, no. 2 (May 1988): 42.

antidiscriminatory rules governing benefits. Workers are becoming more accustomed to working with electronic machinery to gain information, and the application of such a mechanism to benefits administration appears to be appropriate.

Putting in an expensive and complex benefits communication systems can be time consuming. But benefits plans that no one uses or understands are as expensive and time consuming to manage. In addition, they fail to be proactive for high quality output. Time to plan and work on a comprehensive system can mean some very promising results in the years ahead.

SUMMARY

After reading this chapter you will know that:

* *There are a number of interconnected variables that impact productivity. These would include inflation, energy prices, research and development expenditures, employee motivation, changing demographics, and education levels of employees.*

* *Quality and productivity relate to each other in a delicate manner. Increasing output at the expense of quality is damaging to corporate success. Increasing quality can work to enhance productivity.*

* *While there is still some debate as to the extent ESOPs can increase productivity, several studies indicate that it is a good relationship. Surprisingly enough, it is not the pride in corporate ownership that increases output, but rather the ease of tension regarding a sound retirement program.*

* *Recognition programs that tend to single out superstars for rewards and are beyond the reach of the average worker can work to decrease output.*

* *EAPs can increase productivity and help with many company problems, especially those problems caused by troubled employees.*

* *Compensation and benefits systems must be related to job descriptions and performance evaluations. Without the connection, it is difficult to convince workers of the relationship.*

* *The demographic shift in the population is causing pension managers to look for ways to keep workers on the job longer. Pensions can provide this impetus. The payoff for staying extra years may be significant over one's retirement life.*

* *Unions can have a proactive effect on productivity. They have fears and reservations, usually legitimized by years of managerial indifference. Once their fears are resolved, unions can be a strong force toward a successful productivity program.*

* *Perhaps the weakest link in the benefits productivity chain is communications. There are many good software programs on the market to help in this endeavor.*

KEY TERMS

Capital spending	Output
Communications	Productivity measures
Communications barriers	Productivity programs
Employee assistance programs	Patchwork programs
Employee stock ownership	Quality
plans (ESOPs)	Quality improvements
Inflation	Recognition programs
Job mobility	Video disks
Labor shortage	Wage profiles
Motivation	

QUESTIONS FOR REVIEW AND DISCUSSION

1. Explain what is meant by interconnection of variables affecting productivity.
2. How do ESOPs promote productivity improvement?
3. "The pride in being part owner of the company is a major reason for the success stories of ESOPs." Do you agree or disagree with the statement? Explain.
4. What danger lurks in recognition programs?
5. How can we establish EAPs to ensure confidentiality?
6. How can a company publicize its employee assistance program?
7. How can union assistance be secured in productivity improvements?
8. "Unions will constantly fight productivity improvement programs. They are just management's way of reducing union influence in the company." Do you agree or disagree with the statement? Explain.
9. What are the new technologies available to communicate benefits to employees?
10. "Video technology will revolutionize benefits communications." Do you agree or disagree with the statement? Explain.

ADDITIONAL READINGS

ALBERTSON, DAVID.   "Motivation Keeps Employees Human." *Employee Benefit News* 7, no. 6 (September 1987): 22-24.

BROWN, ABBY.   "The Retirement Game." *Personnel Administrator* 31, no. 11 (November 1986): 55.

HOLOVIAK, STEPHEN J., and SUSAN STONE SIPKOFF.   *Managing Human Productivity.* New York: Prager Publishers, 1987.

MITCHELL, OLIVA.   "Employee Benefits in the U.S. Labor Market." *Industrial Relations Research Association Times, Proceedings of the Fortieth Annual Meeting.* Chicago, 1987, pp. 213-19.

"Security and Better Return Is Goal of Investment Retirement Program Under Study." *AFL-CIO News* 32, no. 7 (February 14, 1987); 8.

CHAPTER FIVE

HEALTH BENEFITS

LEARNING OBJECTIVES

After reading this chapter you will be able to:

* *Describe the usefulness of health insurance.*
* *Identify the three major types of health coverage options.*
* *Describe how traditional health insurance operates.*
* *Describe the purpose of a Blue Cross organization.*
* *Describe the purpose of a Blue Shield organization.*
* *Describe the difference between participating and nonparticipating physicians.*
* *Describe how a health maintenance organization operates.*
* *Describe how a preferred provider organization operates.*
* *Describe self-funded health insurance.*
* *Describe how third-party administrators and administrative services only operate.*

INTRODUCTION

Monday morning had arrived. It was the start of the company's open enrollment program. As the benefits administrator briefed her staff on the expected crowd, she wished them luck. Asking for any last-minute questions from her staff about the new health coverage offered by the company, she opened the door to an already forming group.

The first individual in the office was Richard Gerard. Richard, a research scientist in the company, is married and expecting his first child.

Never having to spend much time and thought on what health insurancecoverage would be best, Richard came prepared with many questions to ask. As he met with one of the benefits specialists, he appeared to be confused. It seems that there was so much information for an employee to digest, so many options, that he was lost. What coverage would be best for him? What are the limitations of the coverage, if any? What are the costs involved? How does he enroll? What about the baby coming in a few months? Does that matter? Realizing that Richard needed some answers to those questions before he could make an informed decision, the benefits specialist sat down with him and began to discuss the various aspects of health insurance coverage.

Health insurance means many different things to many different people. Individuals have needs that must be met. Yet organizations are trying to meet as many of those health insurance needs as possible, and probable. No longer may a "one-shop" health insurance package suffice. Employees' needs, cost factors of various coverage, and the like all impact what is offered. In this chapter, we explore this arena and discuss the various types of health insurance programs offered to employees.

AN OVERVIEW

Most organizations today offer some type of health insurance coverage to their employees. This coverage has become one of the most important benefits for employees because of the tremendous increases in the cost of health care. In fact, health care cost the United States almost $450 billion in 1986 — amounting to almost 11 percent of the country's gross national product.[1] Without health insurance, almost any family could be wiped out at any time by the costs of a major illness. Even a major illness is often times misleading. If you consider that one day in a hospital bed costs more than the average suite in most luxury hotels, just a few days in the hospital could deplete one's reserves. The purpose of health insurance is to protect people and their immediate families from the catastrophes of a major illness, or to minimize their out-of-pocket expenses for medical care.

Any type of health insurance offered to employees generally contains provision for coverage that can be extended beyond the employee. An employee, an employee and spouse, an employee with child, or the family can be covered. Coverage included generally focuses on hospital and physician care, and also major medical. Most insurers have regulations that must be followed and communicated to the employee for areas that directly affect them. For example, a health insurer may have specific policies on how or when

---

[1] Stuart Gannes, "Strong Medicine for Health Bills," *Fortune*, April 13, 1987, p. 70.

someone may be added to the policy (open enrollment) or whether some preexisting conditions are excluded from coverage. This means that the employees must be fully apprised of what health care coverage they are getting.

The specific types of coverage offered to employees will vary based on the organization's policies. Generally three types appear more frequently than others. These are: traditional health care coverage, health maintenance organizations (HMOs), and preferred provider organizations (PPOs). All three are designed to provide protection for employees, but each does so in a different way. There are also special employer-operated options available, such as a self-funded insurance, and a third-party administrator.

TRADITIONAL HEALTH INSURANCE

When employers began offering health benefits years ago, there was only one type of health insurance. That was the traditional membership program. A new employee filled out an enrollment card at the time of employment, received a membership card about thirty days later, and did nothing with respect to health insurance unless a change in status occurred (e.g., the employee married, divorced, birth of a child, and so on). This card entitled the employee to coverage at both doctors' offices and in hospitals, and for the most part, covered most of the expenses.[2] The cost of this insurance to the employee was minimal, if any.

The foregoing was a typical rendition of health-care coverage in the United States during the 1940s, 1950s, 1960s, and early 1970s. Most employees had some type of traditional insurance. Table 5–1 is a sample of traditional health insurance coverage. This traditional insurance was generally provided through a Blue Cross and a Blue Shield organization.

TABLE 5 −1   Traditional Health Insurance Coverage

Office Visit for Routine and Preventive Care
   Not covered

Inpatient Hospital Services
   Semiprivate room and board and special services up to 365 days, covered in full.
   Diagnostic services, covered at 100 percent of reasonable costs

Maternity Care
   Covered in full

---

[2] There was a time that if the employee entered the hospital and presented his or her membership card, all the expenses were covered, with the exception of the admission kit (toothbrush, water pitcher, and so on).

TABLE 5 −1   Traditional Health Insurance Coverage   *Cont.*

Physical and Speech Therapy
    Inpatient, covered at 100 percent of reasonable cost
    Outpatient, covered at 100 percent of reasonable cost, 60 treatments within
        180 days

Mental Health Services
    Inpatient, covered in full for 30 days
    Outpatient, covered under major medical

Medical Emergency Services
    Emergency room, if admitted, covered in full. If not admitted, covered at
        50 percent

Major Exclusions
    Services or supplies that are not medically necessary
    Cosmetic surgery
    Custodial Care
    Personal convenience items or services such as telephone and television while
        hospitalized
    Routine or periodic physical examinations and diagnostic services for screening
    Domestic or housekeeping services

Affiliated Hospitals
    No restrictions; however, member may experience greater out-of-pocket
        expenses when receiving services through a nonparticipating hospital

Source: State of Maryland, *1987 Health Insurance Open Enrollment* (November 1987), p. 9.

Blue Cross and Blue Shield Insurance

Since its inception in 1929 at Baylor University, Blue Cross and Blue Shield insurance has served as the dominant health-care insurer in the United States. Blue Cross and Blue Shield plans offer special arrangements to their members in return for a guarantee that medical services will be provided.

Blue Cross Organizations. Blue Cross organizations are concerned with the hospital end of the business. These hospitals contract with Blue Cross to provide hospital services to members, and agree to receive reimbursement from the health insurer for fees incurred. The reimbursement is often paid on a per diem basis for days stayed in the hospital, or as a percentage of the total bill.[3]

Through a Blue Cross arrangement, any member can receive hospital treatment with no out-of-pocket expense, and have peace of mind knowing that the membership card is good throughout the United States. Blue Cross can provide this freedom of choice because of its competitive advantage received through its arrangements with the hospitals.

---

[3] Jerry S. Rosenbloom and G. Victor Hallman, *Employee Benefit Planning* 2d ed. (Englewood Cliffs, N.J.: Prentice Hall, 1986), p. 82.

Blue Shield Organizations.   The other side of the health insurer is the Blue Shield organization. Whereas Blue Cross has special arrangements with the hospitals, Blue Shield tries to achieve the same by signing up doctors to participate in Blue Shield coverage. This participation feature means that a doctor is willing to accept the payment from Blue Shield as payment in full for services rendered. These payments are generally based on what are called usual, customary, and reasonable (UCR) fees. The UCR fees reflect physician fees charged in an area.

Years ago there was little problem in obtaining physician services with little or no out-of-pocket expenses—almost all physicians were participating. Unfortunately, much of that has changed. Many doctors became angry at the long delays in receiving their payments. Many realized that to operate their business required a steady cash flow. The long delays from Blue Shield, coupled with the UCR fees that many doctors complained were unjustifiably low, resulted in many doctors rescinding their participating agreements with the health insurer. In Blue Shield terminology, these physicians are now considered "non-pars." A non-par, or nonparticipating physician, does not preclude any member from using that doctor's services. What it means is that the doctor will not accept Blue Shield payments as payment in full for services rendered; any costs incurred above the repayment schedule set by the health insurer are the responsibility of the patient. This is a critical point that employees must understand. If they have Blue Cross/Blue Shield insurance and decide to go to a nonparticipating physician, they are liable for the difference in fees the non-par charges.   In fact, in many cases, the nonparticipating physician requires payment in full at the time services are rendered, and lets the member process the paperwork to have the money returned from the health insurer. This element alone has added a new dimension of health-care coverage for the average employee.

Why Blue Cross/Blue Shield?   Blue Cross and Blue Shield (which years ago were separate organizations in many cases) offers a freedom of choice to employees that is often unavailable elsewhere. This type of insurance allows members to choose doctors of their liking and provides very good coverage of major illnesses. Many workers grew up in the "Blue Cross/Blue Shield" family, and many still perceive it as the Cadillac of the health insurers. Although, their relationships with hospitals and doctors is strained at times, they still provide some of the best health-care coverage available.

Just as we can list reasons for Blue Cross/Blue Shield insurance, we must also present why workers are leaving the "Blues." First of all is its cost. The cost of Blue Cross and Blue Shield insurance is expensive. On average, a company that has a group plan with the health insurer pays approximately $300 per month for family coverage.   That cost appears to be following the inflationary pressures of medical care, and increasing rapidly. As costs go up to the health insurer, it must pass them on to the members, that is, the company. As costs go up, an organization must pass some of them on to its employees. Accordingly, employees are generally having more deducted out of their paychecks for health insurance premiums.

In addition to having more taken out of their pay, employees are receiving decreased services. Unless one goes to a participating physician, the cost of the visit and services rendered are borne by the employee. Depending on the specifics of the contract,[4] a member may have an out-of-pocket expense of $2,000 to $5,000 each year. To obtain reimbursement for these expenses, it is up to the member to file the paperwork with the insurer under the "major medical" portion of the health insurance contract. Table 5–2 is a sample of major medical coverage and its out-of-pocket expenses.

TABLE 5–2   **Major Medical Coverage**

	STANDARD PLAN	HIGH OPTION PLAN
Deductible	$200/individual $400/family	$100/individual $300/family
Member Co-insurance Deductible for:		
Non-Psychiatric Services	Individual: 20% of $1,500, 0% thereafter	0%
	Family: 20% of $3,000, 0% thereafter	0%
Inpatient Psychiatric Services	50%	0%
Outpatient Psychiatric Services	65%	65%
Out-of-Pocket Maximum Applied to Nonpsychiatric Services	$500/individual $1000/family	$100/individual $300/family
Lifetime Maximum Benefits	$1 million except psychiatric services, which are limited to $500,000	$1 million except outpatient psychiatric services which are limited to $500,000

Source: State of Maryland, *1987 Health Insurance Open Enrollment* (November 1987), p. 9.

---

[4] For instance, each contract has specific deductibles that must be met. For example, an individual deductible may be $100, and total family deductible $400. This means that the first $100/400 of expenses must be paid by the member. After the deductible is met, there is a reimbursement formula. This formula is commonly 80/20, meaning that until the maximum amount of out-of-pocket expense is satisfied, members pay 20 cents for every dollar of medical services rendered. This aspect is generally covered under the major medical portion of the health insurance.

Another reason individuals have veered away from traditional insurance is because "well care" is not included. Under a traditional Blue Cross/Blue Shield arrangement, a routine visit to the doctor for a yearly physical, or for well-baby care, is not covered under the insurance. This means that these services are received at the member's expense. With more emphasis today on health, and expectations that we see our physicians more routinely, these are costs some employees do not want to incur.

Conclusion. Blue Cross and Blue Shield organizations have attempted to revitalize themselves in recent years to regain much of the dominance they had in the health insurance industry. Lately there have been major restructuring efforts at the Blues to merge the two organizations. This action is occurring to assist the health insurer to reduce administrative costs and, with hope, result in more competitive costs.

Blue Cross and Blue Shield organizations are also looking at various alternatives to health-care insurance. Today, working with the Blues is no longer an enrollment process, but one in which a company is looking for creative ways to reduce health-care costs. This means that various education programs, cost-containment provisions, and alternative health-care offerings are available to client organizations.

Commercial Insurers

While Blue Cross and Blue Shield is the most widely known organization for traditional insurance, it is not the only one. Companies like Connecticut General, Monumental Life, and the like all offer health-care coverage that models the approach above. Although they exist, their policies are too numerous for description in this text. There is one notable feature, however. The commercial insurers often do not have the participating agreements with hospitals and physicians that the Blues do. This may affect the universal appeal of the Blue Cross and Blue Shield membership card.

ALTERNATIVE FORMS OF COVERAGE

The traditional health insurance program, whether it comes from Blue Cross and Blue Shield or from a commercial carrier, differs greatly from the alternative forms available. Recognizing the need to meet employees' expectations, while at the same time conforming with the law and containing health-care costs, companies searched for various ways of providing health-care insurance. The better known of these alternatives are the health maintenance organization, and the preferred provider organization.

Health Maintenance Organizations

To comply with the Health Maintenance Act of 1973, a company that offers health insurance to its employees must also offer alternative health-care coverage. The main alternative to health-care that this law created was the health maintenance organization.

HMOs are designed to provide quality health-care at a fixed expense for its members. As mentioned earlier, people's needs have changed, and with these changing needs comes the expectation that they can obtain good health care at a reasonable cost. Under the traditional coverage, well care is not covered, and the costs of such are borne by the employee. To meet this need and provide the desired services to employees, HMOs were created.

An HMO is "an organization that generally delivers broad, comprehensive health care to a specific voluntary enrolled population . . . on a fixed, periodic payment basis."[5] Since their inception, they have grown widely in the United States. It is estimated that there are more than three hundred HMOs operating in the United States, providing services to more than twenty four million members, and growing "at a 25 percent annual pace."[6] Table 5–3 is a sample of HMO coverage.

Health maintenance organizations operate in two basic ways: as a group practice or on an individual practice basis. The main distinction between the two lies in how the doctors work. In a group practice, doctors from various specialties combine their talents and offer their services in one location. These doctors are usually employees of the HMO. Individual practitioners, on the other hand, continue to operate their individual practices. However, under special contract arrangements, the physician agrees to see patients covered under the specific HMO on a fee-for-service basis. Accordingly, no special clinics are needed.

Basis of HMOs.   HMOs operate on the principle of preventive maintenance. With well care provided, a member knows what the fixed out-of-pocket expense will be (typically zero to $5 per visit). As members visit their health-care facility more frequently, potential problems can be discovered, or eliminated, before they become major health threats. If that is accomplished, the HMO can make money by minimizing unnecessary operations and keeping health-care costs down by treating minor illnesses before they become major ones.

It is in the best interest of an HMO to keep its members well. The better and the more frequent care a member receives, the better the chance of ensuring the good health of that individual. If that person stays healthy,

---

[5] Rosenbloom and Hallman, Employee Benefit Planning, p. 89.

[6] Gannes, "Strong Medicine for Health Bills," p. 71.

TABLE 5–3   Health Maintenance Organization (HMO) Coverage

Office Visits for Routine and Preventive Care
  Periodic health evaluations, covered in full
  Routine immunizations, covered in full
  Well-baby care, covered in full
  Allergy testing and treatments, covered in full
  Medical and surgical procedures, covered in full

Inpatient Hospital Services
  Room and board, physician visits, surgery, and special services, covered in full,
    unlimited days

Maternity
  Inpatient and outpatient, including prenatal and postnatal, nursing charges,
    covered in full

Physical and Speech Therapy
  Maximum 20 visits during a 16-week period

Mental Health Services
  Inpatient, covered in full, 30 days per year
  Outpatient, covered at $15 copayment per session up to 50 individual/group
    sessions per year

Medical Emergency Services
  Emergency room and hospital physician and facility services for emergencies if the
    services provided are authorized in advance by a primary-care physician or if the
    condition is at an unanticipated nature and requires immediate attention. $25
    copayment if hospitalization is not required

Major Exclusions
  Any charges in excess of usual, customary, and reasonable
  Experimental and/or investigational medical or surgical procedures/services
  Non-plan sponsored health education programs
  Cosmetic surgery
  Reversal of voluntary sterilization
  Acupuncture
  Whole blood or blood products
  Routine foot care

Source: State of Maryland, *1987 Health Insurance Open Enrollment* (November 1987), p. 13.

health-care costs go down, and the HMO can continue to operate as a viable
alternative. But it is sometimes this emphasis on costs that detracts from the
HMO.

HMO Problems.   For an HMO to operate effectively, it must contain
costs. To do so, many of the HMOs have what are commonly referred to as
"gatekeepers." These gatekeepers are the doctors who must authorize

specialized treatment.[7] In an HMO setting, the member chooses his or her doctor from a slate of doctors active in the practice. That physician becomes the primary health-care physician. While other specialties are generally available in the HMO, it is up to the primary physician to recommend getting another opinion. Accordingly, the member may have a physician who is specialized in one aspect of medicine, but responsible for his or her total care. Desiring to see a specialist, especially one outside the group practice, is often met with a negative reaction. This holding of the "keys" is necessary to contain costs, but is something many individuals do not like.

As individuals become more responsible for their general health, they want more say in what is happening to them. Accordingly, not being able to see a doctor because some gatekeeper says no,[8] only serves as a "cost" in choosing health-care coverage. The answer, then, lies in employees determining what is best for them and what they want out of health insurance. If an employee wants good comprehensive health-care coverage at a fixed cost then an HMO makes sense. If, however, the choice of doctors and hospitals is paramount to the employee, then traditional health-care coverage may be better.

HMOs are not for everyone. Nor do they intend to be. However, if one is looking for a viable alternative to reducing their health-care expenses, HMOs do provide that vehicle.

HMOs and the Employer. From the employer's perspective, providing an HMO is an administrative concept. The costs associated with the HMO may differ from the traditional health insurance costs, but that is of little consequence. Companies decide how much they will pay toward health insurance. Any amount over the set premium is passed on to the employee. Thus, if an organization decides to pay $250 per month for health-care coverage for its employees, then that is all it pays. If traditional coverage costs $300 per month, the employee is responsible, through payroll deductions, to pay the difference. If HMO coverage costs $250 per month, then the employee has no health-care payroll deduction. Aside from the added paperwork and compliance rules, the HMO does not increase benefit costs.

---

[7] One pressing concern for many regarding HMOs is the quality-of-service issue. The method used to compensate the HMO physician provides an incentive to see many patients. This may result in too little time being spent with each. Additionally, in some HMOs, physicians may incur a penalty if the patient is sent to a specialist outside of the HMO. This may result in physicians not referring patients to other specialists when they cannot determine the proper course of action to take.

[8] One point needs to be made here. That is, in an HMO the member has the right to see other specialists if he or she desires. However, unless it is authorized by the HMO, the HMO will not be responsible for the payment for services rendered.

Preferred Provider Organizations

Preferred provider organizations are health-care arrangements in which an employer or insurance company has agreements with doctors, hospitals, and other related medical service facilities to provide services for a fixed fee. In return for accepting this fixed fee, the employer or the insurer promises to encourage employees to use their services. The encouragement often results in additional services being covered. An employee studying what services are offered versus the costs of the different plans may find that the PPO is advantageous. PPOs are a clear-cut case of accepting lower premiums in return for greater quantity of services provided. Table 5–4 is a sample of PPO coverage.

TABLE 5–4   Preferred Provider Organization Health Coverage

Office Visits for Routine and Preventive Care
   Medical office visit, $10 copayment per visit
   Dental exams, not covered
   Well-baby care, including vaccinations, covered in full
   GYN exam, covered in full

Inpatient Hospital Services
   Semiprivate room and board, physician's visits, surgery, and special services, covered in full.
   Diagnostic services (x-rays, lab services), covered in full

Maternity Care
   Covered in full

Physical and Occupational Therapy
   Inpatient, covered in full
   Outpatient, covered in full for 100 visits in calendar year

Speech Therapy
   Inpatient, covered in full
   Outpatient, covered in full for 50 visits in calendar year

Mental Health Services
   Inpatient, covered in full
   Outpatient, covered at 50% of reasonable and customary not to exceed $30 per visit for 100 visits per year

Medical Emergency Services
   Emergency room, if admitted, covered in full; if not admitted, covered at 50%

Covered Services
   Private duty nursing
   Durable medical equipment
   Prosthetic appliances
   Whole blood
   Medical supplies
   Ambulance services
   Deductible: $150/individual per calendar year
   Co-insurance: 20% of reasonable cost up to a yearly maximum of $550

Other Copayment or Fees
   When using nonpreferred providers without a referral from a preferred provider, the benefits are provided subject to copay rate and/or coinsurance.

Source: State of Maryland, *1987 Health Insurance Open Enrollment* (November 1987), p. 10.

PPOs also provide valuable information to the employers. Through utilization review procedures the PPO can provide the employer with data to help the employer determine unnecessary plan use. These "quality" checks can act as the gatekeepers to ensure that health-care costs are contained.

How can a PPO benefit the employee? Through the agreement reached, a PPO can provide much the same service that an HMO provides. The difference is that an individual is not required to use a specific facility, like a hospital. In those cases, the PPO takes the form of traditional health insurance. If an employee decides to go elsewhere for services, then the service fee is reimbursed according to specific guidelines, such as the reimbursement of traditional health-care (80 percent covered by the insurance and 20 percent being borne by the employee).

PPOs are trying to combine the best of both worlds of the HMO and traditional insurance. Their growth in the years ahead is expected to be enormous, especially as people see the benefits they offer. In fact, there is some speculation that HMOs and PPOs will in the decade ahead be the dominant health-care coverage in the United States.[9] PPOs alone are "expected to increase from one percent to an estimated eight percent of the U.S. population by 1990, and to 20–25 percent by 1995, surpassing the growth of HMOs."[10]

EMPLOYER-OPERATED COVERAGE

Although the three types of insurance programs mentioned above are the more popular means of health insurance today, many companies are looking for other options that will assist them in containing the rising health-care costs they incur. To help in this cost-containment measure, some companies have begun reviewing the concept of being self-insured and, in many of those instances, using the assistance of a third-party administrator.

Self-Insured Medical Coverage

A popular twist to health insurance coverage in the 1980s has been the formation of self-funded programs. Many large employers, looking for a means of reducing their health insurance costs, have ventured into the insurance business. Under a self-funding arrangement, an "employer provides a formal plan to employees under which the employer directly pays and is liable for

---

[9] Kenneth S. Abromowitz, "End of Fee for Service," *Employee Benefit Plan* Review 40, no. 9 (March 1986): p. 32.

[10] "Preferred Provider Organizations: The Newest Form of Health Care Delivery," *Small Business Report*, March 1987, p. 20.

some or all of the benefits promised under the plan."[11] This insurance plan is customarily established and operated under an arrangement called a voluntary employees beneficiary association (VEBA). In this case, the employer typically establishes a trust fund to pay for the health benefits used. For the most part, this employer trust fund has received favorable treatment from the IRS.

For employers, by establishing the VEBA, it becomes fully responsible for the health insurance coverage. But by assuming all of the risk, it also eliminates the middleman, the insurance companies. This means that many of the insurance companies' "overhead" charges that are calculated into their premium rates are eliminated. This results in more of the employers' money being spent on what they had intended it to be spent on—health benefits for employees and their dependents.

Depending on the amount of risk an employer is willing to assume, or finance for that matter, the self-funded arrangement may be augmented. This adaptation may be reflected in the purchasing of catastrophic insurance from a health insurer. Generally much lower in cost, a catastrophic insurance plan, commonly referred to as a stop-loss plan, takes effect when a maximum limit is reached. For instance, a company may be willing to pay only the first $50,000 of an employee's claims. In that instance, the 50,001st dollar would engage the catastrophic insurance plan. This same principle can also be applied to aggregate dollars spent by employers, when they are only willing to assume, say, $5 million in insurance risk. Any catastrophic event that arises in any given year above the $5 million will be covered through another insurance source.

The benefits of self-funding are evident. The company assumes the risk, either all or in part, and provides quality health insurance at a lower cost. But this is not something a company can do to "get on the bandwagon." There are many issues an employer must review before such an undertaking, for example, the general health of its employees. What has been the employees' use of health benefits in the past? What costs has the employer incurred? Even though a health insurer has to build that overhead into the premium rate charged, much of the insurer's risk may be spread over many organizations. If utilization at one company is inordinately high, to go self-funded may not be as cost effective. But that does not mean that it is not a viable option, and after careful analysis it may be worthwhile.

Additionally, when an employer becomes self-funded, it must accept the responsibility of handling the claims, paying the bills, and so on. The time and complexities involved in the administrative aspect are sometimes overlooked. Will the company administer the fund itself? Or will it seek assistance elsewhere? If it goes outside the company, there are generally two options available; third-party administrators (TPAs), or administrative services only (ASO) from an insurance carrier.

---

[11] Rosenbloom and Hallman, *Employee Benefit Planning*, p. 91.

Third-party Administrators

A third-party administrator is an independent organization designed to assist employers in managing their health insurance. When an employer operates a self-funded plan, these TPAs act as if they were the insurance company. All administrative activities with respect to the company's health benefits are funneled through the TPA. The TPA is not, however, an insurance company. It is simply responsible for receiving the charges, paying the fees for services, and in many cases providing the self-insured employer with utilization data. Its popularity and growth, however, is directly linked to the number of companies opting for self-funding.

Administrative Services Only

Not to be outdone by third-party administrators, many insurance companies offer services to employers designed to process their health insurance claims. In these insurance companies, like the Blues, they lost some of their business when the companies decided to go with a self-funding arrangement. To try to minimize their loss, and to continue to provide a service, the insurers established provisions whereby they will continue to handle the company's processing of employee health claims. Already capable of handling this aspect of health insurance, many of the ASOs have been able to offer this service to the employer at a lower cost than if the company processed claims itself, or used a TPA.

Generally the services of an ASO are slight. It mainly processes the claims. The utilization review is often lacking or can be added for extra costs.

THE END OF A NIGHTMARE

The demographic and societal changes discussed in Chapter 1 not only brought about the creation of new benefits to meet employee expectations, they also brought about some confusion in administering health benefits. The dilemma arose over coordination of benefits—when both spouses work, where children are present, and when both spouses have health insurance. Whose insurance is the primary payer?

For many years, the rule of thumb was that the husband's insurance was the primary payer. Carrying over from the time when the husband worked and the wife stayed at home caring for children, insurance commissioners, who regulate how insurance operates in each state, believed that the husband's health insurance took precedence. But this was not often working effectively especially when the wife's health insurance provided better coverage. To help alleviate the confusion, the National Association of Insurance Commissioners established in 1987 what is called the "birthday rule" for determining whose insurance coverage is primary. This birthday rule stipulates that dependent health-care coverage will be the primary responsibility of the parent whose birthday falls first in a calendar year.

When dependent coverage is not a concern, the situation is a bit less complicated. Both spouses are primarily covered under their own health insurance plan. However, the spouses plan may engage what the other insurance plan does not cover. The coordination problem here is to ensure that no one is reimbursed or covered for more than the actual expenses incurred. To help assist in this matter, the National Association of Insurance Commissioners established alternative coordination-of-benefits guidelines. These alternatives are provided for the secondary insurer to coordinate benefits as such:

- The total reimbursement from both individuals is not less than 80 percent of allowable expenses, or
- Total benefits are at least equal to what that plan would have paid if it were the primary insurer, and at least 75 percent above any deductible amount.[12]

SOME TIPS FOR RICHARD GERARD

We opened this chapter with the scenario about Richard Gerard. Having given Richard a sampling of what is available in health insurance, it is time to help Richard make a decision. Table 5 − 5 is a quick reference comparison chart of the available coverage. Realizing that Richard is married, his spouse works and has health insurance from her employer, and that a child is due within a few months, the benefits specialist believed she was able to provide some advice. In further discussion with Richard, it appears that both he and his wife have certain health-care goals in mind. They would like to be able to use their doctors of choice, but would also like to find a way to minimize out-of-pocket expenses. Based on this little bit of information, there might be a viable alternative.

First, after checking with the plans the company uses, the benefits specialist noticed that only one insurer has a stipulation for preexisting conditions.[13] Because Richard is expecting a child soon, that option was not

---

[12] Robert M. McCaffery, *Employee Benefit Programs: A Total Compensation Perspective* (Boston: PNS-KENT Publishing, 1988), p. 78.

[13] A preexisting condition is one that currently exists, prior to obtaining/changing insurance plans. For instance, in this scenario, Richard's wife is pregnant. That is a preexisting condition. The one insurance company that lists certain preexisting conditions from exclusion of payments signifies that any expenses incurred for this condition will not be paid through health insurance means.

TABLE 5 −5   Quick Reference Chart Health Insurance

	TRADITIONAL	HMO	PPO
Eligibilty	May live anywhere	May be required to live in HMO's service area	May live anywhere
		Must agree to use the facilities and doctors associated with the HMO	May use the facilities and doctors associated with the PPO or agree to pay additional copayment and deductible
Health-care Provider	The doctor and health care facility of your choice	Must choose from among HMO participating doctors and health-care facilities	May choose any doctor or health-care facility but full PPO coverage only applies to PPO participating physicians and affiliated facilities
Routine Checkups, Preventive Care	Does not cover regular checkups and other preventive services Diagnostic tests covered in full	Covers regular checkups, diagnostic tests, other preventive services	Covers regular checkups, diagnostic tests, and other preventive services, but full PPO coverage only applies to PPO participating physicians and affiliated facilities
Hospital Services and Supplies	Covers doctor and hospital bills	Covers doctor and hospital bills at an HMO affilated or approved hospital	Covers doctor and hospital bills

Source: State of Maryland, *1987 Health Insurance Open Enrollment* (November 1987), p. 4.

viable to meet his immediate needs. It was also learned that both Richard and his wife had similar traditional insurance coverage. It was believed that this duplication was not needed. To help Richard meet his goals, and realizing that open enrollment was not planned for three more months in his wife's company, the benefits specialist suggested that Richard consider changing his coverage to an HMO. In this manner, his wife's family coverage from a traditional insurer would provide them with the opportunity to choose the doctors they desire.

However, for such services as well-baby care, an HMO may provide the quality services for them with a small out-of-pocket expense.

The options were available, the information spelled out in simple terms for Richard to read. He was given a copy of the open enrollment brochure comparing and contrasting the various alternatives available to him and the cost of each. Richard was sent back to his office, with the suggestion that he sit down with his wife, discuss what he has learned, use the brochure as an information source, and come back in a few days. It is believed this will result in an informed choice, one that meets Richard's needs.

SUMMARY

After reading this chapter you will know that:

* *The usefulness of health insurance as a benefit for employees is to protect the worker against the costs associated with a catastrophic illness. Health insurance is designed to assist individuals in obtaining and affording quality health care.*

* *The three major types of health-care coverage are traditional health insurance coverage, health maintenance organizations, and preferred provider organizations.*

* *The purpose of a Blue Cross organization is to establish arrangements with health-care facilities in order for services to be provided to members. The Blue Cross concept permits members to use these facilities and receive health-care services by simply providing the facility with their membership card. Through a Blue Cross agreement, these facilities agree to accept payment from the health insurer for payment in full.*

* *The purpose of a Blue Shield organization is to establish service agreements with health-care providers—namely physicians. Those physicians agreeing to the Blue Shield contract are reimbursed according to usual, customary, and reasonable fees for the services rendered to the patient.*

* *The terms participating and nonparticipating refer to physicians and Blue Shield arrangements. Those physicians agreeing to accept Blue Shield payments in full are considered participating physicians. The nonparticipating physician does not accept Blue Shield payments as payments in full. Accordingly, a nonparticipating physician may hold the patient liable for any expenses incurred over the reimbursed amount received through Blue Shield.*

* *A health maintenance organization operates in one of two ways—as a group practice or as an individual provider. In both instances, an employee pays a set fixed fee for services that the HMO offers. Health maintenance*

organizations are cost containment operations designed to lower health-care costs through preventive measures.

* *A preferred provider organization is an arrangement with doctors and insurance companies whereby the doctors agree to a lower fee for services in return for encouraging employees to use the PPO doctor. To a large extent, PPOs try to combine the benefits of traditional and HMO coverage.*

* *Self-funded insurance programs are designed as a cost containment measure. In this situation, the employer assumes the risk for paying for and administering the health benefits package—bypassing the insurance company.*

* *When a company has a self-funded insurance program, the administrative aspects—processing claims—may be turned over to outside interests. A third-party administrator manages the health insurance benefits for the employer. An administrative services only arrangement is a situation in which the employer contracts with an insurance company to process the health claims only.*

KEY TERMS

Administrative services only	National Association of Insurance Commissioners
Birthday rule	Nonparticipating physician
Blue Cross	Open enrollment
Blue Shield	Participating physician
Catastrophic insurance	Preexisting condition
Consolidated benefits	Preferred provider organization
Commercial insurers	Self-funded insurance
Gate keepers	Third-party administrators (TPAs)
Group practice	Traditional health insurance
Health insurance	Usual, customary, and reasonable (UCR)
Health maintenance organization (HMO)	Voluntary employees beneficiary association (VEBA)
HMO Act of 1973	Well care
Individual practice	

QUESTIONS FOR REVIEW AND DISCUSSION

1. "Employers need to provide only some basic health insurance coverage for their employees. The rest of the coverage desired is up to each employee, and at his or her expense." Do you agree or disagree with the statement? Explain.

2. Compare and contrast traditional insurance, health maintenance organizations, and preferred provider organizations.

3. Describe how the Blue Cross and Blue Shield concepts operate in providing health-care coverage for workers.

4. What are usual, customary, and reasonable fees? Do you believe they are appropriate for use in reimbursing health-care providers? Discuss.

5. Describe the operations of a group practice HMO, an individual practice HMO.

6. If you had your choice of an additional $300 per month in salary or the equivalent in health benefit coverage, which would you choose? Why? What do you think most employees would choose? Why?

7. "Preferred provider organizations, while popular, may result in price fixing on the part of doctors." Do you agree or disagree? Explain.

8. Why would an employer choose to operate a self-funded health insurance program? Discuss.

9. How are TPAs and ASOs designed to assist the company in providing health insurance to its employees?

10. Given the opportunity to choose a particular health-care option at this time, which would you choose? Why? Do you feel that choice would be the same ten years from now? Discuss?

ADDITIONAL READINGS

BRIGHT, HENRY.   "Planning for Prospective Health Care Benefits Regulation."
    Journal of Compensation and Benefits 1, no. 4 (January-February 1986): 197-203.

GANNES, STUART.   "Strong Medicine for Health Bills." *Fortune*, April 13, 1987, pp.
    70-74.

HOSTETLER, JAMES G.   "Buying Group Health Insurance." *Small Business Report*
    11, no. 3 (March 1986): 29.

PERHAM, JOHN.   "Time Bomb in Health Benefits." *Management*, March 1985, pp.
    61-62.

"Preferred Provider Organizations: The Newest Form of Health Care Delivery." *Small
    Business Report*, March 1987, pp. 20-22.

CHAPTER SIX

DISABILITY AND SURVIVOR BENEFITS

LEARNING OBJECTIVES

After reading this chapter you will be able to:

* *Describe the purpose of disability insurance programs.*
* *Describe the various types of short-term disability benefits.*
* *Describe how sick leave is allocated to employees.*
* *Describe the reasons for and ways to overcome sick leave abuse.*
* *Describe temporary disability insurance.*
* *Describe the difference in terms of coverage between short-term disability and workers' compensation.*
* *Describe the purpose of long-term disability programs.*
* *Calculate a long-term disability payment for an employee.*
* *Describe the types of survivor benefits.*
* *Describe the types of group life insurance policies offered to employees.*
* *Describe how employer travel insurance operates.*
* *Describe accidental death and dismemberment coverage.*
* *Describe Social Security survivor benefits.*

INTRODUCTION

In the last chapter, we explored the various health insurance programs available for employees. The purpose of these programs is to provide all employees, and their families, with a means of addressing medical problems.

While several options may be available to the employee, the intent is to assist workers in preventing and/or dealing with health-related problems.

While the majority of workers will find health insurance totally adequate for their needs, there are those whose well-being will require more measures. If the company cannot help the employee get well, then it needs to consider adding the means that will meet their particular needs. In many of the more serious illnesses, this would be a program that provides for the continuation of one's salary. To do so, companies have explored the use of disability insurance programs.

DISABILITY INSURANCE PROGRAMS

Employees today recognize the need for salary continuation for injuries and major illnesses as being almost more important than life insurance. For most employees, there is a greater probability that they will have a disabling injury requiring an extended absence from work of more than ninety days than dying before their retirement.[1] As Table 6–1 indicates, that probability ranges from a low of two times for those age 62, to almost seven times for younger workers.

TABLE 6–1   **Probabilities of Death or Disablement (by Age Category)**

AGE	PROBABILITY OF DEATH	PROBABILITY OF DISABILITY	PROBABILITY OF DISABILITY AS A MULTIPLE OF THE PROBABILITY OF DEATH
22	0.89	6.64	7.46
32	1.18	7.78	6.59
42	2.95	12.57	4.26
52	8.21	22.39	2.73
62	21.12	44.27	2.10

Source: Jerry S. Rosenbloom and G. Victor Hallman, *Employee Benefit Planning*, 2d ed. (Englewood Cliffs, N.J.: Prentice Hall, 1986), p. 29.

The benefits administrator, accordingly, must review various types of disability insurance programs to determine what will offer the best protection for workers. In most cases, these programs can be broken down into two broad categories—short-term disability, and long-term disability programs.

---

[1] Jerry S. Rosenbloom and G. Victor Hallman, *Employee Benefit Planning*, 2d ed. (Englewood Cliffs, N. J.: Prentice Hall, 1986), p. 29.

Short-term Disability Programs

Almost all employers offer some type of short-term disability (STD) plan. Categories under this heading would include the company sick leave policy, short-term disability programs,[2] state disability laws, and workers' compensation. The focus of each is to provide replacement income in the event of an injury or a short-term illness.[3] For many, this short-term period is six months or less.

Sick Leave. One of the most popular types of short-term disability programs is a company's sick leave plan. Most organizations provide their employees with pay for days not worked because of illness. Sick leave is allocated on the basis of a specific number of days a year,[4] accrued on a cumulative basis, or expanded relative to years of service with the organization. In the first case, an individual may take up to a specific maximum number of days off due to illness, while receiving full pay. In the latter case, some organizations expand their sick leave with tenure. Each year of employment may entitle the worker to two additional days' sick leave. Regardless of whether sick leave is used, it would continue to accumulate. Those individuals who have been with the company the longest would have accumulated the most sick leave credit. This recognizes that those employees with the longest tenure tend to be older, and thus have a greater probability of incurring an extended illness.

One of the problems with liberal sick leave programs is abuse. Employees may perceive this benefit to be something they have earned and therefore have coming to them. This perception is also compounded by the belief that you "use them or lose them." It does not take long for that perception to permeate an organization. Take for example two workers, both receiving the same number of sick days per year. Let us suppose that after five years, both leave the organization. Employee one has no accumulated sick days, so he is not upset. But employee two has sixty days accumulated, reflecting twelve days for each year of service. On separating from the company, employee two gives back these sixty days. In essence, she has been punished for not using those days. With all things being equal, employee one

---

[2] Short-term disability programs may be provided through commercial carriers, or through self-funding arrangements. The more popular of the two is purchased coverage.

[3] Before we proceed, there is an important piece of federal legislation that warrants mentioning. Based on the 1978 Pregnancy Disability Act, employers that offer short-term disability insurance to their employees must include pregnancy as part of the policy's coverage. This means that in whatever capacity employers "cover" other disabilities like an extended illness, the coverage for disability due to pregnancy must be the same (see Chapter 2).

[4] The number of sick days offered to employees generally varies according to their position in the organization, and their length of service. Many organizations require a waiting period, approximately six months, before sick leave "kicks" in.

has had an additional twelve weeks of leave with pay.[5] The belief that one should amass sick leave for use later in life is quickly diminishing. That belief may have been popular when a person joined an organization early in life and retired from that company, but with today's mobility, long-term focus has little meaning, especially considering that sick days are not usually transferrable to another organization. Thus the use-them-or-lose-them concept may only hinder productivity.

Recent attempts to combat this potential for sick leave abuse have come in the form of financial incentives to individuals who do not fully use their sick leave for the year. In one instance, a company provides ten days of sick leave to each employee and then gives a $10-a-day premium for each day not taken. Thus an employee who uses only three sick days would receive a $70 bonus. This may result in an employee who will come to work ill so as not to lose the bonuses. Thus employees are rewarded for not taking sick leave, but that may result in longer periods of illness, or the infecting of others in the unit. It is not uncommon to find many people in one department out sick at the same time, especially when something is "going around".

Other attempts have been made to pay an employee, at the time of resignation or retirement, a lump sum for the unused sick days on a two-for-one basis. One problem with this option is that sick days earned during a lower salary year would be paid off at the current higher salary. This increases the cost of benefits administration. Nonetheless, although attempts are being made to correct the abuse of sick leave, as long as workers perceive the reward for not using a sick day to be less than the benefit of an additional day off, abuses will continue. Employees may do so until the employer is ready to pay for sick days not used, day for day. For example, in some manufacturing firms, employers are offering to buy back unused sick leave from their employees. This incentive serves as an end-of-year bonus and encourages judicious use of sick time.[6]

The last aspect of sick leave is its link to a long-term disability program (we will discuss long-term disability shortly). The purpose of accruing sick leave in many cases is to provide a bridge to the time that a long-term disability program would take effect. For instance, if the company has a long-term disability insurance program that becomes effective after the 180th day of extended illness, then there is a need to cover an employee's salary for the initial 180 days. This coverage is provided through a liberal sick leave program. That means employees are permitted to accrue a number of sick days

---

[5] 12 weeks @ 5 days per week = 60 days available.

[6] Other employers are simply doing away with sick leave and are adding the time to vacation or personal days.

throughout their tenure in the organization up to a maximum of 180 days.[7] The onset of an illness extending beyond this time period would be covered under the company's long-term disability program.

The nature of using sick leave as a bridge to a long-term disability program is a critical selling point for employees. They must understand for what sick leave is intended—their personal illness, not a day off from work for any other reason. Also, as they become more involved in their financial planning, they recognize the importance of having salary continuations in the event of an extended illness. This knowledge, coupled with sound sick leave policies, may lead to less abuse in the years ahead.

Short-term Disability Programs.   Many insurance carriers sell a product to companies that provide coverage for an employee's short-term disability (STD). The purpose of this coverage is to "provide a modest level of income replacement for lost wages as a result of a nonoccupational accident sickness."[8] Employees covered under such a plan typically receive between 60 percent and 67 percent[9] of their gross pay. In most cases, there is a minimum waiting period of one week before the benefit takes effect.[10] This waiting period is often required to ensure that the claim of a disability, especially illness, is not fabricated or leading to extreme abuse of the program.

The STD offered to employees is not to be regarded as a permanent, ongoing benefit. In most cases there is a maximum number of weeks that this policy will stay in effect. While the average length of coverage is generally twenty six weeks,[11] coverage may be for periods as short as thirteen weeks or for as long as two years.[12]

State Disability Laws.   Some states have regulations establishing guidelines governing disability coverage. For the most part, these laws, often called temporary disability insurance (TDI), provide for replacement income for individuals who did not become sick or injured because of the job. In these states, eligible workers receive approximately 50 percent to 67 percent of their

---

[7] The time it would take to accrue the maximum number of sick days varies according to the organization's sick leave policy and its coordination with a long-term disability program.

[8] Rosenbloom and Hallman, *Employee Benefit Planning*, p. 219.

[9] Thomas Brown and Howard Hensley, "Disability Benefit Plans," in *Employee Benefits Handbook*, ed. Fred K. Foulkes (Boston: Warren, Gorham, & Lamont, 1982), pp. 18-19.

[10] Waiting periods for an injury stemming from an accident may differ from that for an illness. In these cases, the waiting period for an injury may be shorter, if there is one at all.

[11] Brown and Hensley, "Disability Benefit Plans," pp. 18-19.

[12] Rosenbloom and Hallman, *Employee Benefit Planning*, p. 220.

gross pay, for a duration not to exceed twenty-six weeks.[13] Similar to the commercial STD programs, many of the state disability laws also require a one-week waiting period before benefits commence.

Workers' Compensation. Whereas short-term disability and some state laws focus on nonoccupational injuries or illness, workers' compensation is designed to provide replacement income for work-related maladies. Workers' compensation provides benefits for "income loss resulting from total disability, impairment, medical expenses, and rehabilitation expenses."[14] With respect to income loss, workers' compensation generally requires income replacement at two-thirds of the employee's gross income. Waiting periods for workers' compensation payments usually span three to seven days.[15]

From an impairment point of view, workers' compensation has a schedule of benefits that defines the benefit level for losses of limbs, sight, and so on. In these cases, losses would be classified as permanent total disabilities, and would be compensated accordingly. Compensation for injuries classified as permanent partial (such as the loss of use of an appendage) varies state by state. Impairment compensation is usually provided in excess of replacement income given.

If health insurance coverage was unable to prevent a major illness from occurring, and an extended period of time off work did not provide for ample recuperation, then it may be time to focus on a long-term disability program.

Long-term Disability Programs

The Representative Plan. Similar to their short-term disability counter-parts, long-term disability (LTD) programs are designed to provide replacement income for an employee who is no longer able to return to work and when short-term coverage has expired. The period of time before long-term disability becomes effective is usually six months. Some type of long-term disability coverage is in effect in almost 99 percent of all companies and is provided on a temporary or permanent basis.[16] By definition, a temporary disability is one in which an individual cannot perform the job duties for the

---

[13] In California, the maximum period is thirty-nine weeks. See Commerce Clearing House, *Topical Law Reports: Compensation* (Illinois; 1984), p. 2701; and Brown and Hensley, "Disability Benefit Plans," p. 18-19.

[14] Robert M. McCaffery, *Employee Benefit Programs: A Total Compensation Perspective* (Boston: PWS-KENT Publishing, 1988), p. 51.

[15] Commerce Clearing House, *Compensation*, July 1988, p. 2714.

[16] Commerce Clearing House, *Compensation*, May 1988, p. 2699-7.

first twenty four months after injury or illness. Permanent long-term disability is when an individual is unable to perform in any occupation.[17]

The benefits paid to employees are customarily set between 50 percent and 67 percent, with 60 percent salary replacement the most common (see Table 6–2). In most plans, there is a maximum monthly payment of replacement income. This may be as little $1,000, or greater than $5,000.[18] Table 6–3 reveals a breakdown of the maximum payment offered by many long-term disability policies. In most cases, long-term disability payments continue until the individual's sixty-fifth birthday.[19]

TABLE 6–2   Long-Term Disability Income

PERCENTAGE	TOTAL	WITH MAXIMUM	WITHOUT MAXIMUM
Fixed Percent of Earnings	76	60	16
< 50%	2	2	0
50%	20	15	5
55%	2	2	0
60%	39	30	9
65%–67%	12	11	1
> 70%	2	2	0

Source: Reproduced with permission from *Human Resource Management-Compensation*, Published and copyrighted by Commerce Clearing House, Inc., 4025 W. Peterson Avenue, Chicago, Illinois, 60646.

TABLE 6–3   Maximum Monthly LTD Payments

AMOUNT	PERCENTAGE
< $2,500	5
$2,501–$3,000	6
$3,001–$4,000	11
$4,001–$5,000	24
> $5,000	25

Source: Hewitt Associate's Survey, printed in Commerce Clearing House Topical Law Reports, *Human Resource Management-Compensation* (Illinois: Commerce Clearing House, Inc., May 1988), p. 2699-7. With permission.

---

[17] Ibid.

[18] Rosenbloom and Hallman, *Employee Benefit Planning*, p. 227.

[19] Some disability plans pay benefits for different periods if the disability is due to illness rather than due to injury.

Any time a long-term disability plan is in effect, payments made to the employee are usually reduced by an amount provided through other government sources.[20] That is, if an individual is receiving Social Security Disability Insurance (SSDI), then the combination of the two disbursements may result in excessive payments made to the employee. The purpose of these programs is to financially assist workers during troubling times, not to foster an incentive to become disabled. As such, benefits paid to employees from the long-term disability policy are often integrated to ensure that the employee is replacing 70 percent to 80 percent of income.[21]

For example,[22] suppose an employee makes $36,000 per year. That salary translates into a monthly income of $3,000. The employing organization offers its employees long-term disability insurance benefits at 65 percent of earnings, with a monthly cap at $4,000. The company's LTD is also integrated with Social Security disability payments such that no more than 70 percent of salary is covered. The employee has a verifiable illness, is unable to work in any occupation, and has been covered under the company's short-term disability plan for the past six months. To determine what the payment made to this employee would be, we need to determine the amount of the SSDI monthly payment. For example's sake, let us assume that this employee is entitled to $12,000 in SSDI benefits a year, or $1,000 per month.[23] Now that we have our data we can determine the employee's LTD payment. After the calculations have been completed, we see that this employee, given his specific set of circumstances, is eligible for a payment of $1,000 from SSDI, and $1,100 from the LTD policy. Even though the LTD limit of 65 percent of the employee's salary would be $1,950, when integrated with SSDI, the employee may not receive more than $2,100 (70 percent of monthly salary). Table 6-4 reflects our calculations.

---

[20] The primary government source in this matter is the Social Security Disability Insurance program (SSDI). This federally mandated program provides for subsidized payments to eligible workers (those covered under Social Security) who are unable to continue working. The program offers specific benefit payments to individuals, which increase based on the number of dependents. SSDI payments continue until the individuals sixty-fifth birthday, at which time payments are made through the Old Age Benefits coverage of OASDI. For a comprehensive coverage of SSDI, see Brown and Hensley, "Disability Benefit Plans," pp. 18-19.

[21] The reason for the 70 to 80 percent of replacement income stems from the tax-free nature of some payments. (Payments from an employer LTD are generally taxable; the amount received from LTD based on employee-paid premiums is not taxable income.) If long-term payments were not reduced, it is conceivable that an employee receiving LTD and government disability payments could have a greater income than when he worked. This logic defeats the purpose of the program.

[22] This example was directly influenced by a similar example given in Rosenbloom and Hallman, *Employee Benefit Planning*, p. 225.

[23] Actual benefits received under SSDI vary according to family status, average annual income, and the consumer price index. As such, only an estimate is given.

TABLE 6–4   Calculating LTD Payment

Employee Earnings	$ 36,000	/yr
	3,000	/mo
65 % LTD coverage	1,950	
70 % of monthly income		
for integration with		
Social Security	2,100	
SSDI Payment	1,000	
Proposed total monthly payment		
without integration	2,950	($1,950 + $1,000)
Proposed total monthly payment		
with integration	2,100	(maximum)
Overage	850	($2,950 - $2,100)
LTD payment	1,100	($1,950 - $850)

The above is provided for example purposes only to show how integration may result in the reduction of LTD payments. It is by no means intended as the only means of calculating LTD payments. There are too many extraneous factors that must come into play, such factors as the LTD's maximum, if any, the percentage of replacement income, SSDI or other governmental benefits offered, and so on. The result, however, is a complicated process and calculation for the benefits administrator.

Conclusion.   In a good employee welfare program, a company tries to provide the best coverage possible: a good health care benefit and short- and long-term disability programs. Unfortunately, there are times when these programs are no longer necessary, that is, when the employee dies. While protection for the employee is now a moot point, there are programs that may be extended to the survivors. This is what is called survivor benefits—namely, life insurance, Social Security payments, and accidental death and dismemberment coverage.

SURVIVOR BENEFITS

To provide protection to the families of employees, many companies offer life insurance as a benefit. Life insurance programs offered to employees typically come in two varieties—noncontributory and contributory policies. Our major concern in this context is with the noncontributory variety, for that is the one that is generally totally employer funded.

Noncontributory Plans

Group Term Life Insurance. When companies offer group term life insurance to their employees,[24] the standard policy provides for a death benefit of one to five times their annual rates of pay, with most including a double indemnity provision. That is, should an employee's death result from an accident, the benefit is twice the policy value. Almost 74 percent of all companies provide this coverage.[25]

Death benefits offered are generally linked to one's position in the organization. Generally speaking, the more "valuable" an employee is to the organization, the greater the death benefit offered. Those at the lower levels of the organization typically receive one to two times their annual wages as a benefit, whereas top-level employees may receive as much as two to five times their salary.[26]

The policies offered by employers are limited only by the constraints placed on them by the insurance company underwriting the benefit, and by any state legislation.[27] Typical plans include term insurance policies or Survivor Income Benefit Insurance (SIBI).[28] The more common of the two, however, is term insurance. Term insurance is offered to companies on a renewable basis, and provides for a fixed-amount (lump-sum) death benefit to the designated beneficiary.[29] For tax purposes, the premium on any amount of group term insurance provided in excess of $50,000 is taxable income to the employee.

For the most part, term insurance is a good decision for employers. In most cases this insurance offers "lower premiums for the employer, an absence of medical, age and other restrictions, and is a rarity for contract cancellation."[30] With cost considerations taken into account, term insurance provides an excellent benefit while simultaneously containing some of its cost. Cost figures for term insurance average approximately 60 cents for every $1,000 of insurance.[31]

---

[24] Depending on company policy, there may be a time lag before a new employee's insurance policy takes effect. When waiting periods are used, they typically last about six months. Additionally, eligibility periods may be waived for management personnel.

[25] Commerce Clearing House, *Compensation*, August 1987, p. 2651.

[26] Ibid, p. 2605-3.

[27] Ibid, p. 2524.

[28] Rosenbloom and Hallman, *Employee Benefit Planning*, p. 39.

[29] In most states, beneficiary designation is the prerogative of the employee. However, employers are rarely permitted to be designated as the beneficiary of an employee's life insurance policy.

[30] Commerce Clearing House, *Compensation*, August 1987, p. 2611.

[31] Ibid, p. 2624.

Survivor income benefit insurance is a policy that typically provides for an annuity, rather than a lump-sum payment, to the survivors. According to SIBI plans, beneficiaries are generally designated by the policy, not the policyholder, and include the employee's spouse or dependent children.[32] Although this type of insurance policy has not been as favorable as the group term insurance policy, there is some indication that this may best be "suited as supplement to basic group term insurance."[33]

Variations of other life insurance plans have made their way into organizations. Because of the complexity in their administration, IRS considerations, and the like, many of these policies have never become as popular as term insurance. One plan that was recently touted as an excellent supplemental life insurance policy for employers to offer is the group universal life insurance plan (GULP). This type of insurance permits employees to invest a part of their insurance monies in competitive market portfolios, and have the money accrue on a tax-deferred basis. However, some individuals believe that the GULPs are not as effective as a simple group term insurance policy coupled with a 401(K) program.[34] They reason that ineffectiveness stems from the costs to administer the program, enrollment problems, and investment performance,[35] and they do not receive the same tax-favored treatment as group term life insurance.

Whatever the case may be, there is some indication that employers are always looking for better life insurance products that will help to contain costs while still providing a sound death benefit to survivors. So far, however, the group term insurance policy appears to have the edge.

Travel Insurance.   Another insurance plan offered to many employees is travel insurance. Under this policy, employees' lives are covered in the event of death while traveling on company time. This insurance typically provides a lump-sum payment, from $50,000 to $1 million.

Depending on any unique provisions of a policy, as long as an employee is conducting business-related activities when the death occurs, the insurance will be paid. This means, for example, if a salesperson's day typically begins by traveling to a client's place of business from his or her residence, then coverage begins as soon as this person gets into the car. If he or she were killed in route to that location, then this insurance would be activated. The key element is

---

[32] Rosenbloom and Hallman, *Employee Benefit Planning*, p. 60.

[33] McCaffery, *Employee Benefit Programs*, p. 100.

[34] Commerce Clearing House, *Human Resource Management: Trends and Ideas*, no. 155, November 2, 1987, p. 174.

[35] Ibid., p. 175.

when the death occurs. An employee who normally commutes to work would not be covered if an accident happened on the way.

Contributory Plans

Group Life Insurance. Many companies offer additional life insurance plans to their employees. These plans are typically purchased through the employer so the employee can gain the benefit of group coverage. The plans that are offered to employees are generally supplemental term life insurance and accidental death and dismemberment (AD&D) policies.

Supplemental life insurance policies frequently offer employees the added opportunity to expand their coverage in various increments. For instance, if the employee is provided an insurance policy by the employer that equates to two times salary, that employee is generally permitted to purchase additional life insurance of either one or two times salary. The premiums for these additional policies are borne solely by the employee.

Deciding to purchase additional life insurance from an employer is a matter of personal preference. There are some pros and cons for employees to consider, however. First of all, like the employer-paid life insurance, these policies often rarely require medical examinations. If one is uninsurable elsewhere, this supplemental plan may be cost-effective. Additionally, employers often deduct the premiums from an employee's paycheck. This way, the policy is paid for without much work on the employee's part. Because no medical examination may be required, people who present underwriting risks generally opt for the policy. Accordingly, to cover this added risk, the premiums are generally higher than if the individual purchased a separate plan on his or her own. Whatever the case, supplemental policies provide benefits for many employees, at little cost to the employer. Aside from its administration, this supplemental policy is relatively cost-effective.

AD&D Coverage. Most individuals who are in their twenties, thirties, or forties, who are in generally good health, will probably die due to some type of accident. AD&D insurance is a means of guarding against unexpected deaths and provides a sizable sum, up to $1 million, for the survivors. These policies are inexpensive to purchase and maintain from the employee's point of view, and provide a large amount of insurance money should the family "breadwinner" die accidentally.

Additionally, similar to workers' compensation impairment schedules, AD&D policies provide payment for losses of body parts. These schedules are fixed and communicated to the policyholder on enrollment.

Social Security Survivor Benefits

Employees covered under the Social Security system are also afforded some benefits for their survivors. In this case, Social Security typically provides for a percentage of the employee's salary, approximately 67 percent, to be given to the survivors. The specific amount will vary according to the age of the survivor, the number of dependents, and so on. Table 6–5 is a summary of these benefits.

TABLE 6–5   Social Security Survivor Benefits

Monthly Benefits To

Widow or widower (and/or eligible surviving divorced spouse) age 65 or over (or 60 through 64 at reduced benefits), or disabled and age 50 or older.

Widow or widower (regardless of age) (or eligible surviving divorced spouse) if caring for a child of the deceased worker who is under 16 or disabled and who is entitled to benefits.

Eligible child or children who are unmarried and either under age 18 or a full-time high school student under age 19, or are disabled before age 22.

Dependent parent age 62 or over.

Lump-sum death benefit ($255).

Source: Jerry S. Rosenbloom and G. Victor Hallman, *Employee Benefit Planning*, 2d ed. (Englewood Cliffs, N.J. Prentice Hall, 1986), p. 36.

Conclusion

Employees do not usually think about the possibility of dying during their work lives, especially when other family responsibilities are present. Unfortunately, however, such an event does occur. While it may be little comfort, knowing that one's survivors will be financially cared for is some relief. Earlier we presented an example of a long-term disability payment made to a $36,000-a-year employee. Let us see what kind of survivor benefits this same employee has.

Assuming the company has a group term life insurance policy that pays twice one's yearly salary, with a double indemnity rider, we can show the various calculations for the employee's death benefit. The company also provides travel accident insurance of $100,000. Let us also assume that this employee has a matching contributory group term life insurance, and a voluntary AD&D policy in the amount of $250,000. Table 6–6 is a representation of this employee's survivor benefits package.

TABLE 6–6   Life Insurance Coverage

Employee earnings	$ 36,000	yr
Life insurance coverage	$ 72,000	(2 × $36,000)
if accidental	$ 144,000	(2 × $36,000) × 2
Travel insurance	$ 100,000	
Supplemental life insurance	$ 72,000	
AD&D coverage	$ 250,000	

IF EMPLOYEE DIES OF NATURAL CAUSES	COVERAGE	BY ACCIDENT
$72,000	Employer GLI	$144,000
$72,000	Supplemental LI	72,000
	AD&D	250,000
	Travel	100,000
$144,000	MAXIMUM COVERAGE	$566,000

SUMMARY

After reading this chapter you will know that:

* *The purpose of a disability program is to ensure income replacement in the event of a temporary or permanent disability arising from an extended illness or accident.*

* *The various types of short-term disability programs are sick leave programs, short-term disability programs, state disability laws, and workers' compensation.*

* *Sick leave is generally allocated to employees on the basis of a fixed number of days a year and is accrued on a cumulative basis. In some cases, sick leave is expanded relative to years of service with the organization.*

* *Sick leave abuse stems from the perception that this benefit is something an employee has earned, and that if it is not used it may be lost. To assist in eliminating sick leave abuse, some companies have begun to offer financial incentives to employees who do not abuse their sick leave, including buying back any unused sick leave an employee may have accumulated at retirement or resignation.*

* *Temporary disability insurance programs are usually coupled with mandated state disability laws and provide for replacement income up to approximately twenty-six weeks.*

* *Short-term disability programs provide replacement income for extended nonoccupational illnesses or injuries, whereas workers' compensation is designed to provide replacement income for work-related maladies.*

* *Long-term disability programs are designed to provide replacement income for individuals who are unable to return to work, when short-term disability coverage has expired.*

* *Calculating a long-term disability payment requires knowledge of the employer's plan, its desired income replacement formula, and the amount of integration necessary with Social Security benefits.*
* *Survivor benefit plans can be categorized in two ways: noncontributory plans (group term life insurance, and employer travel insurance) and contributory (group supplemental life insurance, and accidental death and dismemberment insurance).*
* *The types of life insurance programs offered to employees vary in each organization. The more popular include group life insurance (term insurance) and survivor income benefit insurance. Other types of policies may be offered, such as whole life policies, or a combination of the above.*
* *Employer travel insurance provides a fixed sum of insurance should an employee die while performing the duties of his or her job.*
* *Accidental death and dismemberment insurance is a contributory insurance policy available to employees and pays a fixed sum should the employee die or lose one or more a body parts accidentally.*
* *Social security survivor benefits are provided to the survivors of an employee who was covered under Social Security Laws.*

KEY TERMS

Accidental death and dismemberment (AD&D)	Permanent total disability
	Short-term disability
Contributory plans	(STD) programs
Death benefits	Sick leave
Disability insurance programs	Social Security survivor benefits
Double indemnity	Social Security Disablilty
Group life insurance	Insurance (SSDI)
Group universal life	State disability laws
insurance plans (GULPs)	Supplemental life insurance
Impairment	Survivor Income Benefit
Long-term disability	Insurance (SIBI)
programs (LTD)	Temporary disability insurance
Noncontributory plans	(TDI)
Old Age, Survivors, and	Waiting periods
Disability Insurance (OASDI)	Workers' compensation
Permanent partial disability	

QUESTIONS FOR REVIEW AND DISCUSSION

1. What is the purpose of providing short- and long-term disability programs to employees? How much income is replaced?
2. What is the purpose of sick leave? Why is it abused?
3. "If employers want to end sick leave abuse, they should stop offering it to employees. Employers who know their employees know when they are genuinely sick. When that occurs, the employee simply stays home until he or she is feeling better. This way, there is no need for a sick leave policy." Do you agree or disagree with the statement? Explain.
4. How do state disability laws affect short-terms disability programs offered to employees?
5. Compare and contrast short-term disability and workers' compensation. How are they alike? Different?
6. How does long-term disability operate? How are employees determined to be eligible? How much income is replaced? How is it integrated with Social Security benefits?
7. Suppose a company provides a long-term disability plan to its employees. In this plan, 60 percent of income is replaced, with a monthly cap of $2,500. Calculate the monthly LTD payment for a $25,000-a-year employee. For a $40,000-a-year employee. Assume SSDI payment of $250 per month in both cases.
8. What is the reasoning for offering higher-level employees in the organization a greater amount of life insurance?
9. Why should employees buy supplemental life insurance from their employer's plan? Why should they not purchase this extra life insurance coverage?
10. "Disability and survivor benefits should be the responsibility of each worker. Employers cannot be responsible for the financial welfare of each of their employees. Accordingly, this is a benefit that should be reduced in order to contain benefit costs." Do you agree or disagree with the statement? Explain.

ADDITIONAL READINGS

DINIRO, JOHN J.   "Don't Let a Disability Destroy Your Business." *Baron's*, May 11, 1987, p. 42.

"Disability Benefits: How Much, How Long?" *Consumer Guide Magazine*, May 21, 1987, p. 123.

"The Disability Program: How It Works and Who's Eligible.", *Consumer Guide Magazine*, November 1986, p. 86.

HILL, DIANE B.   "Employee Sponsored Long-Term Disability Insurance." *Monthly Labor Review* 110 (July 1987): 16.

MCGRATH, ANNE.   "Protecting Your Earning Power," *U.S. News and World Report*, May 15, 1986, p. 56.

WIATROWSKI, WILLIAM J.   "Employee Income Protection against Short-Term Disabilities." *Monthly Labor Review* 108 (February 1985): 32.

CHAPTER SEVEN

RETIREMENT BENEFIT PLANS

LEARNING OBJECTIVES

After reading this chapter, you will be able to:
* *Discuss the tax reform impact on benefit programs.*
* *Discuss changes brought about by the Consolidated Omnibus Budget Reconciliation Act.*
* *Discuss why payroll-based stock membership plans are seldom used.*
* *Discuss the reasons for funding problems in pension plans.*
* *Describe an employee stock ownership plan.*
* *Discuss some basic elements of retirement planning.*
* *Describe the impact of inflation on retirement accounts.*
* *Discuss the size and impact of pensions on our economy.*
* *Discuss who is covered by pension plans.*
* *Discuss the conventional pension benefit formula.*

INTRODUCTION

When we begin to talk about retirement plans, a whole new jargon emerges. These terms are often unfamiliar to us and typically associated with fears that they may be too technical for us to understand. This fear attacks senior managers with MBAs the same way it grips the employee population.

We hear terms like Keogh plans, IRAs, ERISA, ESOPs, and 401(k). Then if that is not enough, insurance aspects of pensions are typically mentioned. For example, what options do we want for survivor benefits, or annuity payment options if we live?

For many of us, we want to arrive at a point of feeling competent on the topic. Most of us believe that competency in pension plans is achieved by being able to "crunch" or manipulate numbers on any given point of a discussion regarding retirement. That isn't necessary, however. Competency is better achieved by understanding issues. It is achieved by understanding the legal and tax ramifications. Crunching the numbers becomes the easy part, as this activity is typically aided by computer software programs. Without the understanding, however, the numbers examined in the solution are not all that meaningful. All too often, many individuals have made retirement decisions without the understanding, ramifications, and legal implications. The decisions were based on numbers supplied by actuaries or accountants, generally with only superficial detail. The results have been the spiraling costs and the panic currently facing us. This chapter is devoted to raising the level of understanding to where we feel confident enough to use the jargon. The number crunching in this chapter is done to help illustrate points and difficult concepts.

RETIREMENT PLANNING: THE MENTAL STATE

Most of us are not experts in retirement planning. Many of those who offer themselves as experts are from a particular investment area and are understandably biased. For example, the insurance agents, or mutual fund salespeople who counsel us on retirement, present the topic with a "product"-based solution they sell, ready and waiting to fulfill a part of someone's retirement plan.

In corporate work, we rarely have the opportunity to look at retirement benefit planning through the eyes of the worker. The scope is always aggregate cost and global numbers. Our heart may be for the worker, but our bias is elsewhere, similar to the insurance or mutual fund salesperson. Yet we must not forget what we are trying to achieve. We have learned that the transition to retirement years is a necessary and delicate process. The concerns of the retiree's mental state must be addressed. With today's shift in providing continued benefits into the retirement years along with increases in the value of those benefits, keeping retired workers "fit and healthy" is a major concern. One quick look at any demographic projection only confirms the massive project that we must deal with in years to come.

Retirement is not leaving one's employment for the shuffleboard court or craft room. If active people never played shuffleboard or never liked making little crafts before, it is highly unlikely they will in the future.

Retirement is a change in the life stage of activity, not in the phenomenon of mental activity. Our healthiest retirees are not retired mentally or physically. They merely shifted current life energy from one area to another.

There should be no gap in mental usage from one's job to post-career endeavors. The physical stress will be shifted to consciously applied stress for limited duration such as walking, jogging, golf, and other activities. But good retirement planning implies there are pursuits ready for the mind to handle.

The swift removal of people from the productive spheres of society after thirty or forty years of being part of an organization often delivers such a trauma that many can never fully recover their feelings of self-worth and self-respect. The examples of people who die soon after retirement are numerous. All too many are those were nearly dead when they found themselves apart from the "world" as they knew it.

This occurrence is partly management's fault. Lifecycle planning in organizations can prevent this by counseling people all during their careers and encouraging broad areas of mental interest. Granting of sabbaticals is an example of how some organizations reduce turnovers of key people. The sabbatical allows people the freedom to pursue an area of their life's dream. Let us present the retirement years as a sabbatical, a chance to pursue new and different intellectual goals. But this will not occur on its own. We must foster the changing of life stage energy flows so that no lapse of mental sharpness will happen. Retirees will keep their sharp wit and positive energy well into these valuable years.

However, to enjoy these years and pursue this new level of mental existence requires the best mix of financial benefits.

RETIREMENT PLANNING VEHICLES

As the point of retirement approaches, it becomes increasingly important to identify all the sources (and potential sources) of income that may surface during retirement. The alternatives here include one's private pension plan, Social Security, individual retirement accounts (IRAs), self-employed retirement plans, life insurance and annuities, personal investments, inheritances, and any other savings or investments.

Private Pension

There is no legislation mandating companies to provide pension plans for workers. Competition for the best workers, however, union negotiations, and other various professional associations have had the effect of promoting pension plans across the spectrum of organization size. As discussed in Chapter 2, the Employee Retirement Income Security Act of 1974 (ERISA) promises employees will get the benefits of their employer's plan, even in the event of corporate bankruptcy or merger. Additionally, ERISA requires that employees be informed of what their benefits include. But just stating what their benefits include may not be enough. They must be familiar with the various plans offered. There are four broad categories of pension plans. These are defined benefit plans, defined contribution plans, money purchase pension plans, and profit-sharing plans.

Defined Benefit Plans.   In years past the most popular pension was a defined benefit plan. Because of its early introduction and popularity, it is still the most common. This plan specifies the benefits workers will get at retirement. The amount typically revolves around some fixed monthly income for life, or a variation of a lump-sum cash distribution.

The amount and type of benefit are written in the plan, and the company is responsible for contributing into a trust fund an amount each year so that the money will be sufficient to pay the promised benefit levels. The amount contributed each year is figured actuarially. That is, contributions are made by considering variables such as how long plan participants are expected to live, their lifetime earnings, and how much return the trust portfolio will receive annually (5 percent, 10 percent, and so on,). The pension payout formulas used to determine retirement benefits vary widely.

Defined Contribution Plans.   Defined contribution plans are different from defined benefit plans in at least one very important area—no specific dollar benefits are fixed. The plan establishes rules for contributions. The money is invested, and projections are offered as to probable retirement income levels. However, the company is not bound by these projections. Accordingly, unfunded pension liability problems do not occur. For this reason, defined contribution plans have become the popular trend for new qualified pension plans. Additionally, variations in plan administration frequently allow the employee some selection in the investment choices. That is, one may select bonds for security, common stocks for appreciation and an inflation hedge, or some type of money market fund.

Money Purchase Pension Plan.   Money purchase pension plans are variants of defined contribution pension plans. The difference between the two justifies their being listed separately. Under this arrangement, the company commits to put annually into the fund a percentage of the employee's pay. The maximum permitted is 25 percent. With this plan no specific dollar benefits are fixed. Projections of probable income can be made, but the company is not bound to the projection.

Profit-Sharing Plans.   Profit-sharing pension plans are yet another variation of defined contribution plans. Under these plans, the company contributes to a trust fund account an optional percentage of each worker's pay (maximum allowed by law is 15 percent). This, of course, is guided by the profit level in the organization. The operative word in profit-sharing plans here is "optional." The company is not bound by law to make contributions every year. It should be noted, however, that although employers are not bound by law the majority of employers feel a moral obligation to make a contribution. Often they will keep to a schedule, even when profits are slim or nonexistent.[1]

There is another key point to remember in the above discussions of defined contribution plans and their variants. An employee's retirement happiness in terms of financial security is based in large measure on the skill of the people who manage the trust fund into which the contributions are made. Their success or failure determines the benefit payout, as opposed to defined benefits, for which financial security is defined in the plan and guaranteed by law.

Social Security

Social Security is a universal system for providing some minimum retirement benefits. It is just as essential now as when it was first passed in 1935. Unfortunately, for the average worker, the private pension does not provide a sufficient retirement income. In many of those cases, Social Security payments help to augment one's retirement plan. This is why the payments appear weighted toward the lower end of the income mix, emphasizing the first $2,500 to assist workers at the lower end of pay scales to build a sound retirement income.

Social Security is an employee's most portable or vested plan. There are no penalties for changing jobs. To receive benefits implies an employee has have worked the required number of quarters[2] and paid into the plan. The amount employees pay is a certain percentage of their wages up to the "maximum covered wage" with a matching amount paid by the employer.

Benefit Levels.   What are the Social Security benefits? If a married worker retired in 1988 at the age of 65 and paid the maximum amount of Social Security for the preceding three years, the beginning level benefit in 1989 was $733 per month, or $8,800 per year. Suppose the spouse is also over 65, but never worked and is not part of any independent coverage. The spouse benefit is then one-half of the working partner's entitlement, or $4,400 per year. The combined benefit is $13,200 with escalations for inflation.

---

[1] Profit-sharing plans require that there be profits before a contribution can be made. As such, when there are no profits for the period, no contributions need to be made. The only partial exception is that contribution can be made in a year in which there are no profits if there are accumulated profits from prior years. However, should this occur, further restrictions apply.

[2] For everyone born before 1929, 26 quarters (six and a half years) of work are required to be eligible for Social Security. For those born after 1929, the required quarters are 40 (ten years).

If a retired worker decides to work after retirement, there is a penalty clause for the years 65 to 70. Benefits are reduced $1 for every $2 earned above the $8,800 level. (This figure changes regularly with inflation.) In 1990 the ratio changed to $1 for every $3 in earnings.

Benefit Adjustments. There are adjustments made both for postponing benefits and for taking early retirement. After an individual turns 70, that person can earn any amount without penalty. If one defers benefits because work or whatever after the age of 65 there is a 3 percent benefit for each year until age 70 is reached. After 1990 this incentive will also be increased.

If an employee decides to retire early, Social Security benefits can begin at age 62. The reduction in the benefit is 5/9 of 1 percent for each month before age 65 that benefits begin. The conversion of benefits is listed in Table 7–1 with age 65 at the 100 percent level and age 62 at the 80 percent level.

TABLE 7–1   Early Retirement Pay Adjustments

AGE OF RETIREMENT	PERCENTAGE OF BENEFIT
65	100
64	93 1/3
63	86 2/3
62	80

The Status of the Plan. Currently Social Security is exempt from federal taxes provided one's income is under a specified limit. If a single person's income is over $25,000, or $32,000 for a married person filing jointly, then one-half of the amount is taxable. A reoccurring proposal is to tax this income to correct for actuarial problems now being encountered within the system. If this occurs, planned income levels will have to be adjusted after retirement to reflect this change. If it is of any consolation to the reader, the vast majority of the industrialized world pays as much or more for similar social welfare protection. The countries with the least amount in this area are Switzerland and Japan. Japan is currently under significant pressure to increase benefits for its older citizens. While Switzerland may not have a social welfare system at our level, all of their other social welfare programs raise the equivalent tax to an amount roughly equal to that paid by the average U.S. worker.[3]

---

[3] Employee Benefit Research Institute, Dallas Salisbury, ed. *Retirement Income and the Economy: Retirement Income for the Aged* (Washington, D.C.: 1981), p. 13.

Individual Retirement Account

From 1982 to 1986 in an act of "benevolence" for the workers, the Individual Retirement Account (IRA) became the cream of retirement planning. It was a tax shelter for the average person, a way to build a true nest egg. Anyone who had earned income could invest in an IRA, including those who received alimony after 1985.

The limit was $2,000 or 100 percent of earned income—whichever was less. Individuals contributed less if they desired, and employees could choose whatever investment vehicle they liked. The Tax Reform Act of 1986 changed a major part of this tax shelter bonanza. The IRA contribution is deductible only for certain income levels. Some experts believe, however, that although the tax deduction may be lost for higher income earners, it may still worth investing in IRAs for retirement. The miracle of compound interest working in harmony with the tax-free accumulation of interest earnings on the account combines to make the program beneficial. Table 7–2 gives some examples of potential growth. To pick some figures from the table, using the conservative 8 percent growth rate for $2,000 a year for twenty years yields $98,850 to the investor. If a person can save $500 per year in the IRA for twenty years at 8 percent interest, a yield of $24,700 is achieved.

Finally, although there is no lower age limit, the ceiling for contributing is 70 1/2. Taking money out without the penalty tax of 10 percent begins at 59 1/2 (except for disability). All withdrawals must begin, however, at age 70 1/2.

TABLE 7–2   Individual Account Growth Rates

ANNUAL CONTRIBUTION	VALUE AT * END OF YEAR	Annual 8%	Growth 10%	Rates 15%
$2,000	5	$ 12,670	$ 13,430	$ 15,500
500	5	3,160	3,350	3,875
2,000	10	31,290	35,060	46,700
500	10	7,820	8,760	11,673
2,000	20	98,850	126,000	235,620
500	20	24,700	31,500	58,900
2,000	40	559,560	973,700	4,091,800
500	40	139,890	243,425	1,022,975

*Table assumes interest accumulation will be tax exempt and accumulate at the same rate of interest.

Other Retirement Vehicles

There are as many possible retirement instruments available as there are creative people in that industry. We have reviewed the various key plans; however, the following are also in common usage and are included to ensure one's familiarity with them. But, due to their similarity to other programs, which becomes apparent quickly, the discussion will be kept to a minimum.

403(b)s.   The 403(b) is named for the section of the Internal Revenue codes that created the plan. It is a mirror image of the 401(k) plan except for a 20 percent of compensation contribution ceiling. It is designed for educational and various nonprofit organizations.

Simplified Employee Pension Plans.   The simplified employee pension (SEP) plan is a fairly new and, therefore, mostly unknown product that closely resembles an IRA type account.

The key difference is that IRAs limit the annual contribution to $2,000. Contributions to the SEP/IRA are permitted up to 15 percent of compensation or $30,000, whichever is less. The SEP is very simple to establish, easy to maintain, and flexible for the employee—but must be established by the employer. The employee is able to select the type of account into which the contributions are paid. As a nice bonus, having a SEP does not rule out having an IRA account. The handling of the contributions is also similar to an IRA. As this type of account receives more attention, there is little doubt its popularity will continue to grow.

GOVERNMENT INFLUENCES

Chapter 2 provided a review of the laws affecting benefits. However, one piece of legislation has had a major impact on retirement plans and warrants a closer look.   The influence stems from the Tax Reform Act of 1986. In 1984, the Treasury Department called for "tax reform for fairness, simplicity, and economic growth."[4] In 1985, President Reagan sent to Congress a similar echo of the Treasury Department call. During the interim from 1984 to the passage of the Tax Reform Act of 1986, "simplicity" was definitely left out and reform more accurately replaced by the term "overhaul."   In the area of qualified pension plans, both sponsors and participants nededed to make some difficult choices in very complex decision patterns.

The Tax Reform Act of 1986 included both a lowering of the tax rate and the removal of the favorable treatment on long-term capital gains. As a result of this treatment, Congress made the deferral of taxable income less valuable. This posed a serious problem in executive pension perks. In particular, for 401(k) plans, the question of the value of deferring income during a time of low tax rates arose. Additionally, incentives to save through the use of a

---

[4] Dick Raskin and Jay Peters, "Tax Reform's Effect on Qualified Plans," *Personnel Administration* 31, no. 11 (November 1986): 70.

qualified plan are being phased out or removed altogether, with other disincentives added.

Effect on Qualified Plans

The effect of the Tax Reform Act on qualified plans is rather extensive and can be complex. The following discussion is designed to remove the technical language and lay out the key issues that affect the decision-making process in the area.

These changes include:

- With plan year 1989, the hardship withdrawal under the 401(k) plan is limited to the amount yearly deferment. This of course makes the earnings unavailable for use.
- Replacement of ten-year forward averaging with a less favorable five-year forward averaging. Also, this will be only used once in an employee's lifetime after the person reaches age 59 1/2.
- An additional 10 percent penalty tax on taxable withdrawals. (Note that the penalty is not applicable for persons over 59 1/2 or part of early retirement plan, death, disability, or part of an annuity installment.)

For sole proprietors, partners, and high paid corporate executives, other incentives to qualified plans have been removed and disincentives added. This list includes:

- Delayed indexing for the defined contribution annual addition, currently $30,000 until the consumer price index increases by one-third. The benefit is deferred to index for inflation after 1986, thus making 1988 the first year available for an increase.
- The new law includes all after-tax contributions in the maximum annual addition. This point highlights the reason for limiting unmatched after-tax contributions.
- An immediate indexing of a maximum of $7,000 pre-tax contribution to a 401(k) plan that began in 1987.
- A limit of $200,000 on the total annual compensation that may be recognized for plan purposes. This also includes the determination of the deduction, with the limit applied retroactively.
- A 15 percent excise tax on the excess of total annuity income from all plans over $112,500.[5] This includes an IRA plan. The saving grace here

---

[5] This 15 percent excise tax is based on the annual annuity income. This tax applies if the value of all plans exceeded $562,500 on August 1, 1986. The election must be made by filing of the 1988 tax return.

is that benefits that accrued before the effective date of the laws are partially protected by an elaborate "grandfather" procedure.

* A drop from $75,000 to $36,000 (age 55) and $63,000 (age 63) in available deferred benefit for early retirement prior to age 65.[6]

Implications of Plan Changes

The changes identified above will make deferred compensation programs less attractive. Furthermore, they somewhat eliminate the lower-paid worker from enjoying the benefits of deferred income or capital accumulation plans. But before we write off these investment vehicles, let's take a closer look. The results still point to a worthwhile investment medium.

The tax rates now in effect mean that a single individual who has an adjusted income less than $29,750 (1988) falls into a lower tax bracket. Most people who earn $50,000 or more per year, and who are covered by a retirement plan that replaces 60 percent of compensation, will never (working or retirement years) be in a lower tax bracket. What does this mean initially? It means the benefits of automatic tax savings by deferring income are diminished. Yet, if interest rates of 10 percent or more are provided on these deferrals, the program remains attractive even if tax rates increase over the long term. For example, a person deferring $100,000 at 10 percent from the company or other outside investment source would accrue an "after-tax" amount of $185,000 by deferring over ten years. Without deferring the income, the amount generated would be $155,000. Accordingly, the marginal tax rate would have to return to 50 percent at payout for the person to nearly break even.[7]

Even if tax rates move up slowly and with continued moderate inflation, deferrals appear to be an attractive employee investment. But the main issue with 401(k)'s attack by Congress was twofold. It wanted to increase tax revenues and to reduce the discrimination in pension plans. The discrimination is felt mostly by the lower-paid workers who often do not get the same benefit levels. The effect of the Tax Reform Act requires organizations to provide plans that remove this investment discrimination.

---

[6] Raskin and Peters, "Tax Reform's Effect on Qualified Plans," p. 13. Assuming, of course, adjustments to income are insignificant.

[7] John D. McMillan, "Tax Reform: What It Means," *Personnel Administration* 31, no. 12 (December 1986): 97.

THE 401(K) CONTROVERSY

A basic tenet surrounding the 401(k) debate is that the system is inequitable. In fact, there are those who say it is decidedly lopsided in favor of high-income workers. Most people are not surprised by this revelation. Much of society is tipped in favor of high-income individuals. But we forgot society is changing. The highly paid owners and managers did not make available to the workers (especially nonunion workers) any alternative system or plan adjusting for them. This short-sighted view may affect executives in many areas, not just the 401(k). The discrimination rules are extending to all benefit areas. We just keep in mind that today's worker is well educated and will not tolerate issue irregularities.

Studies report that in large nonunionized plans, only about 50 percent of the workers making under $30,000 contribute to deferred compensation plans, with only 2.2 percent contributing for the express purpose of retirement needs.[8]

It is because of the real difficulty lower-income workers have in saving for retirement that the government helped with the growth of company-paid pensions. The cost in terms of tax subsidy to support the $1 trillion private pension system will cost around $39 billion in the next decade in lost revenue to the Treasury.[9]

The Argument to Repeal 401(k)

The critics argue that 401(k) offers little to the low-income wage earner in terms of added retirement security. This too will cost the Treasury approximately $3 billion per year in lost revenue. It is feared that a possible "shift" toward do-it-yourself retirement and away from the company-paid plans may arise. Some even go so far as to accuse employers of using the 401(k) as a convenient substitute for upgrading pension plans for lower-income workers.

Data generated by the Senate Finance Committee indicate that IRAs, 401(k), and similar capital accumulation plans are used primarily by those with incomes above $50,000 per year. In addition, they do little to increase the overall savings rate, and they represent a shift away from other sources of investment. Opponents of IRA go on to point out these plans miss the mass group they were intended to help.

---

[8] Abby Brown, "The Retirement Game," *Personnel Administration* 31, no. 11 (November 1986): 58.

[9] Karen Ferguson and Kenneth Feltman, "Kill the 401(k)," *Personnel Administration*, Vol. 31, No. 11, (November 1986), p. 58.

Critics report that some smaller and medium-size organizations have found 401(k) to be such an appealing escape route from company-paid pensions that they have canceled their pensions entirely.[10]

The Arguments to Keep 401(k)

Those who wish to keep the 401(k) and other capital accumulation plans argue that it may not be perfect, but it does go a long way to meeting some needs. Specifically, these needs are defined as flexibility, portability, and control, which needs are important to lower-income workers. Flexibility is important to a worker employed by a firm that has no qualified pension plan, or cannot afford one. Portability satisfies the problem of the average person moving from job to job. With its lower vesting requirements, it can provide a medium of security. Control is given to lower-income workers to put in the amount they can afford. It can also be used if hardship strikes, or to access the funds to buy a house, finance educations, and pay for medical emergencies. The supporters argue that as the work force becomes more transient, and increases its percentage in more transient service-type jobs, the flexibility of the 401(k) becomes more important.

The Current 401(K) Status

There is no immediate solution to the problem. Prior to the pension reforms in the Tax Reform Act of 1986, there were some decided inequities that hurt the lower-income worker. The two main culprits were long vesting periods and "integration" with Social Security benefits. The Tax Reform Act shortened the vesting period from ten to five years in most plans. The law enables the employer to choose between five-year cliff vesting, which gives 100 percent vesting after five years, or the alternative of 20 percent per year after three years, whereby at the end of seven years the employee is 100 percent vested. This change alone resulted in a 7 percent gain in vested male workers, a 10 percent gain in female workers, and guaranteed pension rights to millions of employees.[11] Unfortunately in pension income accounting, the sum of all the little five-year vested plans left behind by job hopping will not equal all of the benefits received by staying with the organization. Studies show the benefits of the more mobile employee will only be 51 percent of those who hold lifetime jobs.[12]

Theoretically, lump-sum cash costs to workers who retire or change jobs should make up for this. But, again, theory does not necessarily equal reality.

---

[10] Ibid., p. 56.

[11] Brown, "The Retirement Game," p. 59.

[12] Ibid., p. 60.

Most lump-sum distributions are often not directly transferable to the new account, and despite the stiff penalty imposed, there are many workers who spend their lump-sum distribution.

Beginning January 1, 1989, a Social Security offset cannot, in most cases, exceed 50 percent of the worker's accrued benefit. An old common pension formula might have read:

> 50 percent of final average compensation
> less Social Security offset

The new rule is:

> 50 percent of final average compensation
> Less 50 percent of Social Security (provided it is not greater than the 50 percent final average compensation).

Table 7–3 illustrates this change regarding integration with Social Security.

TABLE 7–3   Integration of Social Security Example

	OLD PLAN	NEW LAW CHANGES
Final average income	$14,000	$14,000
50% ($14,000)	7,000	7,000
Deduct Social Security integration	- 5,736 (1986 floor figure)	-2,868 (50% of 1986 floor figure)
Company pension liability	$ 1,264	$ 4,132

Table 7–3 also reflects some changes for benefits administrators. The $2,868 difference in this example will have to be made up by better performance in company pension accounts. Additionally, "it will be increasingly difficult to plan a combined targeted income replacement ration level for all income levels. This fact may be difficult to communicate to employees."[13]

CONSOLIDATED OMNIBUS BUDGET RECONCILIATION ACT OF 1987

The Consolidated Omnibus Budget Reconciliation Act of 1987 (COBRA) incorporates three prior pieces of pension legislation. These were the Pension

---

[13] Frederick I. Schick, "Tax Reforms' Impact on Benefit Programs," *Personnel Administration* 32, no. 1 (January 1987): 85.

Protection Act of 1987, the Employee Retirement Income Security Act of 1974 (ERISA) and its amendments, and the Internal Revenue Code of 1986 (The Code).[14] Let us look at some of the impact of COBRA on retirement plans.

Premium Benefit Levels

With regard to single employer plans, COBRA nearly doubles the annual per participant premium due to the Pension Benefit Guaranty Corporation (PBGC), which is the federal agency that ensures defined benefit plans. In addition, this new law adds a variable rate of premium, which is changed according to plan funding levels. The changes can be substantial. Going from the current $8.50 to a possible $50.00, an increase of $41.50 unfolds. The $41.50 increase would be directed into a new fund. This fund will hold all penalties, interest, and earnings in excess of the prior $8.50 annual participant premium.

We should note another subtle change here with regard to the PBGC premiums. COBRA introduced the term "designated payor." This change will have the effect of increasing the field of responsibility. For a single company, that designee is either a contributing sponsor or a plan administrator.

Changes in Plan Terminations

If a sponsor of a pension plan desires to get a reversion of excess assets on plan termination, one must ensure the plan permits this. If the plan is silent or vague, it needs to be amended immediately. Any plan that prohibits revision should be amended (assuming this right has been retained by the company) in order to begin the five-year waiting period before the change is effective.

Under the prior law, a distress termination of a plan could take place if a substantial member (5 percent control) felt hardship. Hardship was defined as liquidation in bankruptcy, reorganization in bankruptcy, inability to pay debts when due, and unreasonable pension cost because of decreases in work force.[15] This definition of distress has changed to where it is available when each member, not just substantial members of the group, can demonstrate financial hardship. In addition, the standards within the hardship definition have been tightened. The new law makes one liable for the total unfunded benefit and interest from date of plan termination, not just for commitments of benefit guarantees.[16]

---

[14] Judd Albert Rory and Neal Schelberg, "Yet Another New Pension Law: The Omnibus Budget Reconciliation Act of 1987," *Employee Benefits Journal* 13, no. 2 (June 1988): 18.

[15] Ibid., p. 20.

[16] Ibid.

Funding Changes because of COBRA

Prior to COBRA, pension plans could be used as a tax-free savings device for the plans' future liabilities. The changes enacted revised the full-funding limitations definition to mean the lesser of plan-accrued liability or 150 percent of plan's current liability less the value of the assets.

This means that the plan's accrued liability includes projected benefits that will be entitled by normal retirement age. Current liability is defined as the value of all liabilities owed to plan participants and their beneficiaries and any reasonable contingent benefits, all computed as if the plan had been terminated. It appears from comments of experts in the field that the 150 percent of current liability will be less than the total of accrued liability. This fact will decrease the annual tax-free contribution.

COBRA did not overlook anyone in its legislative modifications; even actuaries came under scrutiny. Prior to this law the burden was on the Internal Revenue Service to prove actuarial assumptions were reasonable. Now the burden has shifted to the actuary to justify all assumptions.

Furthermore, interest rate assumptions must be within a permissable range, not more than +10 percent of the average rate of interest on 30-year Treasuries during the four years ending the last day before the new plan year. And when the plan assets are valued, the rule sounds simple, but it is a major shift in emphasis. Now the asset is fair-market value.

Summary of COBRA

COBRA changes go into many more small details, and the inference of some of their points have the possibility of more far-reaching effects. The most dramatic visible impact is the PBGC premium changes. Yet the subtle changes in asset value, quarterly payment intervals, and the like will have significant input on plan sponsors.

STOCK OPTION PROGRAMS

Prior to January 1987 there was a favorable tax treatment associated with long-term capital gains. The Tax Reform Act eliminated this whereby capital gains and ordinary income will be taxed at the same level.

The implications for executives with incentive stock options (ISOs) are significant. Let's give the positive points first. The tax will be deferred until the sale or disposition of the stock. The downside to this change, however, includes both the company and the executive. That is:

- The executive maintains the possibility of being subject to alternative minimum tax on the realized gain at the time of exercise of the option.

(If the option is received and exercised in the same year, it will not be subject to alternative minimum tax.)

- The employer will not be eligible for a tax deduction when the ISO is exercised.[17]

Experts in the field tell management to forget granting any new ISO plans. If an organization has an outstanding ISO, it should consider changing to a nonqualified plan when possible. If the nonqualified plan will not work, it is suggested that executives be offered a bonus to convert. Tax experts indicate the bonus can be "fully funded" by tax savings.[18]

WHAT HAPPENED TO PAYSOPS?

Payroll-based stock ownership plans (PAYSOPs) permit employers to give away stock with up to .5 percent of the company's payroll each year with little attached cost. The only real cost to the company is a minimal amount of administrative fees. The corporate cash donated to the plan to purchase the employer stock is recouped by a corresponding reduction in the company's tax bill. Many times even first-year PAYSOP administrative costs are subsidized by the tax credit.[19]

PAYSOPs replaced the investment tax-credit-based stock ownership plans (called TRASOPs) in 1983. Yet, despite what seems to be a nice program, they have failed to gather both company and worker support. Many believe the gross dollar figures were just too small to serve as an incentive to employees. Employees earning $20,000 would get only $100 (.5 percent of compensation) in the PAYSOP account. This is apparently not enough to serve as a motivator nor a significant contribution to retirement planning. The 1986 Tax Reform Act that killed the tax credit for the part of PAYSOPs, for the most part, put an end to their use in retirement planning.

FUNDING PROBLEMS IN PENSION PLANS

In the 1940s, 1950s, and into the early 1960s, predicting the retirement income level of a worker was not as impossible a task as it is now. Most of the variables in the formula were fairly predictable.

---

[17] Schick, "Tax Reforms' Impact on Benefit Programs," p. 85.

[18] McMillan, "Tax Reform," p. 99.

[19] Richard Stolz, "PAYSOPs Lose Popularity in Wake of Tax Reform," *Employee Benefit News* 3, no. 3 (March 1988): 12.

The salary average level increases were fairly consistent, making amortization easy to compute. The allowance for inflation (not a serious factor then) was easily determined. These factors allowed companies to virtually guarantee some specific percentage of the person's higher years, income or some dollar figure per year as the retirement benefit.

The industrial and economic woes of the 1970s and 1980s combined with periods of rampant inflation changed the funding formula prediction from one of ease to one of concern and difficulty.

Funded versus Pay-As-You-Go Pensions

There are two broad approaches to handling of pensions, both of which face problems. The funded system faces the much publicized investment problem of "unfunded liability." The pay-as-you-go system is faced with demographic problems. The most severe example of this type of system is the Social Security system.[20]

The demographic problem covers the benefit security and intergenerational transfer issue; that is subsequent generations are relied upon to meet benefit payments. The net effect is that our children assume the plan's liability. For private pension plans, the next generation is the following wave of workers and owners. Should the company's fortune go bad and decrease its size, the benefit payments loom large as a percentage of its reduced revenues. Also, the employees' contributions will provide a decreased amount of the cost, and they will be pressured to increase their contribution rate. For the Social Security system, the demographics of the next generation pose some problems: Will it be able to carry the burden of the current retirees?

An interesting point offered by the team at the Employee Benefit Research Institute states that because claimants in funded systems are in a secondary position to creditors and may be stockholders, a funded system may not be the best approach to achieve the goal of retirement benefit security. An unfunded plan in which pension liability has equal claim to corporate debt may be the superior way to achieve benefit security.[21]

In a "funded" plan that is not properly funded, the company is effectively borrowing back money that should have been paid out to meet the plan's cost, hence the unfunded liability.

Problem Disclosure

An unfunded pension liability results when a company's contribution to its plan combined with the fund's investment income are insufficient to fulfill

---

[20] Salisbury, *Retirement Income and the Economy*; p. 84.

[21] Ibid.

future pension obligations.[22]

The Financial Accounting Standards Board (FASB) had been working on the problem of how to properly dispose of this situation when it arises. Certainly stockholders, employees, and interested parties in a fiduciary capacity (bankers, bondholders,and so on) have a right to know the impact of the unfunded liability.

Beginning in 1989 the FASB ruling shifts recognition of pension fund liabilities from the footnotes of corporate financial statements to the balance sheet. The primary organizations affected are heavy industrial concerns, which have the largest amount of the unfunded pension liabilities. However, with the Tax Reform Act of 1986, changes in vesting, pension funding cost, and resultant liability could be adversely affected in many organizations. For some organizations there is a hybrid approach to provide retirement security that includes stock ownership.

EMPLOYEE STOCK OWNERSHIP PLAN

Part of the confusing atmosphere of retirement plans and benefits mentioned earlier is the jargon. For example, management establishes an ESOP, places the money into an ESOT with the qualifying plan a TRASOP, or "Section 301 ESOP." These types of phrases are enough to make most give up trying to follow and understand the benefits field.

Well, it is not that bad. The acronyms above refer to basically the same idea. Recent changes in federal laws have stimulated some interest in employee ownership of the stock in the company. The ESOP will permit the company to take advantage of tax incentives when granting stock to employees. A close relative of the ESOP (the Kelso Plan) has been used in the past with great success in the Sears, Roebuck and Co. organization.[23]

With the ESOP, the money is borrowed from a financial institution, such as a bank, and the stock is pledged as security for the loan. As the loan is repaid, the security used for that portion is placed into an employee stock ownership trust (ESOT). This stock will then be distributed to the workers at no cost to them. This stock may then become a part of the profit-sharing or retirement plan of the worker.

For employees the benefits of an ESOP are that the workers gets the stock when they retire, and they also get special tax credits for the value of the stock bought for them. So then what is a TRASOP, or Section 301 ESOP? It

---

[22] Marilyn Much, "CFOs Strongly Oppose New Pension Rule," *Industry Week* 228, no. 2 (January 1986): 28.

[23] Richard I. Henderson. *Compensation Management*, 4th ed. (Virginia: Reston Publishing Co., 1985), p. 447.

is a plan that qualifies for tax benefits under the Tax Reform Act of 1976. However, since tax changes in 1983, the TRASOP is seldom used.

What is in this for the company? Reality tells us that an ESOP would never be used if all the benefits accrue only to the worker. From the company's point of view, we find the following:

- The company may sell the stock and redeem it without changing the value because it is held only as security.
- The company can increase its working capital, cash flow, and net worth.
- The loan can be paid off and stock redeemed via pre-tax dollars while still enjoying the benefits of special tax credits.[24]
- Many of those who elect ESOPs do so in hopes of attaining higher productivity, thinking the program will enhance identification with the organization. However, there is conflicting evidence as to its use as a productivity measure.

How does this differ from a stock option plan and a stock purchase plan? In a stock option plan, designated employees have the chance to buy a specified number of shares at a certain price within a limited time frame. A stock purchase plan is used to promote savings and help workers develop an estate. Stock is purchased on the open market for the employees, often without a commission charge (giving an immediate savings to the worker) and with matching funds by the company. Also, the program is not dependent on company profits.

A study by the General Accounting Office (GAO) showed that ESOPs covered fewer than 7 percent of workers and less than 1 percent of total stock outstanding. There are more than four-thousand employee stock ownership plans, with the number of ESOPs increasing about 10 percent a year.[25]

The International Foundation of Employee Benefit Plans study indicated there is no pattern among the four-thousand plans currently in existence. That is, there is no trend in size of organization or amount of stock owned by the workers.[26] The growth seems to reflect changes in the law since 1984. For many employers, especially small organizations, fears of control and ownership of their companies seems to be abating with enough time to review the consequences of companies already using ESOPs.

---

[24] International Foundation of Employee Benefit Plans, "Study: Include ESOPs as Benefit," *Employee Benefit News* 2, no. 4 (April 1988): 15.

[25] Ibid., p. 16.

[26] Ibid., p. 15.

PUTTING TOGETHER THE PLAN FOR THE WORKERS

Financial planning for the workers may be the next major course for companies to embark upon. The concept has intuitive merit. The composition of the work force has moved to service-oriented or high-tech workers, for whom the average education for 40 percent of them is some attainment beyond high school.

If we combine that with the tendency to live longer and the desire to stay physically fit, many will begin whole new careers later in life, and work longer. Others prefer not to formally begin thoughts of new careers, but wish to pursue lifetime dreams of travel, hobbies, education, and early retirement, many with a great deal of success.

The key ingredient to all of this is the financial capability. No matter how big or small one's retirement goals, financial planning early in life will make it all seem more successful.

Don't Think in Constant-Dollar Terms

One of the more difficult concepts to convey to those preparing to retire is the elimination of preconceived notions. Too many people believe such myths as:

I'll be in a lower tax bracket.
My expenses will be less.
A fixed dollar will be able to suit my needs fine.
Social Security has a cost-of-living formula built in; therefore I am protected.

The tax changes have made the probability of dropping to a lower bracket remote. Table 7–4 indicates the type of expenses one needs to include in retirement planning. Fixed-dollar income protected from inflation by the Social Security portion is not sufficient. Table 7–5 indicates that even assuming modest levels of inflation, incomes will have to double roughly every ten years.[27] This means if inflation is 8 percent and a person makes $12,000 per year, in ten years there will be a need for $25,896 per year in retirement income just to stay constant in the current life-style. Put in another fashion, one's current $12,000 income will have purchasing power of only $5,500 in ten years. It is this subtle decline over time that produces the high anxiety in retired people. Because Social Security is but a portion of retirement income, it will not change in sufficient quantity to make up for the erosion of

---

[27] Elliot Raphaelson, *Planning Your Financial Future* (New York: John Wiley & Sons, 1982), p. 6.

TABLE 7–4   Expense Item Consideration for Retirement[*]

EXPENSE	WEEKLY	MONTHLY	ANNUALLY
FIXED TYPE			
Housing (rent or mortgage)		$500	$6,000
Electric		80	960
Gas		15	180
Food	$100		5,200
Clothing (mandatory replacement)			700
Transportation			
1. Auto payment		250	3,000
2. Auto insurance		50	600
3. Gasoline	25		1,300
DEBT PAYMENTS			
Income taxes			
Health insurance			
Property taxes			
VARIABLE			
Vacation cost			
Clothing (leisure, fad, etc.)			
Charitable			
Entertainment			
Meals out			
Education			
Investments			
Home furnishings			
Total	Fixed cost$_____		
Total	Variable$_____		
Grand total	$_____		

[*] Figures are hypothetical, put in to demonstrate chart usage.

TABLE 7–5   Inflation and Its Effects on Monthly Income

YEARS[a]	$1,000 INCOME EQUIVALENT[b]	PURCHASING POWER OF $1,000[b]
5	$ 1,469	$682
10	2,158	463
20	4,660	214
30	10,062	99
35	14,785	67

Source: Compiled from Elliot Raphaelson, *Planning Your Financial Future* (New York: John Wiley & Sons, 1982), p. 6. With permission.
[a] Assume inflation rate of 8 percent.
[b] Monthly income level of $1,000.

purchasing power. Also, no one can be sure what limits lawmakers will attach to Social Security to keep it basically solvent. Remember a trite but true adage— "What is given by law can be taken by law." This is suspected by researchers and is already known by workers; and it worries them. There is some support in the research that this concern adversely affects productivity.[28] The benefits administrators' responsibility, then, is to plan employees' retirement as carefully as they would for themselves to relieve this stress.

PENSIONS: HOW BIG ARE THEY?

Almost forty years ago writers in the financial world proclaimed that pensions would be the dominant force in capital markets. Large institutions would dominate Wall Street, and markets would move in response to the megadollar giants. Forty years ago pensions amounted to around $100 billion.[29] Today they are in the realm of a $1 trillion, and the predictions of yesteryear are fairly accurate.

Pension coverage is the most common among government workers, numbering around 90 percent versus around one-half of all private wage and salary workers.[30]

In the private, nonunion sector, the size of the organization plays a major role in determining of pensions. In the unionized sector, company size is not a major determinant. In the smallest organizations (one to twenty-four people) of the nonunion sector, only 16 percent have pensions versus 75 percent for those with one thousand or more employees. There are many possible explanations for this. They range from the high cost for small firms to the fear of union actions for the large ones. However, another factor that is very prominent is the salary scale of workers. The higher the salary scale, the more likely they are to be covered by a pension. In terms of race, there is little difference in pension coverage. The most distressing factor that surfaces in pension research is the economic gulf problem. Younger, less educated, poorer, and female workers have a reduced incidence of participation in pension plans.[31]

Who Receives Pensions?

There is a difference between those who are covered by pensions at their workplace and those who are current recipients. Among pension receivers, the

---

[28] Denise Marors, "Financial Planning for Rank and File Workers," *Employee Benefits News* 1, no. 4, (May/June 1987): 17.

[29] David T. Elwood, "Pensions and the Labor Market: A Starting Point," *Pensions, Labor, and Individual Choice*, ed. David Wise (Chicago: University of Chicago Press, 1985), p. 19.

[30] Ibid, p. 22.

[31] Ibid., p. 25.

benefit payout averages about 40 percent of total income. Across all retired groups we can see that pensions amount to only 15 percent of income for those aged 65 and over. The story is again similar: Those with high working incomes get the high pensions at retirement; those with lower incomes receive little if any pension income. This perpetuates the problem of economic gulf into the retirement years and places a burden on society.

In terms of pension replacement rates, the research work by David Elwood reports that 20 percent of employees' average wage over the final five years of their careers is the replacement rate. This rate changes little by union status, sex, or level of preretirement earnings. Among the younger retirees and persons with more years of service, the replacement rate appears to be higher.[32]

The plethora and variability in complexity of benefit provisions within the deferred plans (85 percent of plans are deferred) are tremendous. This complexity makes them unlikely to be suitable to shelter income from taxes or influence the productivity of the worker on the job. Has the overt legal influence on pensions created an object that is now just a financial burden to the company and an economic disappointment to workers, a no-win situation for both sides? The debate continues.

The Typical Categories

Pension benefits in the deferred benefit fall into two broad categories. Both categories are governed by specific formulas that determine respective income. These are pattern or flat benefit plans, and conventional or unit formula plans.

L. J. Kotlikoff and D. E. Smith estimate the average yearly benefit is $100 per year (with a + 70 factor) for each year of service. As such, if a person has thirty-five years of work, the annual benefit would be $3,500.[33] This type of plan is found almost exclusively in unionized companies in which opportunity for adjustment exists, thus reducing its susceptibility to inflation.

Conventional or unit formula plans are computed as a percentage of some base earnings. The most common (23 percent of these plans) is based on the last five years of service. The figure to use for the final years goes to ten years of service in 4.3 percent of plans, and "others" take a person's career average in 11.9 percent.[34] The percentage grows with service. For example, annual pension benefits may be 1 percent of average salary in the final five years times the years of service. Thirty-year workers would be entitled to 30

---

[32] Ibid., p. 34.

[33] L. J. Kotlikoff and D. E. Smith, *Pension in the American Economy* (Chicago: University of Chicago Press, 1983), p. 78.

[34] Ibid, p. 79.

percent of their salaries. If they made $30,000 during the final five years, the benefit would be $10,000 per year.

Most of the formulas are complex and integrate with Social Security, usually reducing the retirement benefit by some ratio of Social Security income. A very rough rule of thumb about these formulas suggests using 1 to 1.25 percent of earnings times the final five years of service as the base.

Earlier in the chapter we discussed in length the defined contribution plan, which has no such formulas for figuring retirement. It is a safe projection that new plans will more closely model the deferred contribution versus the defined benefit, if for no other reason than to avoid the legal problems of unfunded liability pension payments and the new fines associated with this area.

SUMMARY

After reading this chapter you will know that:

* *Among the many items discussed in the Tax Reform Act of 1986, it was noted that there will be a uniform definition of highly compensated worker for both employee benefit and retirement plans. There will be changes in the traditional normal retirement age of 65 to that of a floating age around Social Security. A statutory limit for figuring compensation has been implemented at the $200,000 level.*

* *The Consolidated Omnibus Budget Reconciliation Act incorporates three prior pieces of pension legislation: (1) the Pensions Protection Act of 1987, (2) ERISA (revised), and (3) the Internal Revenue Code of 1986. The most visible feature of COBRA changes will be in the premium due to the Pension Benefit Guaranty Corporation which nearly doubles the premium.*

* *PAYSOPs have fallen in popularity because of the removal of the tax credit on the Tax Reform Act of 1986.*

* *Funding problems with pension retirement plans occur for a number of reasons. They vary from significant changes in the economic climate of the United States to tax law changes that have tightened up requirements, and mismanagement of the funds and using poor judgment as to portfolio growth.*

* *An employee stock ownership plan is a system whereby money is borrowed with company stock pledged as security. As the loan is repaid, the stock is given to the employees.*

* *When planning for retirement, employees must not assume that they will be in a lower tax bracket or that expenses will be dramatically reduced, or that Social Security will be the variable to offset inflation.*

* *Inflation impacts retirement income. If we face a 6 percent annual rise in inflation, that translates to roughly doubling income every eleven years to stay even with current purchasing power in the retirement years.*
* *Pensions have grown in the past forty years from $100 billion to $1 trillion in size. Certainly, this financial magnitude impacts on the U.S. economy.*
* *Pension coverage is most heavily concentrated in government agencies and nonunionized companies. The recipients of pensions frequently mirror the covered group, but there is a whole segment of society not covered by pensions, a serious problem for us all to face at some future time.*
* *The conventional benefit formula is computed as a percentage of base earnings, typically based on the last five years of service.*

KEY TERMS

Actuaries	Inflation
Consolidated Omnibus Budget	Integration plans
Reconciliation Act (COBRA)	Interest rate assumption
Defined benefit	Internal Revenue Service
Defined contribution	Kelso Plan
Employee stock ownership	Pension
plan (ESOP)	Plan year
Financial Accounting	Profit sharing
Standards Board	Purchasing power
Fixed income	Qualified plan
Flat benefit	Replacement ratio
401(k)	Simplified employee
403(b)	retirement account
General Accounting Office	Social Security
Incentive stock option (ISO)	Vesting
Individual retirement account (IRA)	

QUESTIONS FOR REVIEW AND DISCUSSION

1. What are the two major pieces of legislation that have influenced pension management? What impact have they had?
2. Which piece of legislation has shifted the burden of reasonable interest assumptions from the IRS to actuaries and companies?

3. What is meant by a simplified employee retirement account? Is it available only to persons in large organizations? How does it work with an IRA?
4. How has inflation affected the perception of fixed-income retirement plans?
5. "Pension accounts have helped equalize the wealth distribution in America." Do you agree or disagree with the statement? Explain.
6. What is the relationship between income levels and pension benefit coverage?
7. Which type of plan is expected to grow in future years — defined benefit or defined contribution? Why do you believe it will?
8. What happened to cause the decline of PAYSOPs?
9. What can be done to help funding problems in pensions?
10. How does the conventional formula for calculating pensions operate? Give an example.

ADDITIONAL READINGS

DURKIN, JULIE.   "Social Security Integration after Tax Reform Requires Review and Redesign." *Journal of Compensation and Benefits* 2, no. 5 (March-April 1987): 308-12.

GOTTL, RONALD F. II, and RICHARD D. LANDSBERG.   "The Best Little Qualified Plan in Tax Reform." *Broker World* 7, no. 2 (February 1987): 18-26.

International Foundation of Employee Benefit Plans. "Study: Include ESOPs as Benefit." *Employee Benefit News*, 2, no. 4 (April 1988).

SIEGEL, ANDREW, A. COHEN, and LAURENCE FEIBEL. "ESOPs — The Present and Impending Future — Part I." *The CPA Journal* (January 1986): 14-22.

SIEGEL, ANDREW, A. COHEN, and LAURENCE FEIBEL. "ESOPs — The Present and Impending Future — Part II." *The CPA Journal* (February 1986): 32-36.

CHAPTER EIGHT

EXCLUSIVE BENEFITS: EXECUTIVE PERKS, OUTPLACEMENT SERVICES, AND PERFORMANCE BONUSES

LEARNING OBJECTIVES

After reading this chapter you will be able to:

* *Describe the purpose of executive perks.*
* *Identify the more popular executive perks.*
* *Describe the effect of the Deficit Reduction Act of 1984 on executive perks.*
* *Describe the controversy surrounding executive perks.*
* *Describe the rationale for relocation expenses.*
* *Identify the various relocation expenses covered.*
* *Describe the purpose of golden parachutes.*
* *Describe what is meant by the term outplacement.*
* *Describe what is involved in outplacement services.*
* *Describe why outplacement services are offered to employees.*
* *Describe what is meant by a performance bonus system, and the types of plans that exist.*

INTRODUCTION

Throughout the past few chapters we have discussed benefits that are provided to employees based on membership in the organization. That is, for the most part, those benefits are given to each employee in spite of the employee's level or tenure in the organization. Not all benefits, however, offered in an organization fall into the membership-based category. There are specific benefits that are provided to employees under certain conditions. These would include executive perquisites ("perks"), outplacement services, and performance bonuses (sometimes called performance incentives).

EXECUTIVE PERKS

Executives are frequently offered a smorgasbord of perquisites not offered to other employees. The logic of offering these perks, from the organization's perspective, is to attract and keep good managers and to motivate them to work hard in the organization's interest.

In addition to the standard benefits offered to all employees (e.g., health insurance, disability and survivor benefits, and retirement programs) some benefits are reserved for privileged executives. These perks range from an annual physical, worth several hundreds of dollars, to low-interest loans of millions of dollars, which can be worth $100,000 a year or more to the executive. Popular perks include the payment of insurance premiums and club memberships, company automobiles, liberal expense accounts, supplemental disability insurance, supplemental retirement accounts, postretirement counseling, and personal financial, tax, and legal counseling. Additionally, when inflation was running high, as witnessed in the late 1970s and early 1980s, it was popular to offer transferred executives the opportunity to sell their homes at the appraised value to the company, and have the company assume the increased interest expense resulting from giving up a low-cost 7 or 8 percent mortgage and having to assume a new one at 12 to 16 percent.[1] While the magnitude of mortgage interest rates has decreased somewhat, assisting executives in bridging their old mortgage and new mortgage rates continues. Table 8–1 is a summary of executive perks offered to key managers of an organization.

---

[1] "It takes Big Benefits to Recruit Executives Who Have to Relocate," *Wall Street Journal*, June 3, 1980, p. 25.

TABLE 8 −1   Executive Perks
             (Percentage Found in Survey Organizations)

PERK	PERCENTAGE
Employer-provided automobile	69
Reserved parking	54
Country club membership	42
Luncheon clubs	41
Personal financial assistance	34
Athletic membership	18
Preretirement counseling	12
Personal legal services	5
Loans/mortgage assistance	5
sabbaticals	4

Source: Reproduced with permission from *Human Resource Management-Compensation*,
            Published and copyrighted by Commerce Clearing House, Inc.,
            4025 W. Peterson Avenue, Chicago, Illinois, 60646.

It is interesting to note from Table 8–1 that the most popular perks offered to executives are automobiles, and a reserved spot to park them in. Providing transportation to an executive may appear to be a minor benefit, but taken in its total perspective, the magnitude of these perks increases. For example, companies lean toward the luxury line of cars for their executives. These may include Mercedes, Lincolns, Cadillacs, BMWs, and so on. The cost of these automobiles may range from a low of $20,000 to more than $60,000. The question often asked is, "Can't executives earning $100,000 a year afford to buy their own cars?"[2] The answer is obvious: Yes, they can. But the implications are rooted more deeply. Much of the issue centers on status. Although an executive may be able to afford an expensive automobile, if "everyone knew he bought it, it would not have the same status as when it's given to him."[3] Companies that are interested in offering perks as a means of attracting and keeping good managers in the organization must "play the game." The same rationale also applies to parking privileges. The closer an executive gets to park to the entrance to the building (the least amount of disruption, freedom from the elements), the greater that person's status is in the organization.

With the Deficit Reduction Act of 1984, Congress entered the automobile perk arena by attempting to lessen its benefit to executives. Congress enacted tax legislation that reduced the amount of depreciation a company could write off for "expensive" cars, limiting the depreciation to $16,000 for the first three years. That amount was subsequently reduced to

---

[2] Felix Kessler, "Executive Perks Under Fire," *Fortune*, July 22, 1985, p. 30.

[3] Ibid.

$12,800.[4]   Additionally, tax rules now require the executive to pay personal income tax on the value of the percentage the automobile is used for personal matters. These changes, however, neither lessened the use of automobiles as perks nor discouraged executives from using them. Why? In most cases, the company absorbed the extra costs. As one executive stated, "We've got to do it to remain competitive."[5] That is, to keep these executives from leaving the company, the organization had to look for more creative means of providing the perk. For most, not only did it mean absorbing the costs associated with reduced depreciation and loss of tax investment credits, it also meant reimbursing the executives for much, if not all, of the increase in personal taxes because of the "personal-use" stipulation.

Controversy arises surrounding the outcome of taxing of various perks offered to executives. For one thing, many individuals feel that these "elite" benefits should be taxed because they are not available to the general work force. By taxing their offerings, this is one means of requiring executives to pay for the "extras" they get. But in order to do so, there is a spillover effect. If executives are to be taxed for certain benefits, why not tax the benefits of all workers? The debate on this issue continues. Many people fear that if lobbying continues for more taxes to be paid on executive perks, the ultimate result may be an increase in personal income, and thus taxes, for the average worker. This outcome, unfortunately, will not produce the desired result the IRS is seeking to obtain.

Two Special Perks

Not only do executives receive special benefits while they are employees of an organization, many receive assistance on both the front and back ends of their tenure with the organization. These pre- and post-employment benefits are relocation expenses and outplacement services.

Relocation Expenses.   In an effort to attract qualified applicants, many companies provide payments for relocation expenses to induce the "most" qualified applicant to accept the position. The offer to pay for these costs incurred in a move to a new location is generally not open to all employees—it is reserved for the top levels of management in the company. One must remember that when recruiting for top management positions, the marketplace is not sequestered to a local area. Rather, it is generally viewed as being nationwide. Accordingly, to induce an applicant to accept the position, as

---

[4] Ibid. It should also be noted that tax investment credits for company automobiles were eliminated in the Tax Reform Act of 1986.

[5] Ibid.

generally is the case, most companies offer some assistance in relocating the new employee.

Relocation expenses vary depending on what the company is willing to spend. In general, it is estimated that it requires an outlay of approximately $36,000 to relocate an employee.[6] This money is spent on activities involved in selling and buying a home, and moving expenses. Table 8–2 is a listing of what costs are included in relocation expenses.

TABLE 8 – 2   Items Included in Relocation Expenses

House hunting trip(s) for employee and spouse
Real estate aid in selling old house
Guarantee of purchase price of old home at market value
Temporary living expenses in new area
Payment of closing costs of new home
Subsidies (mortgage assistance) for moving to high cost area

In addition to helping the new executive purchase a home, many companies may also offer assistance in decorator fees. The rationale is that for an applicant to accept the new job, one must not find that the move has resulted in a lower quality of life, or standard of living. As such, a well-decorated old home serves as grounds for negotiating that expenses incurred to pay for the costs of draperies, landscaping, and so on, be borne by the acquiring organization. Additionally, if the new executive has a working spouse (who must leave his or her job because of the relocation), then it is also appropriate for the organization to provide job-search assistance to that individual.[7] That may mean employing the spouse also, or actively seeking placement in the general vicinity.

Golden Parachutes.   A popular perk that accrued to top executives in the early 1980s, and continues today in the midst of takeovers and mergers, is the "golden parachute." The golden parachute was designed by top executives as a means of protecting themselves in the event that they lost control of their organizations. These parachutes provide a severance salary to the departing executive, a guaranteed position in the overtaken or newly created organization, or inducements for early retirement. Whatever the case may be, this elite benefit has provided a comfortable cushion for an outgoing executive to fall back on.

---

[6] "Job Transfers: When and How to Make the Move," *Changing Times* 42 (March 1988): 81.

[7] Ibid., p. 86.

Conclusion

Executives, and other top-level managers are generally offered benefits that are not common to the average worker. While the debate may continue as to whether or not these exclusive perks should be provided, the fact remains that for an organization to attract and retain quality top-level employees, certain expectations must be met. Until the fundamentals of our society change, if ever they should, we will have the "haves and the have-nots." There is no reason to believe our culture will change, for becoming one of the "haves" is the apex that has inspired such greatness in our country.

For the remaining nonexecutive work force, such a benefit as a golden parachute is not applicable. However, for some, outplacement services are.

OUTPLACEMENT SERVICES

If there is a phrase that can describe U.S. companies in the 1980s, that phrase would be the "downsizing of corporate America," retrenchment efforts on the part of companies to achieve a "lean and mean" status. The 1970s were difficult for many organizations. There was a marked shrinkage of the once-strong smokestack industries—steel, auto, and rubber. Competition in the high-tech industries soared, giving rise to massive layoffs at such companies as Apple, DEC, and Wang. Conglomerates were shedding less profitable business units or closing down altogether. And foreign competition steadily increased, causing more problems for U.S. manufacturers.

Human resource planning, as noted in Chapter 3, tended to ignore the strategic directions of the company. In most cases, there was no linkage between the strategic plan and human resource planning. Managing the declining organization proved a major feat. Going bankrupt, divesting holdings, and eliminating unprofitable product lines were activities not prevalent in growing enterprises. Almost every major newspaper ran front-page stories of the problems in our organizations. News of the 1985 DuPont efforts to reduce its employee base by 11,200, AT&T attempts to eliminate 24,000 jobs by the end of 1986, or cited reports from *Business Week* that through 1986 more than 128,000 jobs were lost in Fortune 500 companies[8] only touched the tip of the iceberg. Downsizing was here to stay. It was not something to weather for a short period, and then return to the "old ways." As such, these problems had a major impact on the employee population— at all levels. Employee numbers had to be reduced in companies. Not haphazardly, though, but after careful analysis and linkage to a new strategic direction. To assist in this effort, outplacement services became popular.

---

[8] Ron Zemke, "Delayed Effects of Corporate Downsizing," *Training*, November 1986, p.67.

Outplacement is a term used for describing a process, typically provided by consultants, to assist dismissed workers in marketing their services in locating a new position outside their current organization. This assistance includes helping the dismissed worker with the psychological aspects of losing a job, retraining workers to develop new, in-demand skills, and conducting personal assessments to determine a worker's ability and job preference, in addition to aid in resume writing, interviewing techniques, career counseling, and job searching. These services typically begin at the moment the layoffs commence.[9]

It needs to be emphasized that outplacement services are generally provided for workers at any level, including executives, who are dismissed from the organization through no fault of their own. There is often a perception that downsizing efforts target the nonexempt population more than the managerial level. Downsizing efforts know no boundaries. While it is true in a layoff more employees than managers may be dismissed, the fact is their numbers in the organization are greater to begin with, thus leaving a disproportionate base from which to draw. But make no mistake about it. Even though more than two million jobs have been lost in major companies,[10] the downsizing of corporate America has been greatly felt in the managerial ranks. While the exact number of managers outplaced is not known, the lean and mean efforts have concluded in restructuring of organizations, resulting in a greater span of control for managers.[11]

Why Outplacement Services?

When one considers the legal ramifications of layoffs, there is really little more for a company to do than to provide employees with their severance pay

---

[9] Depending on the outplacement firm contracted, these services may begin prior to the actual layoff. In these cases, an outplacement firm may begin to search for positions, prepare for psychological counseling sessions, and in some cases, prepare for medical emergencies that may arise when the layoffs are announced.

[10] Dyan Machan, "Pink Slip Time," *Forbes*, February 9, 1987, p. 118.

[11] By span of control, we mean the number of direct reports a manager has reporting to him or her. A span of six means that manager has six employees working under his or her direct supervision. As an example, suppose that two departments perform similar work, and one department is considered expendable. If the managers of both departments had six workers each, by increasing the span of control to twelve, one managerial position could be eliminated. Typically, however, not only would one manager be dismissed, but the organization would also look at the work being performed and make a decision on how many employees are needed. Maybe only seven workers are needed. In this case, five workers could be outplaced. Our span of control of twelve comes back into play when we consider combining departments. If we further assume that another department that did related work had a manager and five workers (all needed), these two departments could be combined. The result; two managers and five workers outplaced, a reduction in size of the organization.

(according to company policy)[12] and say thank you and good-bye. That may be the most cost-effective means of laying them off. But there are other factors that enter into the picture. And these factors point to more emphasis on outplacement services. Such considerations as employee well-being are taken into account, as well as protecting the company from age discrimination and unfair employment practice suits.[13] To many organizations implementing outplacement services, the potential costs from lawsuits, as well as the intangible costs associated with psychological effects on dismissed employees, outweigh the costs of the program. And these programs are inexpensive. On average, outplacement services cost between $1,000 and $4,500 per day, with added costs required for the outplacement of executives.[14]

Who Is Affected?

All employees in all organizations may be subjected to layoffs. Through concerted outplacement efforts, there appears to be a pattern that has arisen. The typical employees found using outplacement services are individuals in their forties, earning between $50,000 and $200,000 annually, and who have approximately fifteen years of service in the company.[15] By these characteristics, it is easy to determine who receives outplacement services more often. Individuals earning over $50,000 are considered in managerial or highly regarded professional ranks and, for the most part, are harder to place elsewhere. It is not that outplacement services are unavailable for lower-level employees; they are more easily placed in local job markets, especially with unemployment rates at its lowest point in over a decade. The point that is clear is that of the vast numbers of employees affected in downsizing efforts, the majority may well have been in the higher ranks of the organization.

For these individuals, outplacement services provided a means for them to find gainful employment. Some were placed elsewhere in other companies, some took advantage of early retirement incentives, and some started their own ventures. Whatever the case may have been, statistics on placement of dismissed workers reveal that in three to six months, these individuals found new jobs, most of which paid higher salaries than the ones they left.[16]

---

[12] Severance pay varies widely in organizations. A general rule of thumb, however, is one week of severance pay for every year of service in the organization, usually with some minimum stipulated.

[13] Edmund B. Piccolino, "Outplacement: The View from HR," *Personnel*, March 1988, p. 24.

[14] Ibid., p. 26.

[15] Piccolino, "Outplacement," p. 26.

[16] Elaine M. Duffy, Richard M. O'Brien, William P. Brittain, and Stephen Cuthrell, "Behavioral Outplacement: A Shorter, Sweeter Approach," *Personnel*, March 1988, p. 28; and Dyan Machan, "Pink Slip Time." p. 117.

The Ethical Dilemma

Laying off workers was a reality in the 1980s, one that will surely continue into the 1990s. While services like outplacement tend to lessen the impact of being "let go", there are some very serious questions that remain. Most notably, should a worker be told of the pending downsizing? In much of the latter part of 1987 and early 1988, a congressional debate centered on the Plant Closing Bill, which requires employers to notify workers sixty days in advance of a pending plant closing or a major layoff. Most businesses and then President Ronald Reagan believed that this bill was an added burden to place on companies. The intent of the bill — notification — appeared not to be the main issue. Businesses claimed that there were circumstances that did not permit for this advanced notice to be given. In cases in which no special conditions arose, employers cited that they were willing, and had given plenty of advanced notice. These employers believed that they did not need this added government regulation. On the other hand, workers wanted the added protection. They had witnessed, some firsthand, being notified the morning of a plant closing. They believed that such action was wrong. In the workers' view, and that of their supporters, they felt that the reason management did not want to give advanced notice stemmed from the fear that for sixty days, employees could do much damage. Whether or not that perception is correct, the fact remains that the sixty-day plant-closing notice was passed in the summer of 1988.

A similar feeling is perceived when individuals get laid-off. It is not uncommon for workers who will be laid off to be herded into an auditorium, told of the company's decision, and escorted out of the building. In this instance, personal belongings of the employee may not be retrieved immediately — typically management has contracted to have all personal belongings packaged and sent to the employee. There is no doubt in areas where security is a concern that this is a preventive mechanism, but in other areas, the rationale may be hard to find for some individuals. Many workers feel hurt and betrayed by such action, especially when one considers that many of these employees have good work records that span several years in the company. Yet how are the company's interest and the employee's dignity protected at the same time? Would employees sabotage a computer program? Would executives jeopardize their integrity and take sensitive materials and "use" them to obtain employment with a competitor? Therein lies the dilemma.

Throughout the past few pages, we have delved into an area of special benefits that is sometimes seen as gruesome. There is no easy way to separate an employee from the organization. Even in the best of efforts, emotions will run high. It is time now to turn our attention to a different focus, that is, of rewarding productive work. While each worker is paid a certain amount of money to perform the job, some workers are afforded the opportunity to earn performance bonuses. The idea behind a performance bonus, or incentive, is to create an atmosphere in which workers perform above what is typically accepted as "standard" productivity. In these cases, the organization makes a larger profit from the increases in productivity. To provide some incentive for workers to increase their productivity, some of the gains the company attains are shared with the workers. In the next section, we will explore this area of performance bonuses.

PERFORMANCE BONUS SYSTEMS

There are individuals who may say that a discussion of performance bonuses, or incentives, is inappropriately placed in a discussion of benefits. And for the most part we would agree. It belongs more to the area of compensation administration. However, a case can be made to extend the discussion of exclusive benefits to this area, because performance bonuses, especially at the top management level, are perks that are not available to the work force in general. Accordingly, we believe it is important to discuss this specific area briefly.

A performance bonus system is one that offers employees an opportunity to achieve greater monetary gains through increased productivity. They are, correctly so, extensions of one's compensation for any given year. These performance bonus plans may be established under one of three categories— individual, group, or organization-wide performance.[17]

Individual Performance Bonuses

Individual performance bonuses come from a variety of methods. For the work force population, these types of plans would correspond to a piecework system, or one built on commissions. The better known of the two, however, is clearly the piecework system.

Under a piecework plan, the employee is typically guaranteed a minimum hourly wage rate for meeting some preestablished standard output. For output over this standard, the employee earns a set amount for each piece produced. Differential piecerate plans establish two rates — one up to standard, and another when the employee exceeds the standard. The latter rate, of course, is higher to encourage the employee to "exceed standards."

Sales personnel frequently work on a commission basis. In addition to a low wage rate, called a draw, they get an amount that represents a percentage of the sales price. The percentage received varies depending on the product

---

[17] Much of this material has been adapted from David A. De Cenzo and Stephen P. Robbins, *Personnel/Human Resource Management* (Englewood Cliffs, N.J.: Prentice Hall, 1988), pp. 434-39.

sold. That is, the percentage of sales commission on a $6 million city sewer system would be lower than for selling a $225 maintenance agreement to accompany a video recorder.

A relatively new aspect of individual performance bonus plans that has made its way into corporate America for many executives is the performance agreement. These agreements, a modified version of the popular management-by-objectives system, clarify specifically what the executive is expected to achieve over a period of time — usually one year. They set clear and measurable tasks against which the executive's performance is evaluated. Incentive clauses are often written into these agreements, for achieving the specific goals established will result in a monetary bonus for the executive. For example, Table 8–3 is an example of a performance agreement for a human resources executive. Notice that only some of the items have been tagged as ones that will enter the performance bonus equation. This typically means that these are the most critical items to accomplish in a given year. Not only are monetary rewards (based on some formula the board of directors has agreed to) tied to their completion, oftentimes, punitive measures will be taken if these specific items are not met.

**TABLE 8–3   Sample Performance Agreement
                (for Human Resources Executive, Selected Items)**

FINANCIAL
> Establish, operate, and manage the human resource function of the organization within plus or minus 5 % of $6,598,000.*
> Control expenses contracting for external human resource services not to exceed 15 % of total budget.

PERFORMANCE DUTIES
> Establish corporate culture programs for implementing/communicating new corporate strategy to the work force by June 30.*
> Create decentralized units to provide full human resource services to strategic business units by September 1.*
> Continue active campaign of promoting positive employee relations programs. Conduct attitudinal surveys of employees by December 15.
> Recruit and select candidates for employment such that no more than 3 % of all jobs go unfilled past 90 days.
> Implement and have operating a human resources information system by December 31.

OUTSIDE ACTIVITIES
> Provide community service by serving on three boards of voluntary organizations.
> Provide leadership in company's role in United Way Campaign.*

SELF DEVELOPMENT
> Pursue development efforts as outlined in past performance evaluation.
> Take an active role in local Human Resource Professional Society.

> *
> identified as performance bonus items

The concept behind any individual performance bonus is to establish the conditions under which "standard" performance will be met. What these do is to identify clearly the specific work to be done. However, that in itself can lead to problems. If these incentives lead to excessive competition among workers, or encourage them to cut corners, the work environment promotes just the reverse. Additionally, you may get only what you pay for. Because one's bonus is tied to a particular set of activities (which, we add, generally cover only part of one's total job), workers may not perform the unmeasured, and unrewarded activities. For example, if the human resources executive is not being measured on subordinate development (which takes money to do) but clearly on his or her budget cost center, there may be an incentive to save a few dollars by not sending the subordinates to appropriate training programs.

All in all, despite their potential for abuse and misdirection, individual performance bonuses are widespread in practice.

Group Performance Bonuses

Each of the individual performance bonus systems discussed above may be used on a group basis. That is, two or more employees can be paid for their combined work.

When are group bonuses desirable? They make the most sense when employees' tasks are interdependent and thus require cooperation. This would describe, for example, the conditions that exist in a computer factory assembly line.

One of the problems with group bonuses, however, is that employees often do not see their work being directly linked to the groups bonus. The bonus for the group is influenced by the productivity of others within it. This can lead to internal conflict, and ultimately lower productivity.

In the case of the human resources executive, the performance standards cannot be achieved without help. The executive should have similar agreements with his or her direct reports, each focusing on a major performance standard. In such a case, there may be performance bonuses provided to this next layer of management. Accordingly, all of this executive's team is working toward, and sharing in, the rewards. It should be noted, too, that in some cases not only do executives get performance bonuses for completing their work, they may also receive a percentage of the bonus given to their direct reports. The incentive here is to ensure that all parties are "pulling their weight."

Organization-wide Performance Bonuses

Our last type of performance bonus system is the organization-wide category. Under this arrangement, the bonuses offered are compelling the efforts of all employees toward achieving the organization's goals. Typically in this arrangement, the bonuses are provided based on organization-wide cost reduction or productivity gains. These savings are then disbursed to employees as bonuses, profit sharing, or stock ownership.

Many of these types of plans have been around for years. Kaiser Steel, for example, developed in one of its plants a cost reduction plan that provides monthly bonuses to employees.[18] The amount of bonus was determined by computing one-third of all increases in productivity attributable to cost savings as a result of technological change or increased effort. Additionally, Lincoln Electric has had a year-end bonus "ranging from a low of 55 percent to a high of 115 percent of annual earnings."[19] The Lincoln Electric plan pays off handsomely for employees beating previous years' performance standards. Because this bonus is added to the employees' salaries, it had made Lincoln Electric workers the highest-paid electrical workers in the United States.

One of the better-known organization-wide performance bonus systems is the Scanlon Plan,[20] which seeks to bring about cooperation between management and the employees through the sharing of problems, goals, and ideas. Under Scanlon, each department in the organization has a committee composed of the supervisors and employee representatives. Suggestions for labor-saving improvements are funneled to the committee, and if accepted, cost savings and productivity gains are shared by all, not just the individual who made the suggestion. Typically about 80 percent of the suggestions prove practical and are adopted. The thrust behind this plan is its cooperative philosophy, employee involvement, and sharing of the gains.[21]

Profit-sharing and stock ownership plans are also organization-wide bonus systems. They allow employees to share in the success of the company by distributing a part of the profits back to the workers. The logic behind these plans is that they increase commitment and loyalty to the organization. Workers are more likely to be cost conscious if they have a share in the benefits.

On the other hand, employees may find it difficult to equate their work to the profits, or stocks being shared. Their individual effort has a relatively small impact on total organization productivity. Additionally, external factors such as the economy, competition, and so on, may have more of an impact on the company's bottom line than the efforts of the employees themselves.

---

[18] Harold Stieglitz, "The Kaiser Steel Union Sharing Plan," *National Industrial Conference Board Studies in Personnel Policy*, no.187 (New York, 1963).

[19] Richard I. Henderson, *Compensation Management*, 5th ed. (Englewood Cliffs, N.J.: Prentice Hall, 1989), p. 353.

[20] Ibid.

[21] Gary Dessler, *Personnel Management*, 4th ed. (Englewood Cliffs, N.J.: Prentice Hall, Inc., 1988), p. 404.

Another problem is that these types of plans suffer from a time-lag effect. Payoffs are distributed at wide intervals. A bonus paid in January 1990 for the efforts in 1989 loses a lot of its reinforcement capabilities. Finally, we should not overlook what happens when organization-wide bonuses become both large and recurrent. When this occurs, it is not unusual for employees to adjust their spending habits and anticipate and expect the bonus. Employees see the bonus as something that has some certainty to it. As such, the bonus loses its impact, for it becomes perceived as a membership-based benefit, just like sick leave and vacations.

Conclusion

In this section we have attempted to discuss performance bonuses and how they may be viewed as exclusive benefits. The intention was not to usurp bonus or incentive systems under the benefits umbrella, but to show how the two may be related. These programs carry costs with them, which must be borne by the employer. And anytime an employee cost is realized, one can make the case that another benefit for employees has been established.

SUMMARY

After having read this chapter, you will know that:

* *The purpose of offering executive perks is to attract and keep good top-level managers, and to motivate them to work hard in the organization's interest.*
* *The more popular executive perks include insurance premiums, club memberships, company automobiles, liberal expense accounts, supplementary disability insurance, supplemental retirement accounts, postretirement counseling, and personal financial, tax, and legal counseling.*
* *The Deficit Reduction Act of 1984 had a questionable impact on executive perks. The act intended to lessen these benefits to executives by taxing them as personal income. Among others, the Act focused on company automobiles, decreasing the amount of depreciation a company could expense, reduced tax investment credits, and required employers to include in W-2 income statements that part of the automobile used for personal matters. The greatest impact of the act was felt by the companies, which, for the most part, increased their perks to include paying for the increased taxes.*
* *The controversy surrounding executive perks centers on taxing these benefits. The proponents of this action cite that these are exclusive benefits, not available to all employees. Thus they should be taxed. The opponents cite that this could lead to taxing of all benefits for all workers.*

* *The rationale for relocation expenses is to induce top-level candidates to accept offers of employment.*
* *Relocation expenses covered vary according to each company. However, the more popular relocation expenses are house hunting trips, assistance in selling one's old home, temporary living expenses, subsidized mortgages in high-cost areas, payment of closing costs, and job search assistance for spouse.*
* *The purpose of a golden parachute is to protect top executives in the event of a takeover or merger. This perk provides certain guarantees to the existing executives.*
* *Outplacement is a term used for describing a process to assist dismissed workers in marketing their services in locating a new position outside their current organization.*
* *Outplacement involves psychological assistance for the terminated employee, retraining, conducting personal assessments, resume writing, interviewing techniques, career counseling, and job searching.*
* *Outplacement is offered to employees for many reasons. Among them are the well-being of employees, and protecting the company from age discrimination and unfair employment practice charges.*
* *A performance bonus system offers employees an opportunity to achieve greater monetary gains through increased productivity. The three types of performance bonus plans are the individual, group, and organization-wide systems.*

KEY TERMS

Career counseling	Mortgage assistance
Club memberships	Organization-wide performance
Company automobile	bonus
Corporate downsizing	Outplacement services
Deficit Reduction Act	Performance agreement
of 1984	Performance bonus system
Golden parachutes	Perks
Group performance bonuses	Piecerate plans
Individual performance	Plant Closing Bill of 1988
bonuses	Psychological assistance
Kaiser Steel Plan	Relocation expenses
Lean and mean organization	Scanlon Plan
Lincoln Electric Plan	Spousal job search

QUESTIONS FOR REVIEW AND DISCUSSION

1. Why is the company-provided automobile such an important perk for executives? Why should the company provide one?
2. "All executive perks should be taxed dollar for dollar. Because the average worker does not get them, the top managers should pay for their extras." Do you agree or disagree with the statement? Explain.
3. How has the Deficit Reduction Act of 1984 affected benefits offered to executives? The company bottom line?
4. What are the advantages of providing relocation expenses to top managers? Are there disadvantages for not providing them? Explain.
5. How do golden parachutes work? Do they motivate executives to "go down" without a fight? Explain.
6. What are the advantages and disadvantages to offering outplacement services to employees who are terminated from the organization?
7. "Outplacement services are another service designed by managers to protect managers." Do you agree with the statement? Explain.
8. "Workers should not be notified in advance pending a major layoff or plant closing. Doing so would create havoc—something not needed during this tumultuous time." Do you agree or disagree with the statement? Explain.
9. How are performance bonuses and benefits related?
10. Compare and contrast individual, group, and organization-wide performance bonus systems. How are they alike? Different?

ADDITIONAL READINGS

DUFFY, ELAINE M., RICHARD M. O'BRIEN, WILLIAM P. BRITTAIN, and STEPHEN CUTHRELL. "Behavioral Outplacement: A Shorter, Sweeter Approach." *Personnel*, March 1988, pp. 28-33.

"Executive Compensation Means Cash, Stock, Perks." *Employee Benefit Plan Review*, February 1988, pp. 58-61.

HAMERSTONE, JAMES E. "How to Make Gainsharing Pay Off." *Training and Development Journal* 41 (April 1987): 80-82.

PERKINS, DONALD S. "What Can CEOs Do for Displaced Workers?" *Harvard Business Review*, November-December 1987, pp. 90-93.

PICCOLINO, EDMUND B. "Outplacement: The View from HR." *Personnel*, (March 1988), pp. 24-27

CHAPTER NINE

COSTING EMPLOYEE BENEFITS

LEARNING OBJECTIVES

After reading this chapter you will be able to:

* *Identify why companies do not get the return on investment they desire from benefits.*
* *Determine the cost-per-hour calculation technique for benefit costs.*
* *Cost holiday pay benefits.*
* *Cost paid vacation benefits.*
* *Cost pension and profit sharing benefits.*
* *Cost life insurance benefits.*
* *Cost health insurance benefits.*
* *Cost sick pay benefits.*
* *Cost legally required benefits.*
* *Determine the final benefits cost to an organization and its percentage of total payroll.*

INTRODUCTION

The decision to offer particular benefits is often a function of the organization's ability to pay for the benefits. The benefits offered to employees do not come cost free. Accordingly, the benefits specialist must understand the impact benefits have on the bottom line of the organization. The benefits offered should be packaged in such a way that there is some return on investment for the organization.

Research in the field suggests, however, that companies may not be getting the return they expect on this form of investment. One reason for this may be that employees often place minimal value on the benefits they receive, taking them for granted, and not considering them as incentives for increased productivity.[1] This phenomenon may be due to a failure of management to communicate in a detailed and clear manner to their employees regarding the value of benefits they receive. The reason little or no communication regarding benefits takes place may reveal that many companies do not perform sufficient cost analyses of the benefits offered and, therefore, do not have accurate figures to convey to their employees.[2] Knowing the cost of a benefit package is essential before benefit communication with employees can be effective — not to mention the long-range impact of benefit costs on company operations.

In order to determine the impact of benefit offerings, their costs to the organization must be calculated. While costing the benefits may vary, the remainder of this chapter will focus on a cost-per-hour calculation technique that can be used to cost economic benefits.[3]

CALCULATION TECHNIQUE: A COST PER HOUR

The examples of costing benefits that follow in this chapter will stem from a costing technique that translates the total cost figure of a benefit into a comparable base. The most frequent term used for comparison purposes on labor costs is dollars per hour. Accordingly, to achieve some common ground to assist in our comparison, the benefit costs will be translated to this base.

This is done by dividing the total cost of the benefit by the number of hours involved. The most frequently used figure for the total number of hours for which an employee is paid (counting vacations, holidays, sick time, and so on.) is 2,080 hours per year.[4] These hours are generally referred to as "hours worked." Research in the use of the 2,080-hour figure suggests its usage because it covers the benefits of paid leave time. If we want to know more precise figures that exclude such hours, the adjustments are simple

---

[1] Richard I. Henderson, *Compensation Management and Rewarding Performance*, 5th ed. (Englewood Cliffs, N.J., Prentice Hall, 1989), p. 410.

[2] Ibid., p. 434.

[3] The following costing material is adapted from Stephen J. Holoviak, *Costing Labor Contracts and Judging Their Financial Impact* (New York: Praeger Publishers, 1984).

[4] The annual hours per year, 2,080, is derived from the following formula: 52 weeks of work X 40 hours of work per week.

subtractions of hours from the 2,080 figure. For those who work for straight salary, including unpaid overtime in the denominator is necessary. The contracted time is 2,080. If one needs to work longer to complete the task, that becomes a personal choice or a corporate culture decision. The more accurate dollars-per-hour figure is achieved by using the constant hours for salaried employees.

To calculate our specific examples throughout this chapter, we will be using the following formula:

$$\text{Cost/hour benefits} \quad = \quad \frac{\text{Total cost of benefit}}{\text{Total number of paid hours}}$$

Keep in mind that this calculation does not include any cost increase for organizational overhead. There is an indication that employees costs are roughly three times their direct salary cost.[5] This tripled figure is intended to capture significant levels of organizational overhead, personal benefits, and other components of "full costing" that would be helpful in calculating the cost-benefits analysis of a training program, or the like. However, the technique is very specific, and for our purposes of calculation it is not useful. The inclusion of the "full cost multiplier" however, "provides a useful rule of thumb for estimating human resource program costs,"[6] but not the individual employee cost.

With the above formula as our starting point, let's take a look at costing benefits in our ficitious company.

VOLUNTARY BENEFITS

In this section, we'll take a look at applying the above formula to the benefits we offer. For our purposes, we need to establish some parameters about our organization. Our total organization has two-hundred employees. The job titles of these employees and their pay levels are shown in Table 9-1. Using this information, we will be calculating benefit costs for the following benefits we offer: holiday pay, vacation, pension, life insurance, health insurance; and sick pay.[7]

---

[5] Lyle M. Spencer, Jr., *Calculating Human Resource Costs and Benefits* (New York: John Wiley & Sons, 1986), p. 45.

[6] Ibid.

[7] It should be noted that some organizations are increasing vacation and sick leaves for executives as a means of increasing their compensation without them having to pay taxes. In some situations, the increase leave may be accumulated, and sold back to the company at retirement.

TABLE 9 −1   Company Statistics

JOB CATEGORY	NUMBER OF EMPLOYEES	PAY RATE/HOUR
Computer specialist	10	$18
Accountant	20	$14
Customer service representative	100	$12
Claims examiners	70	$9

Holiday Pay

It is common for companies to offer employees from nine to thirteen paid holidays per year. Prior to the recession in 1982 there was a trend toward increasing the number of paid holidays. Yet lately the trend has somewhat reversed. The trend in the late 1980s appeared to focus on decreasing the number of employee holidays, while simultaneously offering from one to three floating or personal holidays. These personal days are to be chosen by the employee and mutually agreed to by the employer. Table 9–2 lists the seven most commonly observed holidays, and the other commonly recognized holidays that employees may receive as paid time off from work.

TABLE 9 −2   Holidays Observed

MOST COMMONLY OBSERVED	
New Year's Day	Labor Day
Good Friday	Thanksgiving Day
Memorial Day	Christmas Day
Independence Day	
OTHER HOLIDAYS POSSIBLY OBSERVED	
Presidents' Birthday	Friday after Thanksgiving
Columbus Day	Christmas Eve
Veterans Day	New Year's Eve

Aside from paying employees their wages for the holidays, there are other expenses that may be involved (as there are with sick pay and paid vacations) that are frequently overlooked.[8]   Many of these costs deal with the costs associated with replacement workers. If the entire organization is closed for the holiday, these costs can be minimized.[9] However, with respect to personal

---

[8] Michael Granoff, *How to Cost Your Labor Contract* (Washington, D.C.: Bureau of National Affairs, 1973), p. 24.

[9] With service-sector work, there can be similar problems. For example, food in a busy twenty-four-hour establishment must be cooked and served, and dishes cleaned. Yet some areas may have a more "seasonal" configuration, and float holidays and vacations accordingly. These considerations are taken into account for our particular business.

holidays, a replacement worker may be needed. Costs, then, may be slightly higher. A list of these potential replacement costs are shown in Table 9–3.

TABLE 9 — 3   Possible Replacement Costs

Advertising	Company badges and safety equipment
Reference checks	Orientation and training
Employment agencies	Security and credit investigations
Break-in time	Severance pay
Letter of application	Extra Social Security taxes
Application blanks	Insurance costs
Interview by personnel	Increased unemployment insurance

Computing the Cost of the Paid Holiday. The cost of a holiday for our company, which allows ten days of paid holiday time a year at regular pay levels, is computed using the data in Table 9–4. No allowance was made for replacement costs, for the entire organization is closed on these holidays. In actual work settings where this may not be the case, estimates may need to be made on the applicable costs. Even so, without these added items, the straight-time cost per hour of this benefit approximates 40 cents per hour. In other words, for each additional holiday offered, our company will spend about 4 1/2 cents per employee hour. The reverse, however, holds true for cutting back on holiday offerings.

TABLE 9 — 4   Calculating Holiday Pay Costs

JOB CATEGORY	NUMBER OF WORKERS	RATE OF PAY	NUMBER OF HOLIDAYS	HOURS PER DAY	TOTAL COST
Computer specialist	10	18	10	8	$14,400
Accountant	20	14	10	8	22,400
Customer service representative	100	12	10	8	96,000
Claims examiner	70	9	10	8	50,400
Total holiday benefit cost					183,200

$$200 \text{ workers} \times 2{,}080 \text{ hours} = 416{,}000 \text{ hours}$$
$$\text{Cost/Hour benefit} = \frac{\text{Total cost}}{\text{Number of hours worked}}$$
$$= \frac{\$183{,}200}{416{,}000 \text{ hrs}}$$
$$= 44 \text{ cents/hour}$$

We can expand this discussion and arrive at another way to view the cost of this benefit. The question that arises is, How much will we need to generate in sales to cover the costs of the holiday benefit? If our gross margin is assumed to be 25 percent, then $732,800 in additional sales would be needed to offset this cost.[10] To arrive at this dollar figure, the total cost of the benefit is divided by the gross margin figure. Our calculation is shown in Table 9–5.

TABLE 9 −5   Gross Margin Calculation

$$\begin{aligned} \text{Sales required to} \quad &= \quad \frac{\text{Total cost of benefit}}{\text{Gross Margin}} \\ \text{offset benefit cost} \quad & \\ &= \quad \frac{\$183,200}{.25} \\ &= \quad \$732,800 \end{aligned}$$

Conclusion.   Any additions to the holiday benefit would also increase the required sales figure. Benefits administrators need to understand the long-range sales forecast and economic data to be sure that the benefits offered are in line with sales projections. Break-even analysis may relate to this issue. The added sales figures, however (units produced to reach this dollar amount), based on current operating methods may not be as applicable. Depending on the industry, the use of other figures than gross margin may be more appropriate. For example, in the grocery business, sales turnover figures may present a more accurate result than gross margin.

Costing Paid Vacations

A major benefit in the area of pay for nonproductive time is the granting of annual vacations to employees. Any method of computing the cost for this benefit depends on how the employees are compensated. Those who receive a regular salary will receive this as their vacation benefit.[11] Those who are paid on an incentive basis may receive only what would be their "draw" amount, or have their pay based on some average earnings for some time frame before the vacation.

Eligibility for vacations is normally based on tenure periods of each employee. For example, one may receive one week of vacation after six months of service, two weeks for one to three years of service, and so forth. The time each employee receives is called vacation entitlement. It becomes necessary to keep accurate records of the employee work force in terms of the length of service on the job and pay rates to compute the vacation benefit cost

---

[10] For example purposes, we use the dollar increase in sales needed to generate income to cover the expense of benefits. We are assuming that general and administrative (G & A) expenses remain constant, even though to increase sales a case can be built that G & A expenses will also increase to achieve that desired result.

[11] Henderson, *Compensation Management*, p. 459.

accurately. In addition, it is necessary to know how vacation periods are determined and the length of benefit for each employee.

To determine the cost of this benefit, it is necessary to know whether vacationing employees will be replaced with temporary help. This implies the cost per hour of the replacement — which involves such costs as recruiting, plus any benefits the temporary worker may receive — must be figured into the formula. To determine the long-run cost implications of this benefit, certain questions must be answered. Among these are: Can an employee accumulate vacation time over a period of years and receive the benefit at a later time (another time period or at retirement)? Can the employee receive extra pay by working instead of taking the vacation? Do part-time workers qualify for vacation benefits?

To determine the costs of the vacation benefit, the information in Table 9 − 6 will be used. Note the derivation of total cost for the benefit. In this example, vacation entitlement varied (by length of service) and as such, impacted our overall costs. Because of different vacation entitlement, we cannot take a standard pay rate times number of workers time weeks of vacation for our calculation. To achieve our total cost, we multiply the number of employees in each job category times their vacation entitlement, and add across the row. This provides us with a standard unit for measurement—hours of vacation entitled at a specific pay rate. For example, vacation costs for our computer specialists can be computed as follows: Three have 2 weeks of vacation, or 240 total vacation hours; four have 3 weeks of vacation, or 480 total vacation hours; and three have 4 weeks of vacation time, or 480 total

TABLE 9 − 6   **Calculating Vacation Costs**
                  (Without Replacement Costs)

JOB CATEGORY	# OF WORKERS	PAY RATE	2 WEEKS (80 HRS)	3 WEEKS (120 HRS)	4 WEEKS (160 HRS)	# OF H.T.*	TOTAL COST
Computer specialist	10	$18	3	4	3	1,200	$21,600
Accountant	20	14	6	8	6	2,464	34,496
Customer service representative	100	12	30	40	30	12,000	144,000
Claims examiner	70	9	25	20	25	8,400	75,600
Total vacation benefit cost							**$275,696**

$$\text{Cost/Hour} = \frac{\$275,696}{416,000 \text{ hrs}}$$
$$= 66 \text{ cents/hour}$$

*H.T. = Hours of Entitlement

vacation hours. Thus, 240 + 480 + 480 = 1,200 total vacation hours for the computer specialists. These 1,200 hours now serve as the basis of determining our vacation benefit cost for this job category. The other vacation benefit costs are calculated the same way for our remaining three job categories.

To determine our vacation cost per hour, using our calculation formula, we find that these vacation entitlements are costing us 66 cents per hour. As we indicated before, this cost would require sales of $1,102,784 to offset the cost, again assuming our 25 percent gross margin. These figures, cost per hour and total sales, however, are understated to the extent that the costs reflect only straight-time pay at current levels, with no replacements. Should replacements be needed, or if vacation entitlement is taken in later years when the pay rate is greater, we will incur more costs at that time. For our purposes, we are only looking at current costs and assume that the vacations are taken in the year that they are entitled.

Costing Pension and Profit Sharing

Pension and profit sharing are areas for which the counsel of specialists is more than helpful; it is mandatory. Early pension and profit-sharing plans were not as complicated as they are now. Currently, they must provide decent retirement benefits and simultaneously satisfy requirements of both federal and state agencies.

For pension cost to be a legitimate deductible business expense to the employer, it must qualify according to various Internal Revenue Code sections. In addition, the Employee Retirement Income Security Act of 1974 (ERISA) and many subsequent amendments mandate that many tough provisions be included. If the company is unionized, then the employer must also permit its union to have a voice in the plans's administration.

Generally, the cost of any proposed changes in defined pension plans is given to consulting or staff actuaries. Companies provide the necessary demographic data, and the cost of the plan is based on the traditional techniques used by actuary companies and quoted in terms of total annual cost or a cents-per-hour figure. What the company outlay will be depends on the actuarial cost method used, and the expected rate of earnings on the contribution. The "entry-age normal method," which assumes a standard entry age, is the most widely used technique. Benefits are usually amortized over a three-year period.[12]

Companies must always be careful in adjusting benefits without a thorough examination of all the ramifications. Two examples reinforce this

---

[12] Granoff, *How to Cost Your Labor Contract*, p. 19.

aspect.[13]   First, if a company decides to help retired persons by changing the plan to allow for postretirement adjustment to reflect consumer price index increases, it may be difficult to project accurate costs.   This sort of change makes it hard for consulting actuaries to give the company accurate figures as to what pension costs will be in the future.   Second, any automatic wage adjustment added to help current employees keep pace with changes in economic conditions will make it very difficult to predict wage levels at retirement.   The wage-level prediction at retirement is the key point of information in determining both future benefits and company contribution level to provide such benefits.

In addition to the above, various other questions that should be considered when costing pension benefits are:

1. Will the employee share in pension cost?   Will the employer's contribution be vested immediately and be "portable" to go with the employee when leaving the company?
2. What is the relationship of benefits to tenure?   Are there any provisions for early retirement?
3. When will the employee have full right (vesting) to the contributions made by the employer?[14]

When answers to these questions become clear, the organization can begin to calculate its pension costs.   In our organization, we are going to vest our employees immediately and make contributions on their behalf equal to 10 percent of their base wage rate.   Table 9–7 shows how the calculations are generated.   Our cost per hour for this pension benefit is $1.15.   To have some idea as to what we would need in sales to recover the cost of this benefit, we'll apply the same gross margin formula.   In this case, we will need an additional $1,905,280 in sales revenue.

Actuaries tend not to offer opinions on the efficacy of company policy. Their input is of a technical nature.   They figure the cost of company pension plans and any plan changes.   The company must decide, for example, whether it will provide continuing benefits when senior employees are laid off.   Company policy also tends to dictate the minimum plan benefits, how Social Security benefits received will enter in to one's retirement benefit, and so forth.   In other words, it is up to the company on how retirement benefits will be paid.

---

[13] W. D. Heisel and Gordon S. Skinner, *Costing Union Demands* (Milwaukee: Public Employee Relations Library, 1976), p. 34.

[14] Ibid.

TABLE 9 −7   Calculating Pension Costs

JOB CATEGORY	NUMBER OF WORKERS	WAGE RATE	TOTAL WAGE[a] PAID	TOTAL[b] COST
Computer specialist	10	$18	$374,400	$37,440
Accountant	20	14	582,400	58,240
Customer service representative	100	12	2,496,000	249,600
Claims examiner	70	9	1,310,400	131,040
Total Pension Costs				$474,320

$$\text{Cost/hour} = \frac{\$476,320}{416,000 \text{ hrs}}$$
$$= \$1.15/\text{hour}$$

[a]Total wage paid = Number of employees × the wage rate × 2,080.
[b]Total cost is generated by multiplying the total wage paid by 10 percent.

Costing Life Insurance

Life insurance protection for employees is provided by virtually every company. Many types and varieties of insurance plans are available. Regardless of the type or variety, however, one needs to make precise judgments about the financial impact of this benefit.

For the most part, life insurance plans are offered as part of a group plan. In doing so, this benefit is usually obtained at a lower cost than if employees were to pay for similar protection on their own. The amount of life insurance to carry on an employee varies; as a general rule of thumb, companies give a benefit equal to two times the employee's total wage or yearly salary with a customary $50,000 maximum.

Table 9–8 shows the calculations for costing our life insurance benefit. We assume that employee life insurance premium cost is not constant.[15] It will vary based on the amount of coverage we have. For our current wage levels, offering a death benefit of two times an employee's salary would cost us approximately 4 cents per hour; requiring $66,240 in sales to offset.

Should we be considering increasing pay rates, we must realize the impact this may have on our life insurance cost. A 10 percent wage increase will raise our life insurance benefit cost more than $4,900, or from just under 4 cents an hour to a little over 5 cents an hour. This occurs because our employees will move up a premium cost category as a result of the wage increase (see Table

[15] This assumption may differ in companies that have a maximum level of life insurance coverage for their employees.

9-8). The point raised, and one that is not just isolated to life insurance, is that any change in wage structures will ultimately affect our benefit costs.

TABLE 9 — 8   Calculating Life Insurance Costs

		CURRENT PLAN COST			WITH 10% PAY INCREASE	
ANNUAL SALARY	NUMBER OF WORKERS	PREMIUM PER MONTH	YEARLY COST	NUMBER OF WORKERS	TOTAL COST	
Under $20,000	70	6	$5,400	0	$	0
$20,001-$25,000	100	7	8,400	70		8,400
$25,001-$30,000	20	8	1,920	100		9,600
$30,001-$35,000	0	9	0	20		2,160
$35,001-$40,000	10	10	1,200	0		0
Over $40,000	0	11	0	10		1,320
Total life insurance cost			$16,560		$	21,480

$$\text{Cost/hour} = \frac{\$16,560}{416,000 \text{ hrs}}$$
$$= 4 \text{ cents/hour}$$

$$\text{Cost/hour with 10\% increase} = \frac{\$21,480}{416,000 \text{ hrs}}$$
$$= 5 \text{ cents/hour}$$

Costing Health Insurance

Costing our health insurance premiums serves as a challenging activity. There are so many types of health insurance offerings that it is difficult to find some common ground for calculation purposes. Companies either pay the entire amount or some specified portion of the cost. However, irrespective of the type of plan that we offer, in the example we will only fund them at a particular level. That is, whether an employee chooses a plan that costs $160 per month, or one that costs $215 per month, our policy is that we will only subsidize health insurance at the $195-per-month level. Any costs above that level will be passed on to our employees as copayments.[16]

For our company, then, our calculation is shown in Table 9-9. At our current level, our health insurance coverage is costing us approximately $1.17 per hour, and accordingly, will require $1,944,000 in sales to offset.

---

[16] We assume the company's expense for coverage to be a fixed expense across the board. Variations of coverage (i.e., employees with family coverage) will be subsidized at the fixed level, with the excess charges being taken out of the employee's pay each week.

TABLE 9 – 9   Caluculating Health Insurance Costs

NUMBER OF WORKERS	EMPLOYER CONTRIBUTION PER MONTH	TOTAL COST
200	$195	$486,000
		(200 × $195 × 12)

$$\text{Cost/Hour} = \frac{\$486,000}{416,000 \text{ hrs}}$$
$$= \$1.17/\text{hour}$$

Health-care costs in organizations are major benefit expenses. While we look for ways to keep these costs down, we must realize the importance of this benefit to our employees and continue to look for the lowest cost means of providing the benefit.

Costing Sick Pay

Many companies have a policy that allows employees to take time off for being sick without loss of pay. Most are funded by the company up to a point, after which, commercial insurance plans, for which we pay premiums, will often take over continuing one's salary for an extended illness (see Chapter 6). To calculate our sick pay costs, we need to know the number of hours of sick leave all employees have accrued, and their pay levels. Table 9 – 10 shows the calculations for our company. In our example, five sick days per year per employee costs us 22 cents per hour. We would need an additional $366,400 in sales to offset this benefit.

TABLE 9–10   Calculating Sick Pay Costs

JOB CATEGORY	NUMBER OF WORKERS	RATE OF PAY	NUMBER OF SICK DAYS	NUMBER OF HOURS	COST
Computer specialist	10	$18	5/employee	400	$ 7,200
Accountant	20	14	5/employee	800	11,200
Customer service representative	100	12	5/employee	4,000	48,000
Claims examiner	70	9	5/employee	2,800	25,200
Total sick pay benefit cost					**$91,600**

$$\text{Cost/hour} = \frac{\$91,600}{416,000 \text{ hrs}}$$
$$= 22 \text{ cents/hour}$$

While we can expect that not all employees will use all of their sick leave, we must be aware of accumulated leaves. A sick day today for an $18-an-hour employee is less than one a year later, when our $18-an-hour employee is making $19.80. For example, let's assume we can show accumulated costs through pay increases. If there was a 10 percent across-the-board wage increase, and each employee rolled over one sick day from the previous year, our calculation results are shown in Table 9–11. In the rollover year, a sick day benefit now costs us 29 cents per hour. While we saved some costs in the previous year, because not all accrued days were taken, the year in which the sick benefit is used is bound to reflect a higher cost. Accordingly, accumulated sick days are usually capped at some limit (e.g., to bridge the gap between a short-term and a long-term illness). Care must be taken in the administration of this plan to ensure cost effectiveness. Buying back sick leave in some format is one means of achieving this end.

**TABLE 9–11   Calculating Sick Pay Costs
(Sick Days with Rollover)**

JOB CATEGORY	NUMBER OF WORKERS	RATE OF PAY	NUMBER OF SICK DAYS	NUMBER OF HOURS	COST
Computer specialist	10	$19.80	6	480	$ 9,504
Accountant	20	15.40	6	960	14,784
Customer service representative	100	13.20	6	4,800	63,360
Claims examiner	70	9.90	6	3,360	33,264
Total sick pay benefit cost					**120,912**

$$\text{Cost/hour} = \frac{\$120{,}912}{416{,}000 \text{ hrs}}$$
$$= 29 \text{ cents/hour}$$

*Six sick days per employee assumes five sick days granted and one rollover sick day for each employee.

Benefit costs accumulate quickly even though the individual costs for some appear negligible. Collectively, they increase to about 40 percent of straight-time pay.

Not every possible economic benefit has been discussed. To cite so would be incorrect; to attempt to would be a major feat at best. Jury duty, wash-up time, uniforms, paid lunches, and so on, are examples of other benefits that were not discussed, but would follow the same calculations for costing. The cost for the principal ones, however, was calculated, and their summary costs are shown in Table 9–12.

TABLE 9 — 12   Cost of Voluntary Benefits

BENEFIT	TOTAL COST	COST/HOUR
Holiday pay	183,200	$ .44
Vacations	275,696	.66
Pensions	476,320	1.15
Life insurance	21,480	.05
Health insurance	486,000	1.17
Sick pay	91,600	.22
Total cost of voluntary benefits	**$1,534,296**	**$3.69**

How did our company fare in the examples used? Based on the six benefits discussed above, our company spends $3.69 per worker hour on benefits, requiring a sales revenue of $6,137,184 to offset the costs. We spent $1,534,296 on the benefits package thus far, which accounts for approximately 32 percent of our total wage bill. Unfortunately, we've only addressed a few of the voluntary benefits. Lest we forget, the legally required benefits impact our benefit costs, too.

LEGALLY REQUIRED BENEFITS

Obvious by their absence from the above examples are the legally required benefits. If you recall from Chapter 1, those that fit this category are Social Security, workers' compensation, and unemployment compensation. Because of the precise government requirements set forth in these areas, most companies are aware of their specific costs. However, to be complete in our benefit-costing analysis, these must be added to our benefit costs because of their significant impacts. Legally required benefits now average about 9 percent of total payroll costs. The example below will use figures close to current cost for calculation purposes. The cost implications for some of these benefits may vary because of state statute or because of the frequency of their use. Table 9–13 shows the calculations for costing the legally required benefits for our company. Note that statutory benefits raise our cost per hour an additional $1.45. Because these are legally required of most organizations, these costs must be assumed to be a quasi-fixed expense. The only variance is the actual dollar amount spent. To recoup this expense, we will need to generate a sales revenue of $2,410,180.

TABLE 9 — 13   Cost of Legally Required Benefits

BENEFIT	COST	EXPLANATION
Social Security	$364,385	7.51 percent of the first $48,000 of wages. All workers fall into category.
	7.65 X $4,763,200 =	$364,385
	=	88 cents/hour
State unemployment insurance	$142,896	Contribution of three percent of total payroll.
	$4,763,200 X .03 =	$142,896
	=	33 cents/hour
Workers' compensation	$95,264	Contribution rate of two percent of total payroll.
	$4,763,200 X .02 =	$95,264
	=	23 cents/hour
Total cost of legally required benefits	**$602,545**	= $1.45/hour

THE FINAL COSTS

Throughout this chapter, we have tried to show a means of costing employee benefits. By converting all costs to cents per hour we are able to compare the benefits offered in like terms. Because of this comparison, should we decide to embark on a cost-containment venture we will be able to determine what a small benefit change may produce.

How much have we spent? While we don't profess to say we've included all of the benefits possible, we have calculated the costs of the major ones offered. For these benefits, our organization is spending $5.14 per hour,[17] which translates into 45 percent of our total payroll (see Table 9 — 14). By offering these benefits, we'll need $8,547,364 in sales revenue to offset our benefit costs. Appear expensive? Yes, it is. In fact in our small company, our benefits are above the national average of approximately 39 percent of total payroll. We need to reduce their impact on our bottom line.

---

[17] For comparison purposes, it is interesting to note that in 1987, the national average for per hour benefit cost was $5.13. (See Commerce Clearing House, Human Resource Management: Trends and Ideas, no. 188, February 8, 1989, p 17.)

TABLE 9 −14   Total Benefit Costs

BENEFIT	COST	COST/HOUR
Holiday pay	$183,200	$ .44
Vacations	275,696	.66
Pensions	476,320	1.15
Life insurance	21,480	.05
Health insurance	486,000	1.17
Sick pay	91,600	.22
Social security	364,385	.88
State unemployment Insurance	142,896	.34
Worker's compensation	95,264	.23
Total benefits expense	2,136,841	5.14
Total payroll expense	4,763,200	
Benefits as a percentage of total payroll	= 2,136,841	
	4,763,200	
	= 45 percent	

In our next chapter we'll look at some ways to hold benefit costs down, what we call managing benefit costs.

SUMMARY

After reading this chapter you will know that:

* *Many companies do not get the return on investment they expect from benefits because employees often place minimal value on the benefits they receive. This perception may be explained in part by management's failure to communicate adequately to employees the value benefits bring.*
* *The cost-per-hour calculation is the total cost of a benefit divided by the number of paid hours. The number of paid hours is determined by multiplying the number of employees involved by the standard work-year hour multiplier, 2,080.*
* *To determine the holiday benefit cost, multiply the number of workers involved by their pay rate times the number of holidays offered times eight hours per day. This provides the total cost of the benefit, which is then divided by the number of worked hours to generate a cost-per-hour figure.*
* *To determine the cost of paid vacations, first determine entitlement hours at each pay level. Once these hours are determined, they are multiplied by the pay rate to determine a total cost. The total cost is then divided by the number of worked hours to generate a cost-per-hour figure.*

* To determine pension costs, formulas will vary. For example purposes, the total wage bill is multiplied by a percentage that is determined by company policy.
* To determine the cost of life insurance, one must know the premium costs associated with salary levels. Once determined, multiply the number of workers in each category by the respected cost to generate a total life insurance premium. This is then divided by the number of hours worked to generate the cost-per-hour figure.
* To determine the cost of health insurance premiums, company policy must dictate how much the organization will spend. This flat monthly amount is multiplied by the number of workers to determine the total cost. The total cost is then divided by the number of hours worked to generate the cost-per-hour figure.
* To determine the cost of the sick pay benefit, multiply the number of workers times their pay rate times the number of sick days accrued times eight hours per day. This will generate the total cost of the benefit, which is then divided by the number of hours worked to arrive at the cost-per-hour figure.
* The legally required benefits are determined by using a multiplier times the total wage bill. For Social Security, the multiplier in 1990 is 7.65 percent of the total wage bill, up to the prescribed maximum 3 percent for unemployment insurance, and 2 percent for workers' compensation. These costs are summed and divided by the number of hours worked to generate the cost-per-hour figure.
* The final benefit cost to an organization is determined by adding the costs of each benefit offered. The same holds true for the cents-per-hour figure. When a total cost figure is determined, this is divided by the total payroll cost to determine the percentage of the total wage bill that is added on for benefits.

KEY TERMS

Actuaries	Health insurance cost
Break-even analysis	Holiday pay costs
Consumer price index	Hours worked
Cost containment	Labor costs
Costing benefits	Legally required benefits costs
Cost of benefits	Life insurance cost
Full-cost multiplier	Pension costs
Gross margin	Replacement costs
Sick pay costs	Total benefits costs
Straight-time pay	Vacation pay costs

QUESTIONS FOR REVIEW AND DISCUSSION

1. What three factors have influenced the higher costs of benefits?
2. What may managers do to enhance the awareness of employees to the costs of benefits?
3. Describe the cost-per-hour calculation technique.
4. Describe a standard means of calculating voluntary benefits.
5. Describe the full-cost multiplier and its usefulness in costing benefits.
6. Describe what is included in replacement costs.
7. What are some of the hidden ramifications of changing retirement plans for postretirement increases?
8. Describe the process for calculating the total benefit cost to an organization.
9. "Benefits are valued by most employees." Do you agree or disagree with the statement? Explain.
10. "Offering benefits to employees is too expensive. Accordingly, many should be cut because they go unused by the employees. A company should only offer benefits that most of its employees will find beneficial." Do you agree of disagree with the statement? Explain.

ADDITIONAL READINGS

CAIN, CAROL M. "New Laws Adding to Cost of Benefit Administration." *Business Insurance* 21, no. 7 (February 16, 1987): 21-22.

"Court Case Spotlights AIDS" Benefit Cost," *Employee Benefit News* 1, no. 1, (January-February 1987): 17.

"Employer Outlays for Benefits Rise," *Employee Rights Notes* 8 no. 1, (January 1987): 7-9.

RAPPAPORT, ANNA M. "Flexible Compensation for Effective Benefit Management," *Topics in Health Care Financing* 12, no. 4, (Summer 1986): 74-83

CHAPTER TEN

BENEFIT-COST MANAGEMENT

LEARNING OBJECTIVES

After reading this chapter you will be able to:

* *Understand the concern surrounding the increasing trend in benefit cost to employers.*
* *Discuss who should be responsible for benefit decisions.*
* *Discuss various programs to control health-care cost, such as utilization review and case management.*
* *Determine relevant questions of potential health insurers or plan administrators that will generate cost savings as the plan progresses.*
* *Identify the hidden problems present in early retirement programs.*
* *Identify the problems of fraud and indifference in short-term disability payments.*
* *Discuss new approaches to benefits planning from the argument of rate of return on investment, and discounting.*

INTRODUCTION

When we think of cost management, or cost containment, a whole assortment of ideas come to mind. But these are usually directed by our area of interest and specialization. Production managers often see it as reduction in waste; industrial engineers see it as more efficient plant layout. When it comes to cost management of benefits, there is no similar rational trail to follow. One may want to concentrate on health-care costs while another on pension plans; yet there is no readily apparent consistency.

We do know that benefits are getting more expensive, and in Chapter 9 the lesson was presented on how to compute their cost. A recent Chamber of Commerce survey reported benefits averaged 39.3 percent of payroll with a range of 18 percent to 60 percent. In dollars it is about $10,000 per year per employee ranging from $3,500 to $13,000. These figures compare to 1985 figures of $8,166 per employee, or 37.2 percent of payroll.[1]

The Chamber study researched several industry categories and found there was a significant variance in benefit cost depending on the group. For example, in the textile and apparel industry benefits averaged almost 29 percent; while in the rubber and plastics industry, the figure was closer to 57 percent. The Chamber report also indicated differences between areas of the country. Firms in the northeast central region paid the highest benefits, partly because of larger-than-average pools of retirees and their related health-care cost. Manufacturing firms averaged 42 percent of payroll, or $12,035 per year ($5.71 per hour added to the cost per worker). This compares to $8,917 for nonmanufacturing organizations. The difference was largely attributable to health-care cost.[2]

In the Second and Third World countries, where wages are lower and benefits rare, the phenomenon is lessened. Does that imply that we should offer benefits at a level consistent with Third World countries or go back to our own early days and have sweat shops? Certainly not, although we may whimsically tease about cutting out benefits and the "shot in arm" that it would be to the bottom line. Human dignity directs us to be different. The trick is to manage the costs of benefits and be sure to give the "best benefits for the buck."

WHO MAKES BENEFIT DECISIONS?

This is a somewhat rhetorical question. But it is the foremost part of the benefit-cost management problem. There often is no focus of responsibility in the average organization. Depending on the level or corporate rank of the personnel manager, he or she may have the authority to make these decisions, not just implement programs and administer them. However, there is no buck-stops-here person in an organization when it comes to benefits.

In many organizations, the controller or equivalent financial officer is the person who is often vested with this decision-making power. Yet the controller's position is often the less than optimum location for this power.

---

[1] Anita Bruzzese, "Benefits Cost 39.3% of Payroll," A report of the U.S. Chamber of Commerce, *Employee Benefit News* 3, no. 3 (March 1988): 1.

[2] Ibid., p. 31.

Few persons who occupy this post have training in human resource management, productivity, and efficiency, or the time to devote to this topic. They may be sympathetic or sensitive to these issues, but in today's competitive environment, that is not enough. We certainly will not lay the blame for the high benefit cost at the feet of controllers. However, their training is to understand fiscal terms; the incremental increases that come along are handled differently by the fiscal officer versus the personnel officer or benefits specialists. If the incremental cost can be absorbed or passed through to an end user of the product, without undue hardships on the bottom line in the short term, then the fiscal officer's training does not call for throwing a "warning flag" to everyone who should then watch out for the cost.

VIGILANCE AND MAINTENANCE OF COST INFORMATION

If we are trying to avoid what appears on the surface to be a logical choice of candidates to "watchdog" benefit cost—then who should? The exact title of a position could vary by type of industry, profit/nonprofit status, and size of organization. However, across all of these categories is the basic pressure that someone handles personnel and is concerned and trained in productivity, compensation, and benefit issues. Small organizations may have this responsibility spread across several people. This will not work as well. There needs to be either an official person such as a benefits specialist (if the company can afford it) or have the responsibilities consolidated in another person away from the controller or fiscal officer.

The watchdog tactics are important. In this chapter, as we describe successful programs used to manage cost, the watchdog role begins to crystalize. This person challenges the validity for any benefit-cost increases. He or she meets with the company fiscal officers to assess short- as well as long-term impact increases. Impact in this case refers to:

- Bottom-line impact—total impact on profits and earnings per share now and into the intermediate-term planning cycle.
- Any effects on product price — does it need to be increased?
- Market share impact — can the organization raise price of product without losing market share to competitors?
- Employee perspective — do the employees value the benefit enough to justify the organization keeping it in its current state? Employees must be included in these discussions.

- It is our contention that the benefits specialist should become the reference point for changes brought about by federal laws, employee benefit needs and desires, and new trends in benefits. More than these, the benefits specialist shall become the organization's buck-stops-here person for benefit decisions.

AREAS OF BENEFIT PROGRAM COST MANAGEMENT

Approaches to managing benefit costs have taken many avenues— committees have evolved made up of academics, business lenders, and insurance people; consultants have multiplied; and the federal government has indicated concern. Most of these groups have ended with a focus that is too narrow for our needs. This is not to indicate they are not making inroads; they are typically centering on one area, usually health care. They do this to the exclusion of a host of other issues that contribute to the problem. The topical coverage of this chapter will range from health-care to planning. Our mission differs significantly from the narrowly focused groups. We must touch on many areas because of the broad nature of the problem. Finally, many of these special committees conclude by suggesting that the burden of costs should be shifted to the worker. For example, many suggest maximum coverage ratios in health-care whereby the company pays 80 percent, the worker 20 percent. These types of programs were around twenty years ago. Most were abandoned because the employee's 20 percent share could still cause financial ruin.

Health-Care Cost

We start talking about cost management with the subject of health-care benefits. It is not uncommon, although not necessarily pleasant, to find this costs the organization more than $3,000 per employee. Experts in the field predict that by the turn of the century health-care costs will reach 15 percent of this nation's GNP. Currently it is at 10.9 percent of GNP and rising. To contribute more to the rise, in 1988 all the major health-care providers increased their prices from 15 percent to 20 percent.[3]

This news becomes a grim reality for the corporate decision maker entrusted to hold down the cost. Most organizations report little success in what has been termed a "war" on cost. Yet, if faced with 20 percent price increases from health-care providers, internal programs to control cost are seldom successful. At best, the cost-management programs show minor progress. However, with these pressures, minor progress or just holding even becomes, in reality, a victory.

Health maintenance organizations, once thought to be the savior of health-care cost containment, will face the same fate as their membership ages.

---

[3] "Nation's Health-care Tab Continues to Skyrocket," *Employee Benefit News* 1, no. 5 (July/August 1987): 10.

The chief obstacle to ever winning the battle on health-care management is demographics.

Market Approaches

One of the special focus committees that offered cost-containment ideas in broad categorical areas in health-care was the Center for Economic Development (CED). This nonpartisan committee comprises two-hundred academics and business leaders. Their suggestions in the report entitled "Reforming Health-care: A Market Perception" were keeping in mind that health-care reform needed to meet frequently conflicting goals. These conflicting goals included:

- Controlling cost
- Increasing access to care even for those with no insurance
- Enhancing the quality of care via technological development[4]

As a result of their efforts, the CED did propose a number of programs. Some of the proposals are of a nature that shifts the burden of insurance cost unfairly to the worker. This plan was to encourage workers to choose the more efficient health-care providers. Unfortunately, most people would not know an efficient provider from an inefficient one. This is not solely the fault of the worker; few companies have programs that teach workers this. Yet there are means to bring about this goal. Various programs have shown that they have some value in managing benefit costs. Other programs suggested that do merit review are:

- Making utilization review (UR) a part of the health-care plan
- Encouraging private insurance for long-term and catastrophic-type-care providers.
- Encouraging healthy worker life-styles via wellness programs

At the national public policy level, the CED encouraged major reform. These programs include:

- Introducing to Medicare and Medicaid a system of vouchers allowing beneficiaries to purchase private insurance
- Streamlining the drug approval process

---

[4] "Market-Oriented Reform Seen to Control Health-care Costs," *Employee Benefit News* 1, no. 5 (July/August 1987): 11.

- Reforming current tax incentives that foster the use of inefficient systems[5]

Implied from the above suggestions is that organizations conduct a regular review of programs and that they know what is being purchased up front. Let's take a closer look at these topics to see what they offer in managing health-care costs.

Utilization Review

The objective of a utilization review program is straight forward—to be sure that proposed treatment by both the physician and the hospital are medically necessary. For nonemergency hospital work, the employee or a physician first calls the insurer or independent review consultant. The reviewer evaluates the appropriateness of the care and length of stay. Any changes to the agreed to items require the physician or hospital to call back and justify the reasons.

Are the programs successful? Yes, there are reports of success. The savings for companies varied 5 percent to 15 percent over what had previously been spent on physician and hospital fees.[6] Companies with aggressive copayment plans and large employee deductibles ($300–$500), however, saw less savings.

The advantages of utilization review procedures are best for companies in which the medical plan is "rich" and pays for even elective or cosmetic-type surgery, and has no deductibles; it has a high proportion of female employees; and where health-care costs are out of control.[7]

UR programs vary widely in cost from $1.25 to $2.50 per person per month and for services that are used. Comparison shopping of utilization review groups is mandatory because there are some potentially negative aspects. That is:

- They must be in the same geographic location. In catastrophic cases the first forty-eight hours are critical treatment time. Having to conduct the program "blind" via the phone in an unknown area is a negative factor.
- What is the liability protection of company based on utilization review suggestions? There are lawsuits because of their actions. If possible, get a "hold harmless" agreement relieving the company of responsibility if the third-party administrator is charged with gross negligence.

---

[5] Ibid., p. 11.

[6] Lynn Densford, "Utilization Review: The Win-Win Benefit," *Employee Benefit News* 1, no. 5 (July/August 1987): 19.

[7] Ibid., p. 21.

- The UR organization can be insensitive to the employees. Harassment of employees brings turnover. Turnover of well-trained people costs more than health-care benefits.[8]

The best approach to the benefits manager is to consider UR on the front side, pre-admission review for elective surgery. This area reflects 50 percent of average admissions. Continuous and post reviews may not produce the dramatic type of cost savings desired, and the dollar outlay may be prohibitive.

Certainly UR plans appear as if they are here to stay. Insurers report 80 percent to 90 percent of new plans purchased involve some sort of program review. If good cost savings can be achieved by pre-admission programs on elective items and the program merits the "trouble" (positive benefit-cost analysis), then purchase should be considered.

Cost-Containment Issues in the Purchase of (Health-Care) Insurance for Employees

In the 1980s the world of health insurance was turned upside down. In the 1960s and 1970s employers knew what to ask when buying health insurance and what to expect. Now 90 percent of the cost of health-care claims is beyond both the organizations' and the insurance providers' control.[9]

In the past few years the old reliable financial-based questions have lost most of their merit and can be misleading. Unfortunately, most benefit specialists don't know what to ask any more. But there are some rules of thumb that can help. First, companies must be sure of their own objectives. Determining this, they can proceed to question the provider-care issues. Table 10 − 1 lists questions for benefits administrators to give the direction we need.[10] The slant of these questions is to replace the former financially oriented group.

Not too many years ago fast turnaround time and nice brochures were important issues. Now quality of care equaling the price charged is a key factor along with being sure that "too much" or fraudulent charges are detected. In addition, the question of self-insurance is no longer tied only to size of the organization. With the ability to eliminate virtually any item on special insurance coverage, even small organizations can self-insure, if all the other figures are "right."

---

[8] Ibid.

[9] Laurence Hicks, "Evaluating Your Health-care Insurer," *Personnel Administrator* 31, no. 12, (December 1986): 79.

[10] Ibid., p. 80.

TABLE 10–1   Interorganizational Questions to Purchase
Health-Care Insurance

QUESTION	COMMENTS
Self insuree or conventional?	Rules of thumb on size are not as valid today as 5 years ago. It is a question of risk aversion and laying off risk with special insurance protection.
If self-insured, do we use TPA or an insurance company to handle the plan?	With the advent of mini and micro computers, Third Party Administrators (TPAs) can often be as efficient with less cost than big insurance companies. Note: be careful of TPA quality — check references.
When we put the plan out to bid, what is important to include?	If it's for conventional insurance, or TPA, the first point is ability to control the number of claims. Second, to insure that quality of care equals the prices charged. (Note, not just fast turnaround in claim time).

Source: Material extracted from Laurence Hicks, "Evaluating Your Health Care Insurer,"
Personnel Administrator 31, no. 12 (December 1986). With permission.

It goes without saying that the first group of questions to a potential insurer should be from the old reliable mix of financial type information data. This would mean exploring such questions as:

• What is your experience, ranging from broad administrative categorical down to my industry specific?
• How are you funded? Or give me the straight facts on your financial strength to handle our business.

However, companies must move beyond those if they are going to save money. They are informative, but the 1980s showed us that new variables exist that can affect cost employers never believed would be so important. The data in Table 10 − 2 provide a quick review of the questions that must be answered when sending proposals out for provider bids. Yes, out for bid, not just to call Blue Cross/Blue Shield and buy. It is amazing how many organizations still just call a provider and buy without comparison shopping.

The first question is very important and falls in on the area of utilization review. We mentioned it earlier in the chapter as an add-on item if the organization already had a plan without this type of service. However, many administrators and insurers are picking up on the UR trend and including it as part of the service package. If it is available and the price is competitive with others that do not provide UR, the choice of whom to buy from is simplified. The items of interest in the first question include:

TABLE 10 — 2   What to Ask Potential Insurers

Question

Are there programs to control benefit utilization? These would be, for example, offsets for pre-certification participation, discharge planning, case management, payments for alternatives to in-patient hospitalization.

Do you handle auditing of claim utilization? Are the claims audited? Any minimums for an audit to be conducted? If contracted, what is subcontractor experience? Will I be notified of audited plan savings?

Can the plan administrator or insurer generate savings through: (1) coordination of benefits, (2) charge control, (3) subrogation or right of reimbursement? The savings generated through these efforts can be sizeable.

Will the data I receive help me know if the workers are having good health care at a fair price?

Will the plan administrator provide information on overall worker utilization of the health care plan?

Source: Material extracted from Laurence Hicks, "Evaluating Your Health Care Insurer," *Personnel Administrator* 31, no. 12 (December 1986). With permission.

- Are there precertification programs for hospitalization?
- Are there programs for continuous review and discharge planning?
- Are there case management programs? Is there flexibility in the plan to consider alternatives to traditional hospitalization?
- If conventionally insured, will there be offsets to premium increases for participation in precertification programs?[11]

The second question (Table 10 — 2) covers the area of claim auditing. Will it be handled by the insurer or, in the case of a self-insurer, a plan administrator for the program? Attention should focus on the following areas:

- Is there a minimum audit amount?
- Where will audits take place?
- Will insurer handle audits or are they given to a subcontractor or UR consultant? Is the subcontractor/consultant experienced?
- Do I get a copy of the report on savings realized?[12]

According to Laurence Hicks, many large organizations do not know the answers to the above questions. Yet the savings realized from auditing can be substantial.

---

[11] Ibid., p. 82.

[12] Ibid., p. 83.

The third question (Table 10 − 2) deals in three areas where substantial company savings can occur. These three areas are:

- Coordination of benefits — a savings of 6 percent of claims is a reasonable figure to achieve.
- Control on charges—a savings of 2 percent to 3 percent of claims. These are charges beyond which are "reasonable and customary."
- Subrogation (right of reimbursement) — a savings of 1 percent of claims. This is careful follow-up where someone else is legally at fault and responsible for the bill, which has been settled by the company's insurance. Many insurers and administrators fail to track such claims. We want providers who are zealots about such things.[13]

The final question (Table 10 − 2) deals with reasonable expectations we have of the type of data we are to receive (on a regular basis) from the provider. Hopefully, it will be complete to the point where a determination of the plan's capability to deliver high-quality care at a fair price for the worker is taking place. Listed below are some examples of data to ask for those organizations that are unaware.

- Hospital days/1,000 covered people
- Admissions/1,000 covered people
- Average length of stay
- Rank-order cost by diagnosis
- Admissions/discharges by day of week and length of stay
- Rank-order amount paid to top providers
- Average room/board charged by hospital
- Average per diem by hospital
- Average cost/stay by hospital
- Outpatient visits/1,000 covered people
- Ratio of out-patient to in-patient
- Unplanned admissions after out-patient visit

To better judge the quality of provider care use this data:

- Readmissions within fourteen days of discharge
- Repeat visits to emergency room within seven days of discharge
- Number of deaths against severity index
- Cases of cardiac arrest

---

[13] Ibid., p. 84.

- Number of heart attacks within twenty-four hours after surgery
- Number of hospital transfers
- Hospital acquired infections
- Number of repetitions of routine tests[14]

With the possible substantial savings eluded to, it makes the new and challenging talk of purchasing health-care insurance worth the price of learning a new behavior pattern—asking the correct pertinent questions. The current economic environment is also causing us to be aware of other problems, such as an aging work force and its benefit cost. In addition, can we let workers retire early any longer?

The Cost of Retired Workers

It is not a news scoop that our population is aging. Much has been written about the huge numbers entering the retirement years. Many of these individuals will leave the work force before the traditional age, causing further aggravation to the dual problem of worker shortages and benefit cost.[15] Many companies report that a major contributor to the rising health-care cost is caring for the increasing retirement population. As we live longer and the demographics come into full view, a problem for which we have little control will increase in magnitude. Of course, as labor economists indicate, the problem will go away in roughly three decades by natural attrition, much like the teenage unemployment problem of the mid- to late-1960s and early 1970s. The baby-boomers grew up and the problem disappeared. But in the wake of this large group of retirees is a drought of qualified workers to fill the void. Companies will be faced with new recruiting problems resulting in the emergence of yet more benefit needs.

Not only will organizations need to provide child care to entice younger workers, but also elder care for those who must care for elderly relatives. Having these mechanisms in place early may benefit the organization by, among others, reducing future recruiting costs.[16]

Early Retirement. In the past, early retirement was used as a way to trim the work force and boost earnings in the short term. This practice could prove very expensive in the long term and be more problematic than companies ever

---

[14] Ibid., p. 86.

[15] "Early Retirement: The Hidden Costs," *Employee Benefit News* 1, no. 5 (July/August 1987): 9.

[16] "Employers to Feel Burden of Aging Society," *Employee Benefit News* 2, no. 6 (June 1988): 23.

believed. Some advice offered by experts before making future early retirement offers to employees includes the following:

- Make a long-term study of pensions, health-care benefits, and social benefits (e.g., health clubs).
- Figure more people will accept the offer than anticipated (the national trend is to want to retire early).
- Figure your rehire needs. Will there be crucial shortages in skill areas? Where will you get replacements?
- Be sure offer doesn't "smack" of age discrimination in a way to rid yourself of older workers.[17]

A subtle point is worth mentioning here. If the organization's pension is a deferred benefit, the actuarial costs are predicted on a different set of assumptions. If a lot of employees accept the open invitation to retire early, it could suggest some substantial contributions need to be made to be sure the plan is funded and sound. This is true especially in light of the "tax reform" penalties in effect.

Use Financial Planning for Potential Retirees.   It is not uncommon for corporate benefits administrators to report the uneasiness that workers have about retirement planning and benefits usage. Good planning can alleviate this worry and contribute to a healthier retired work force. This in turn helps control benefit costs. Many organizations report that they find positive results by conducting seminars for retired workers on financial planning, wellness, and benefits utilization. Any type of arrangement that makes the retired worker more informed reduces the necessity to make dramatic changes.

NONTRADITIONAL BENEFIT ANALYSIS

Most of the literature on benefits discusses it in terms that are not consistent for executive decision making. The topic of benefit protection lends itself readily to discussions that are best described as "soft" analysis. To discuss benefits in terms of hard analysis may cause one to come across as uncaring and unfeeling. Therefore, companies go through exhaustive efforts to try to offer the most complete benefits package they can without going into the traditional management decision-making area.

If they decide to purchase machinery, buildings, and the like, their analysis would take on the jargon of rate of return on investment. They focus on whether the rate of return will meet their hurdle rate (a minimum standard

---

[17] "Early Retirement: The Hidden Costs," p. 26.

return for acceptability as an investment). Discussions of discounted cash flows would be included, and the project would be subject to prioritization along with the other alternatives for organization dollars. Yet, benefits retain a "semiholy" state. Despite the fact that pensions alone are in the realm of 6 percent of corporate revenues, companies continue to use soft techniques to make the decision on their acceptability.

No one expects to change the other variables in this process. But the introduction of the traditional analysis technique into the system can strengthen the decisions. In its basic form we are talking about the financial theory of capital budgeting when figuring benefit decisions. This technique offers genuine potential for analysis of comparative options. As computer software programs expand, capital budgeting models are becoming more "user friendly."

With the cost of benefits analysis, the process becomes one of measurement of costs associated with particular benefits extended into the future (i.e., contract life with a provider). These costs are then discounted back over the life of the item using the internal rate of return (hurdle rate) of the company as the percentage factor. An internal rate of return is a percentage figure that the company believes is necessary to achieve on its invested funds, or it may be the cost of borrowed money. Alternative options on various benefit plans can then be ranked using present value tables or a standard formula.

The standard formula is $PV = V/(1\text{-}i)^N$ where PV is the present value, V is the equivalent future value in N periods to come, i is the discount rate or company cost of capital figure, and N is the number of years of expected length of the plans. Fortunately, tables exist that can be used to find present values at various interest rates. An example of such is shown in Table $10-3$. Present value tables tell how much money must be set aside today to have a designated amount later.

TABLE 10–3   Present Value of $1 at Compound Interest

Period Hence	7%	8%	10%	12%	14%	15%
1	0.935	0.926	0.909	0.393	0.877	0.870
2	0.873	0.857	0.826	0.797	0.796	0.756
3	0.816	0.794	0.751	0.712	0.675	0.658
4	0.763	0.735	0.683	0.636	0.592	0.572
5	0.713	0.681	0.621	0.567	0.519	0.497
6	0.666	0.630	0.565	0.507	0.456	0.432
7	0.623	0.584	0.513	0.452	0.400	0.376
8	0.582	0.540	0.513	0.452	0.400	0.376
9	0.544	0.500	0.424	0.361	0.308	0.284
10	0.508	0.463	0.386	0.322	0.270	0.247
15	0.362	0.315	0.239	0.183	0.140	0.123
20	0.258	0.215	0.149	0.104	0.073	0.061

For example, assume the cost of capital is 12 percent and one is looking at a five-year period. What will the current value of a $100 return be in five years? Look at Table 10–3, go down the left column marked periods hence to five, read over to the 12 percent column, and record the figure 0.567. Multiply this figure by $100 and the present value of the return is $56.70. Calculating the present value of future money flows is often referred to as "discounting."

Costs associated with particular benefits may be difficult to pinpoint because they vary with respect to how far into the future they extend. Do they extend for the life of the current benefits provider contract or several successive contracts? Does the analysis use the same long-term planning horizons as the company? Costs in each case could have the same present value during the current contract period, but could vary if extended to several contracts.

The concept of discounting has potential in figuring alternative offers and requests in the cost-management process. For example, management can make several offers of benefit packages to the employees. Various combinations of benefits in discounted form that result in the same net percentage value may be offered to employees. If one of these alternative forms is acceptable, both the employee and company are happy.

The potential use of discounting in flexible benefit package situations is significant. That is, each employee will get the best package of benefits for the dollar, and the company won't have to overspend on each package to ensure everyone is happy. (We will look at flexible benefits in the next chapter).

Consider a basic example of a company with a two-year contract with providers. The internal rate of return or company cost of capital is 15 percent. The amount management can afford is a 75-cent increase for each year of the two-year contract. This is based on an assumed average base rate of a $5 per hour/per employee current value in benefits.

**TABLE 10–4　　Initial Package Cost
　　　　　　　　　(Using present value table in the 15% column)**

First year	($5.00 + $.75 increase) × .870	=	$5,002
Second year	($5.00 + $.75 increase) × .756	=	4,347
Total present value of the benefit increase		=	$9,349

For the purpose of simplicity we are assuming the benefits package for the average employee adds $5 per hour to the compensation. It, of course, has the mandatory items and probably some variety of health-care plan, pension plan, and so on, all adding to a value of $5.00 per hour. The company wishes to limit its spending in the next two years by 75 cents an hour in benefits. This can be absorbed in many fashions (e.g., all health-care or pension). Management is indifferent to where it is absorbed but not indifferent to the limit of the expenditure amount.

The example will cost an initial variety package offered in Table 10–4 and an alternative benefits package arrangement in Table 10–5. For management, either choice is generally acceptable because of the same discounted present value.

The present-value computations for the initial benefits package yield a value to the company of $9,349. The goal of the benefits specialists is to find alternatives for the various workers with different needs they will accept yet with the same present-value cost to the company.

To judge the alternative package, its total present value must equal $9,349, the amount management is able to afford. To find alternatives acceptable to the parties, the following format is used: ($5.00 + I).870 + ($5.00 + 2 I).756 = $9,349. If I stands for the increase the first year and 2 I the second-year increase, the present value figures from the table are used in the formula to solve for I, the increase amount. When solved, I equals .512, and the alternative package may be computed that will have the same present value as the prior offer but may satisfy some different needs via flexible benefits offers. The benefit package value to the worker becomes $.512 or $5.12 ($5.00 + .512) for the first year and $1.024 or $6.024 ($6.00 + 2[.512]) for the second year (see Table 10–5).

TABLE 10–5   Alternate Package Cost

	BENEFITS PACKAGE COST
First Year	$5.512 x .870 = $4.795
Second Year	$6.024 x .756 = <u>$4.554</u>
Total Present Value of Alternative Benefit Package	= $9.349

The alternative package to the workers ($.512 + $.1024 = $1.536) results in an added 3.6 or 4 cents above the first offer ($.75 + .75 = $1.50) but has the same present value cost to management. As pointed out earlier, the company must decide if it wishes to have a total benefit provider cost of $6.54 ($5.00 + 1.536 = $6.536 or 6.54 from the alternative package) per hour versus $6.50 ($5.00 + $1.50 = $6.50 initial package). The 4-cent difference does obviously influence future contract negotiations because this will be the new starting point for figuring future package cost.

There is of course a slight difference for the employees. Those who choose the combination of benefits worked out in Table 10–5 do end up with 3.6 cents above those who choose the initial package in Table 10–4.

When the time value of money is a factor in management decision making, discounting or present-value calculations can provide a framework for making benefit-cost-containment decisions using the same decision-making criteria as that in other areas of the company.

The key point is that companies can make numerous combinations to suit employees with special needs. Younger workers may choose packages with higher maternity benefits and child care; while others with older children may choose dental and vision plans. With discounting, companies can equalize the packages to avoid the problem of some people getting more than others. More importantly, it adds a sense of order to flexible benefits orientation that has been lacking. Traditional orientations have centered on traditional cost techniques and failed to convert these costs to a base for comparison.

SUMMARY

After having read this chapter you will know that:

* *Benefit costs have risen dramatically in recent years and average about 39 percent of payroll cost. This level is expected to increase as the retirement pool of people grows.*
* *The typical organization lacks a focus of responsibility in benefit decisions. There needs to be a person in charge of these decisions, not necessarily the controller.*
* *Health-care cost continues to climb faster than GNP. Several organizations have resorted to referrals to specialty facilities, consultants, case management, and the like to help. For the most part, little has worked to the extent envisioned. UR programs can only work in geographic proximity to the organization and health-care providers.*
* *In prior years, it was a simple process to purchase insurance. But in the past five years this has changed. Companies must now ask new sets of questions that can generate real dollar savings.*
* *Early retirement programs are a short-term shot in the arm for bottom-line improvement but, can be a big long term expense. These expenses range from recruitment cost of rehires to the extra pension cost and health-care cost for the employees.*
* *It is a new concept in regard to benefit discussion, but it has been around for years in terms of other company investments. Rate of return and discounting are two techniques that we have introduced here to show a new ware to consider benefits. Certainly human dignity and other arguments come first, but putting benefits into the traditional language of business may precipitate more cost-saving ideas.*

KEY TERMS

Benefits specialists	Hurdle rate
Case management	Medicaid
Controller	Medicare
Conventionally insured	Precertification
Discharge planning	Rate of return
Discount rate	Self-insured
Gross national product	Short-term disability (STD)
Health maintenance	Third-party administrator (TPA)
organization (HMO)	Utilization review (UR)

QUESTIONS FOR REVIEW AND DISCUSSION

1. Explain why managers feel benefits can no longer be referred to as "fringe."
2. Where should the locus of control for benefit decisions rest? Why?
3. What can the benefits specialists do to help control health-care cost?
4. As the population ages, what is the outlook for HMOs?
5. What is utilization review? How does it work?
6. "Utilization review procedures should be implemented in every organization." Do you agree or disagree with this statement? Explain.
7. Discuss the dual-edge argument concerning early retirement.
8. Why is it costly for employees to retire early?
9. Why does the use of discounting have potential practical applications for purchasing and offering benefits to employees?
10. What is the formula for present value? What is the present value of $1,000 at 10 percent twenty years from now?

ADDITIONAL READINGS

HOLOVIAK, STEPHEN, and SUSAN STONE SIPKOFF. *Managing Human Productivity: People Are Your Best Investment* (New York: Praeger, 1987), pp. 115-35.

JOHNSON, RICHARD E.   "How to Select a UR Program Tailor-Made for Your Company." *Employee Benefit News* 2, no. 6 (June 1988): 25-28.

RUSH, L. BRIAN.   "Controlling Benefit Costs." *Risk Management* 34, no. 4 (April 1987): 30-34.

STEVENSON, DOUGLAS F.   "Employers Carrying Benefit Load." *Business Insurance* 21, no. 16 (April 20, 1987): 24.

WISEMAN, MARK G.   "An Overview of Flexible Compensation" *Topics in Total Compensation* 2, no. 1 (Fall 1987): 9-14

CHAPTER ELEVEN

FLEXIBLE BENEFITS

LEARNING OBJECTIVES

After reading this chapter you will be able to:

* *Describe the purpose of flexible benefits.*
* *Describe the history of flexible benefits with emphasis on ERISA and the 1978 Revenue Act.*
* *Describe what is meant by the term core coverage.*
* *Describe the advantages of flexible benefits to both employees and employers.*
* *Describe the disadvantages of flexible benefits to both employees and employers.*
* *Describe flexible spending accounts.*
* *Describe modular flexible benefits plans.*
* *Describe core-plus options flexible benefits plans.*
* *Describe add-on flexible benefits plans.*
* *Describe flexible credits and their relationship to flexible benefits programs.*

INTRODUCTION

When an employer considers offering benefits to employees, one of the main considerations is to keep costs down. Traditionally employers attempted to do just that by providing a slate of benefits to their employees — whether employees wanted or needed any particular benefit, or used it at all. The thrust behind this action came from retention of employee factors — without a good benefits package good employees could not be attracted and kept.

Companies learned, however, that these benefits offered did very little to motivate the employees, or to produce an incentive for them to be more productive. Employees viewed benefits as a "given," a membership reward that was granted to them simply because they worked for the company. That fact, coupled with the rising costs of benefits and a desire to let employees choose what they want, led employers to search for alternative measures of benefits administration. The leading alternative to address this concern was the implementation of flexible benefits. The term flexible benefits refers to a system whereby employees are presented with a menu of benefits and are asked to select, within monetary limits imposed, the benefits they desire. While used in this context the focus is solely on employee benefits. We must, however, keep in mind that such a system may be implemented as flexible compensation programs.[1] In fact, when we talk about flexible benefits, many different terms are used to express this concept — cafeteria benefits, cafeteria plans, flexible compensation, supermarket compensation, and smorgasbord compensation.[2] For our purposes, we prefer to use the term that is becoming more acceptable in benefits circles, and focuses specifically on the freedom of choice of employee benefits (as opposed to benefits and cash contributions) — flexible benefits.

A BRIEF HISTORY OF FLEXIBLE BENEFITS

If the clock would turn back some three decades in our benefits departments, one would witness very little concern and action regarding flexible benefits. Part of the reasoning for this inactivity lay in the premise that employers were more concerned with providing benefits that covered "each major area of economic risk, including death, disability, retirement, and incurrence of medical expenses."[3] Until these vital areas had adequate coverage, attempts to focus on providing flexibility in selection would have proven ineffectual. Besides, the demographic composition of our work force (husband working, wife/homemaker and children at home) dictated this action.

---

[1] Flexible compensation programs allow workers to choose the total compensation package that best satisfies their current needs. Specifically, where flexible compensation programs exist, employees are informed of their total compensation for the next period, and they can choose a mix of direct salary, life insurance, deferred compensation, and other benefits to suit their particular needs.

[2] Jerry S. Rosenbloom and G. Victor Hallman, *Employee Benefit Planning*, 2d ed. (Englewood Cliffs, N.J.: Prentice Hall, 1986), p. 473.

[3] Thomas H. Paine, "Flexible/Cafeteria Plans," *Employee Benefits Handbook*, ed. Fred K. Foulkes (Boston: Warren, Gorham, & Lamont, 1982), p. 25-3.

These demographics, as we noted in Chapter 1, were changing. With these changes in work and marital status, the influx of nontraditional workers, came the impetus for rethinking our benefits offerings. Yet it was not until the early 1970s that rudimentary flexible benefits programs arrived in such companies as the Educational Testing Service of Princeton, New Jersey, and the TRW Company.[4] In spite of their attempts to "revolutionize" benefits administration, many of these early programs were not well received. In fact, the press they received was more negative than anticipated due to the increases in administrative requirements.

Early flexible benefits programs were also dealt a severe blow by the enactment of ERISA in 1974, which prohibited choices to increase benefits that appeared to be on the pretense of salary reduction because they discriminated against the lower wage earners.[5] The result was that existing flexible benefits programs could continue if they desired in spite of the administrative problems, but no new programs could be implemented. For four years, further expansion of flexible benefits programs were stalemated.

Then in 1978 with the enactment of the Revenue Act, specifically Section 125 (later amended by the Miscellaneous Revenue Act of 1980 permitting deferred income programs and the Tax Reform Acts of 1984 and 1986),[6] the amended Internal Revenue Service Tax Code permitted employees to make selections between receiving cash or benefits without having to pay taxes on those chosen benefits. This was acceptable even in cases where employees were reducing salaries to obtain greater benefit levels. The main stipulation of Section 125 was that this action was permitted as long as the plan was administered in a nondiscriminatory manner.

Shortly after the tax changes came into effect, some movement toward implementation of flexible benefits appeared. One of the earliest and better-known organizations to do so was the then American Can Company (sold and renamed in 1987 to Primerica).[7] At American Can, all employees got core benefits coverage (economic risk areas) and then chose from optional benefits, the amount of which was determined on the "basis from benefit reductions in medical coverage and the pension plan, and from a service factor."[8] What was witnessed in this case was that flexibility in benefits could be successful in

---

[4] Robert M. McCaffery, *Employee Benefit Programs: A Total Compensation Perspective* (Boston: PWS-KENT Publishing, 1988), p. 171.

[5] Paine, "Flexible/Cafeteria Plans," p. 25-3.

[6] Rosenbloom and Hallman, *Employee Benefit Planning*, p. 473., and International Foundation of Employee Benefits Plans, *Employee Benefits Digest* 25, no. 7 (July 1988): p. 2.

[7] Andrew D. Szilagy, Jr., *Management and Performance*, 3d ed. (Illinois: Scott, Foresman, and Co., 1988), p. 240.

[8] Mitchell Meyers, *Flexible Employee Benefit Plans: Companies' Experience*, Report no. 831 (New York: The Conference Board, 1983), p. 8.

meeting employee needs, and simultaneously, some of the rising costs associated with benefits could possibly be contained. Other large companies soon followed. TRW reenergized its plan, now permitting employees to restructure their compensation package each year with diverse sets of choices. For instance, employees could choose among four health-care and eight death benefit options.[9] The growing nature of flexible benefits programs into the 1990s rests on two factors. That is, they are a "means to better meet the needs of a changing work force, as well as [a means] to achieve cost effectiveness."[10] While we will hold off on the debate on its cost-effectiveness for a moment, the fact remains that flexible benefits programs have found their way into the mainstream of benefits administration.

ADVANTAGES OF FLEXIBLE BENEFITS PROGRAMS

The aim of flexible benefits programs is to provide advantages to both the employee and the employer. Let us look specifically at what may accrue to each.

To the Employee

Employees gain some advantages by having the opportunity to choose their benefit selections. As we noted earlier in our changing demographic society, each employee has specific needs that change over time, driven by many factors. These are often based on an individual's age, marital status, sex, and number of dependents.[11] By having the freedom to choose benefits that are tailored to their specific needs, employees are ensured that the money the employer spends will be spent on items that they want. And in a day and age when having specific needs met by the company is important and often demanded, these flexible systems appear to provide a "motivating" vehicle. The liberty to choose how those will be met reflects a concern on the behalf of employers that provides a "positive employee relations" effect in organizations, one that is repeatedly welcomed by the work force. As a result, the employees feel more in control of their benefits, which in some cases leads to increased employee morale.[12]

---

[9] Ibid., p. 24.

[10] *Employee Benefits Digest*, p. 2.

[11] Gary Dessler, *Personnel Management*, 4th ed. (Englewood Cliffs, N.J.: Prentice Hall, 1988), p. 448.

[12] Mary Allen, "Benefits, Buffet Style," *Nation's Business* 75, no. 1 (January 1987): p. 45.

To the Employer

When one hears how flexible benefits are communicated to employees, one often wonders why an employer would take such action. Is it that employers are truly concerned with the human resources in the organization? Is it because company focus places the worker as the foremost asset in the organization? Promising, at best, but probably not the compelling reasons behind flexible benefits programs.

First, and most important, flexible benefits offer a unique opportunity to employers. While giving workers the opportunity to have control over what is spent, benefits-wise, on them, these programs are designed to assist in managing benefits costs. Anytime some action provides such dual benefits, to both the employer and the employee, failing to implement one is probably the issue of focus. There is nothing inherently wrong with looking for ways to contain benefit costs. Not doing so would be fiduciarily irresponsible on the part of the organization. To have a win-win situation is clearly an advantage.

Additionally, flexible benefits programs take some of the responsibility off the shoulders of the benefits administrator. Recognizing that worker needs are different, without such a program, this specialist would be charged with the enormous chore of deciding what is best for all workers. Despite the quality of individual choice, there is some evidence that not all employees would believe that the benefits they receive are the best possible. Even if they were the "best" for all today, there is no guarantee that tomorrow one could make the same claim. By implementing flexible benefits programs, employees can tailor their benefits to fit their specific needs at any given time. This may result, from an attitudinal point of view, as a "maximized perceived value"[13] of an employee benefit. Thus complaints generated from the work force regarding whether particular benefits are offered or not can be minimized.

Flexible benefits plans may also serve another vital role in organizations. In their attempt to attract and keep quality employees, flexible benefits programs assist in achieving this goal. During recruiting efforts, there is evidence that applicants tend to favor organizations that have flexible benefits programs.[14] As shown in Chapter 3, if an organization can increase its likelihood that a qualified applicant will accept the job offer if one is made, then mechanisms that promote that goal attainment are beneficial.

While extolled as a promising feature of any human resources department, flexible benefits programs are not without their critics. There is a belief that realizing the advantages are not cost free. There are disadvantages that must be calculated into the cost/benefits formula of these programs.

---

[13] Paine, "Flexible/Cafeteria Plans," p. 25-6.

[14] Elisabeth K. Ryland and Benson Rosen, "Attracting Job Applicants with Flexible Benefits," *Personnel*, March 1988, p. 72.

DISADVANTAGES OF FLEXIBLE BENEFITS PROGRAMS

To the Employee

When employees consider what their benefits will be under a flexible benefits plan for each coming year, there are some problems that may arise. The more common of these problems for the employees are adverse selection and poor choice selection.[15]

Adverse Selection. Adverse selection refers to a situation in which those in greatest need of a particular benefit choose that benefit more so than the average employee. For example, if employees with medical problems, which place them at greater actuarial risk, select the life insurance offered through the flexible benefits program in greater numbers than those who present less of an actuarial risk, then there is a tendency for that benefit cost to increase. This heavy utilization may result in fewer "well" employees choosing that benefit. Accordingly, this results in a situation in which those with "a greater chance of incurring that risk select the option, while those with a lesser chance will spend their money elsewhere."[16] In such a case, either these risky employees pay more for their benefits (or are able to select only a few critical benefits), or the company has to find a means of keeping the cost of the benefit constant for all employees.

To help address the adverse selection problem, companies may consider implementing a variety of strategies to keep the disadvantage to a minimum. These strategies include such measures as a defined core coverage (minimum coverage offered by the employer, at the employer's expense, for all employees), restricting employee's eligibility (requiring physical examinations, for example, before employees can opt for "maximum" coverage), tailoring price for the risk covered (employee charges for a benefit in accordance to that employee's risk and coverage), and subsidizing payments for lower-risk employees (providing inducements for those at lower risk levels to take the benefit and lower the overall utilization).[17]

Poor Choice Selection. Employees often have a short-range perspective when selecting benefits in any open enrollment period. This tendency is often fostered by selecting benefits that have "some meaning" to the employee now, those things that can be used in the forthcoming period, those that provide the greatest advantage — in many cases, time off from work. This occurrence does

---

[15] Paine, "Flexible/Cafeteria Plans," p. 25-13 — 25-15.

[16] Ibid., p. 25-13.

[17] Ibid., and McCaffery, *Employee Benefits Program,* p. 187.

not make it easy for managers when they have to tell an employee's widow that her husband chose longer vacation periods in lieu of life insurance. To protect against this problem, management may need to tailor its flexible benefits plan to ensure that a minimum level of coverage is provided for all of the "risky" areas — medical, life, and disability.

Additionally, employees who never have had the opportunity to decide on their benefits packages may be somewhat overwhelmed at first. Just what coverage should be taken? How do you know what is best? How do you make your selections? This is probably one of the more critical areas of concern for the benefits administrator. The answers to the employees' questions often lie in communications.

Employees should not be expected just to complete their benefits forms and return then to personnel. Employees need to understand exactly what each benefit is, its intended coverage, and any options within categories. This process is generally best facilitated through meetings or seminars (generally piloted and refinements made) with employees, explaining exactly what is involved. During such seminars, employees are told about the new benefits, their costs, and so on, and are given the opportunity to make sample selections. The key here is to let employees have a "dry run" at selecting their benefits, seeing how they would spend their benefits credits and ensuring that these are really the benefits they want. By permitting sample selection far enough in advance of enrollment, this allows employees ample time to change their minds, should they desire, or to make changes because of some other factors—such as efforts to coordinate benefits with a spouse. Furthermore, brochures need to be made available to the employees for them to take home and study in order to make an informed choice when enrollment time arrives.

By providing a minimum core coverage to address the risky areas, and communicating the flexible benefits program to employees, many of the problems of poor selection can be eliminated. Clearly not all will be, however. In those cases, the guiding light is the realization that any benefit selection is only binding for one enrollment period. If one makes a poor selection today, or if during the benefits period factors change,[18] new selections may be made during the next open enrollment.

To the Employer

When employers consider implementing a flexible benefits program, two major problems appear: the costs of establishing and operating the program and the administrative complexities involved.

---

[18] In most programs, certain changes may be made during the benefit period. For example, if one marries, has a child/dependent, or divorces, changes in status are usually permitted.

Cost Factors.   For many employers the impetus for implementing flexible benefits programs is to help manage or contain benefits costs.   Yet to do so does not come cost free.   In fact, it has been estimated that the initial start-up costs for such a program "can run from $500,000 to $1.5 million, for a complicated computer program to keep track of all the trading of benefit options."[19] Add to that figure the costs of "communicating, enrolling, training the administrators, securing legal approvals, and negotiating insurance arrangements" and quickly another $500,000 may be realized.[20] The bottom line is that these systems are not cheap to install, or to maintain.

Yet companies do decide to make such an expenditure.   While the jury is still out as to whether flexible benefits do help all companies contain benefits costs, the fact remains that in some cases they are able to save the company money.   Master Chemical Corporation, for example, has cited that from a $10,000 outlay, coupled with self-insured medical coverage, it has achieved benefits savings of $47,000 and $65,000 in the first two years of its operation. Additionally, because of their size, some companies have also found that the administrative cost for on-going operation has been minimal.[21]

Whatever the verdict, one factor is apparent.   Flexible benefits programs are becoming more prevalent today.   The start-up costs appear to be decreasing, partly because companies are investing in human resource computer systems for reasons other than just flexible benefits.   And as changes in tax laws and worker expectations occur, those companies that are already equipped to offer such programs may need to make only minor adjustments to meet the challenge.

Administrative Complexities.   Operating flexible benefits programs requires countless hours of preparation and implementation.   The old days of providing a set level of benefits for employees minimized the amount of administrative involvement for the benefits specialist.   Today, however, with more complicated systems and processes, minimizing is not the result.

Without repeating what was said above with respect to costs, someone must ensure that the employees understand this program, be made aware of the program and its process, and have an opportunity to ask questions.   With large programs, there may be countless combinations of benefits packages that are possible, and the benefits administrator must be able to explain any combination.   This information must be entered onto the computer to ensure that each worker's "plate" is filled appropriately and registered accordingly.

---

[19] "Cafeteria Benefits Plans Let Employees Fill Their Plates, Then Pay with Tax Free Dollars," *Wall Street Journal*, May 9, 1983, p. 58.

[20] Paine, "Flexible/Cafeteria Plans," p. 25-15.

[21] Allen, "Benefits, Buffet Style," p. 45.

Yet once again, with the assistance of advanced computer programs, this concern can be held to a manageable minimum. There is no denying that the administrative portion of flexible benefits programs may be the most trying, but with proper tools and assistance, the once-perceived nightmare can be lessened.

Conclusion

Flexible benefits programs have made their way into the mainstream of benefits administration. In spite of their inherent problems, the advantages of such programs clearly appear to outweigh the costs. The wave of the future in benefits is one that is flexible in nature. There is no reason to believe otherwise. Yet, when we talk about flexible benefits, we are not talking about one single type. In fact, there are many variations of flexible benefits programs offered. In the next section we will explore four of the more popular plans—flexible spending accounts, modular plans, core-plus options plans,[22] and add-on plans.[23]

TYPES OF FLEXIBLE BENEFITS PLANS

Flexible Spending Accounts

A flexible spending account is a special type of flexible benefit that permits employees to set aside a specified amount of their gross income to pay for particular services. This enables employees to pay for such items as health-care premiums, certain medical expenses (like dental), dependent-child-care premiums, and specific group legal services with pre-tax dollars.[24] By placing a specified amount into a spending account, the employee is permitted to pay for these services with monies that are not included in W-2 income. This may result in a lower tax rate for an employee, and may increase the amount of take-home pay. Table 11–1 is an example of the calculation of the benefits of a flexible spending account.

Flexible spending accounts are approved and must operate under Section 125 of the Internal Revenue Code. This Section illuminates many stipulations that must be adhered to. First of all, each account established must operate independently. There can be no crossover from one account to another. For example, money set aside for dependent-care expenses may only be used for that purpose. One may not decide later to seek reimbursement from one

---

[22] Richard E. Johnson, "Flexible Benefit Plans," *Employee Benefits Journal*, 11, no. 3 (September 1986): p. 3–6.

[23] Paine, "Flexible/Cafeteria Plans," p. 25-9.

[24] Johnson, "Flexible Benefit Plans," p. 4.

TABLE 11-1   Sample Flexible Spending Account Calculation[a]

ANNUAL SALARY	CURRENT	WITH SPENDING ACCOUNT
	$20,000	$20,000
- taxes	-3,415	N/A
- Pre-tax		
health premium	N/A	- 735
Net pay	$16,585	$19,265
- taxes	N/A	-3,195
After-tax		
health premium	- 735	N/A
Yearly take-home		
pay	$15,850	$16,070
Additional take-home		
pay due to spending		
account	N/A	$ 220

Source: State of Maryland, *The Benefits Menu* (November 1987), p. 3.

[a]Note: Assumes a 30 percent tax (includes federal and state, and Social Security), and $735 yearly contribution for employer provided health premiums.

account to pay for services where no account was established, or to pay for services from another account because all monies in the dedicated account have been withdrawn.   Additionally, money that is deposited into these accounts must be spent during the period, or forfeited. Unused monies do not revert back to the employee in terms of a cash outlay. In forfeited cases, the monies typically revert back to the company.   This point must be communicated carefully to employees in order to avoid misconception of the plan requirements.

How are these accounts administered?   Typically an employee who has established an account provides the employer with a voucher of expenses, and either the employee is reimbursed or a check is sent directly to the provider for services rendered.

Modular Plans

The modular plan of flexible benefits is a system whereby employees choose a complete package of benefits.   As opposed to selecting "cafeteria style," modular plans contain "a fixed combination of benefit plans put together to meet the needs of a particular segment of the employee population."[25] Additionally, by packaging these modules appropriately, these plans also help to eliminate adverse selection.[26]

---

[25] Ibid., p. 4.

[26] Ibid., p. 5.

Table 11–2 is an example of a modular plan. Notice that each plan carries with it certain additional costs. Where there are no additional costs, the cost for the entire module is borne by the employer. For those desiring extended coverage, there is typically some copayment involved.

TABLE 11–2   Sample Modular Plan

	MODULE 1	MODULE 2	MODULE 3	MODULE 4
	HEALTH PLAN A	HEALTH PLAN B	HEALTH PLAN C	HEALTH PLAN A
Dental	No	No	No	Yes
Vision	No	Yes	Yes	Yes
Life*	1 × AE	2 × AE	3 × AE	3 × AE
Dep. care	Yes	No	No	No
Cash back	Yes	No	No	No
Cost to employee	None	$$	$$	$$$

*
Annual earnings.

Source: Reprinted with permission from vol. 11, #3 *Employee Benefits Journal*, published by the International Foundation of Employee Benefit Plans. Statements or opinions expressed in this publication are those of the author and do not necessarily represent the views or position of the International Foundation, its officers, directors, or staff.

Core-Plus Options Plans

A core-plus options flexible benefits plan exhibits more of a menu selection than the two programs mentioned above. Typically under this arrangement employees are provided with coverage of core areas—usually medical coverage, life insurance at one times annual earnings, minimal disability insurance, a pension program, and standard time off from work with pay.[27] With these minimum in place, not only are employees provided basic coverage from which they can build more extensive packages, the core-plus option helps to eliminate adverse selection.

Under this type of plan, employees are afforded the opportunity to select other benefits. These additional benefits may range from more extensive coverage of the core plan to other benefits, such as spending accounts. Employees are generally given credits to purchase additional benefits. These credits are often calculated according to an employee's tenure in the company, salary, and position. As a rule of thumb in first-time installations, the credits given to an employee equal the amount needed to purchase the identical plan in force before flexible benefits arrived. That is, no employee would be worse off. If employees decided to select what was previously offered, they would be able to purchase such benefits with no added out-of-pocket expenses

---

[27] McCaffery, *Employee Benefit Programs*, p. 176.

(copayments) that they had previously paid. (We will come back to an example of core-plus-options plan shortly.)

Add-on Plans

The add-on plan of flexible benefits is where current benefit levels remain in effect. For whatever reason, the employer has determined that benefits levels should be raised for the employees. Yet, rather than redesigning the entire system, the add-on plan provides employees with a menu of benefits to purchase or to extend coverage. For instance, if an employee prefers to have an additional week of vacation, then that employee may purchase that additional benefit with flexible credits provided by the employer. In such cases, benefits may be improved while not eroding the existing benefits structure.

Employees also have two other options under this arrangement. Should they decide not to spend their flexible credits on benefits, they can return them to the employer and be reimbursed accordingly. However, under this case, the reimbursement becomes taxable income to the employee. On the other hand, if employees desire to purchase more benefits than the flexible credits they received, they may do so, but must pay the difference.

Additionally, by maintaining the current benefits package, such disadvantages as adverse selection and poor choice selection may be minimized.

AN EXAMPLE OF CORE-PLUS OPTIONS

To provide some exposure to flexible benefits, we would like to work through a couple of examples. In these examples we will have two employees. Employee A has been with the company for eighteen years. This employee is currently earning $40,000. Employee B has been with the company for two years and is currently earning $22,000 annually. Furthermore, we are going to assume for example purposes the following:

- All flexible credits are earned based on 37 percent of current earnings.[28] The total credits available will be off-set by the cost of core coverage. These core benefit costs are shown in Table 11–3. The remaining credits may be used to purchase benefits only.
- Yearly costs for health care coverage are estimates, based on $225 per month for HMO family coverage. Life insurance is calculated at 60 cents per $1,000 of life insurance. Disability insurance costs are

---

[28] We are assuming, of course, that current salary is a reflection of tenure and position in the organization.

estimates. Retirement costs are calculated at 16 percent of total earnings, while 401(k) estimates are generated from a percentage of a maximum 12 percent contribution. Vacation costs are calculated at 1/52nd of annual earnings. Paid holidays and personal holidays use a cost-per-day calculation based on annual salary.

- Both employees are married and have dependents. The health insurance plan will assume family coverage.
- The sample sheets shown are a reflection of a newly designed benefits package. Items included as core benefits may or may not have been included in the old benefits package.

With these assumptions in mind, let us explore what happens to each individual.

TABLE 11-3   Cost of Core Benefits

BENEFIT	COST (CREDITS) EMPLOYEE A	EMPLOYEE B
Health insurance	2,700	2,700
Life insurance	288	158
Disability insurance	96	53
Dental coverage	0	0
Vision coverage	0	0
Retirement noncontributory plan	6,400	3,520
Vacation	769	423
Paid holidays	1,078	592
Personal holidays	462	254
TOTAL COST OF CORE BENEFITS	11,793	7,700

Employee A

Employee A, with a current earnings of $40,000, is granted 14,800 flexible credits by the organization. However, she does not have full access to all of the credits. The core costs of 11,793 to this employee result in 3,007 flexible credits available to purchase additional benefits. The benefits available to purchase, and their associated costs, are presented in Table 11–4. With this information, employee A has the freedom to choose those additional benefits, or extended coverage, as she desires. This tailoring permits this employee to select and purchase the additional benefits that best meet her expectations.

TABLE 11–4   Sample Core-Plus Option Sheet and Benefit Costs for Employee A

NAME:	Employee A	YEARS OF SERVICE:	18
ANNUAL EARNINGS:	$40,000	CREDITS TO SPEND:	3,007
HEALTH CARE		RETIREMENT	
HMO	Core	Noncontributory plan	Core
PPO	500	401(k) with 1% match	48
Traditional	900	401(k) with 2% match	96
		401(k) with 3% match	144
LIFE INSURANCE		401(k) with 4% match	192
1 × AE	Core	401(k) with 5% match	240
2 × AE	288	401(k) with 6% match	288
3 × AE	576		
4 × AE	864	VACATION	
5 × AE	1152	1 week	Core
		2 weeks	769
DISABILITY INSURANCE		3 weeks	1,539
50% AE	Core	4 weeks	2,308
55% AE	96	5 weeks	3,077
60% AE	116		
65% AE	136	PAID HOLIDAYS	
70% AE	156	7 days	Core
DENTAL		PERSONAL HOLIDAYS	
No Coverage	Core	3 days	Core
PPO	150	4 days	154
Tradational	170	5 days	308
VISION			
No Coverage	Core		
PPO	258		
Traditional	312		

Employee B

Similarly, employee B, with a current earnings of $22,000 is granted 8,140 flexible credits by the organization. He, too, does not have full access to all of the credits. The core costs for employee B are 7,700, resulting in 440 flexible credits available to purchase additional benefits. The benefits available to purchase, and their associated costs are presented in Table 11–5. Employee B may choose those additional benefits, or extended coverage as he desires. As with employee A, this tailoring permits the employee to select and purchase the additional benefits that best meet his expectations.

TABLE 11–5   Sample Core-Plus Option Sheet and Benefit
             Costs for Employee B

NAME:	Employee B	YEARS OF SERVICE:	2
ANNUAL EARNINGS:	$22,000	CREDITS TO SPEND:	440

HEALTH CARE		RETIREMENT	
HMO	Core	Noncontributory plan	Core
PPO	500	401(k) with 1% match	26
Traditional	900	401(k) with 2% match	52
		401(k) with 3% match	78
LIFE INSURANCE		401(k) with 4% match	104
1 × AE	Core	401(k) with 5% match	130
2 × AE	158	401(k) with 6% match	156
3 × AE	316		
4 × AE	474	VACATION	
5 × AE	632	1 week	Core
		2 weeks	423
DISABILITY INSURANCE		3 weeks	846
50% AE	Core	4 weeks	1,269
55% AE	53	5 weeks	1,692
60% AE	106		
65% AE	159	PAID HOLIDAYS	
70% AE	212	7 days	Core
DENTAL		PERSONAL HOLIDAYS	
No Coverage	Core	3 days	Core
PPO	150	4 days	84
Traditional	170	5 days	168
VISION			
No Coverage	Core		
PPO	258		
Traditional	312		

Conclusion

This simple rendition of core-plus option was intended to show how various benefits may be purchased by employees. The interesting point to note is that because of many factors, (years of service, salary, position, and so on) credits available will vary. While certain costs such as health insurance have a tendency to remain fixed within categories (i.e., family coverage, employee only coverage) other benefit costs increase as in proportion to salary. For example, to purchase additional vacation weeks, the employee must buy them at the current cost, calculated on the basis of salary. Accordingly, in the next period when salaries may be higher, employees will find that it is now more expensive to purchase the same entitlement. Credits, however, will also increase to facilitate the purchase.

Lastly, a question of fairness may arise. Just looking at available credits one might assume that the higher-paid employees are able to purchase more benefits. In our example, employee B has very few credits to spend. In fact, he may not be able to afford, with the credits given, traditional health insurance. Yet we must remember that many factors enter into this picture. First of all the length of service. Typically newer employees initially do not get much more than a week of vacation. Aside from that, the core benefits provide ample coverage. Additionally, one factor often overlooked by employees when making selections is the current deduction from their paychecks. For instance, while employee B does not have enough credits to purchase the traditional health-care coverage, considering that this employee is currently having $30 deducted every two weeks from his paycheck for health insurance changes the picture. If our employee must make up the difference of $460 (the difference between core coverage and traditional insurance, less available credits) and divide that into a twentyfour pay deduction,[29] he is now paying just over $19 for the same coverage. That means if he is accustomed to having $30 taken out of his paycheck, there is an additional $10 per pay that can be used to purchase additional benefits. So for about the same money, he could purchase, among other things, additional personal holidays. It is in this context that the fairness issue weakens. Besides, we must remember that systems like these are implemented to help manage costs. Should employees decide to purchase more benefits than credits allow, they do so at their own expense. This sharing of benefit costs is one of the main purposes of flexible benefit systems.

SUMMARY

After reading this chapter you will know that:

* *The purpose of flexible benefits is twofold. First of all it is designed as a means of assisting an organization in managing its benefits package. Second, these programs permit all workers to choose total compensation packages that best satisfy their current needs.*
* *Flexible benefits are recent phenomena in today's organizations. With changes occurring in demographics of the work force, benefits needed to be altered to meet the changes. The first flexible benefits programs began in the early 1970s. However, the passage of ERISA significantly curtailed their widespread use. The Revenue Act of 1978, however, permitted deferred income and ultimately, with other tax reform acts, permitted employees to*

---

[29] In a twenty-six-week pay system (biweekly) there are two months each year when employees receive three pays. This third paycheck generally does not have health insurance deducted from it. Thus, even though under this system one gets paid twenty-six times per year, health insurance premiums are deducted in only twenty-four of them.

make benefit selections between receiving cash or benefits, without having to pay taxes on the benefits received. The thrust of the Revenue Act fostered continued growth of flexible benefits programs.

* *Core coverage refers to a benefits system whereby those benefits that typically provide coverage of risky areas—medical, life, and disability—are afforded to all employees to ensure some minimum level of protection.*

* *Advantages accrue to both the employee and the employer when flexible benefits programs are implemented. From the employee standpoint, these advantages reflect a freedom of choice, tailoring benefits to employees' specific needs. For the employer, such programs assist in managing benefits costs, aiding in attracting and keeping quality employees, and taking much of the responsibility off the benefits administrator's shoulders for providing the "best" possible benefits package for all employees.*

* *The disadvantages that may arise because of a flexible benefits program are adverse selection and poor choice selection for the employee, and cost factors and administrative complexities for the employer.*

* *Flexible spending accounts permit employees to set aside a specific amount of money, on a pre-tax basis, to be used to pay expenses incurred for medical and dental reasons, dependent care, and qualified legal services. Specific IRS guidelines direct such accounts.*

* *A modular flexible benefits plan is one in which employees must choose among various packages that are offered by the employer. In these instances, employees must choose an entire package in its total, not just choose select items.*

* *A core-plus options flexible benefits plan is one in which employees are afforded core benefits coverage, and then may add to this coverage by spending their accrued flexible credits. These credits may be used to purchase additional benefits or to extend coverage, or they can be sold back to the employer for cash.*

* *An add-on flexible benefits plan is one in which current levels of benefits remain in effect, and employees are permitted to purchase other benefits to augment their benefits packages. This type of plan is typically used when an employer wishes to increase benefit levels for employees, yet keep the existing benefits structure intact.*

* *Flexible credits are monies that are afforded to an employee to purchase "extra" benefits. These credits are typically earned on the basis of salary, tenure, and level in the organization. Based on these credits, employees may spend part or all of them on the menu of benefits offered by the employer.*

KEY TERMS

Add-on plans	Flexible benefits
Administrative complexities	Flexible compensation
Adverse selection	Flexible credits
Biweekly pay systems	Flexible spending accounts
Cafeteria benefits	Membership rewards
Cafeteria plans	Modular plans
Core coverage	Pay deductions
Core-plus options plans	Poor choice selection
Cost factors	Supermarket compensation

QUESTIONS FOR REVIEW AND DISCUSSION

1. Why should a company consider implementing a flexible benefits program?

2. How did the 1978 Revenue Act and subsequent tax reform acts affect the spread of flexible benefits programs?

3. List and identify five companies that are currently operating a flexible benefits program. How does each work?

4. "Employees are being fooled by what appears to be a promising tool—flexible benefits. These plans are just masquerades for reducing employee benefits in an organization." Do you agree or disagree with the statement? Explain.

5. Why is it important for employees to have a choice in the benefits offered to them? Why would it not be such a good idea? Explain.

6. How do flexible benefits plans affect recruiting and selection?

7. What is meant by the terms adverse selection and poor choice selection? How can these be avoided?

8. "Employees really do not have the information nor the ability to effectively choose their benefits package. To do so requires a professional benefits administrator. To be expected to make a selection in a matter of days is just not feasible for any employee." Do you agree or disagree with the statement? Explain.

9. Present an argument for not establishing and implementing a flexible benefits program. Now present ways that counter your argument.

10. List and describe four types of flexible benefits programs. How does each work?

ADDITIONAL READINGS

"Changing Work Force, Acquisitions, Mergers Fuel Growth of Sec. 125 Cafeteria Plans." *Employee Benefit Plan Review*, (April 1988): 14–18

"Flexible Benefits Provide Strategies for Change," *Employee Benefit Plan Review* 41, no. 9 (March 1987): pp. 10-11.

"Flexible Compensation: Plans Fared Well Under Tax Reform Act; Continued Growth Likely, Conference Told." *Benefits Today* 4, no. 3 (January 30, 1987): p. 47.

JOHNSON, RICHARD E. *Flexible Benefits: A How To Guide*, 2d ed. Wisconsin: International Foundation of Employee Benefits Plans, 1988.

RAPPAPORT, ANNA M. "Flexible Compensation for Effective Benefit Management." *Topics in Health Care Management* 12, no. 4 (Summer 1986): 74 83

CHAPTER TWELVE

THE FUTURE: TRENDS IN BENEFITS

LEARNING OBJECTIVES

After reading this chapter you will be able to:

* * Understand the interconnectedness of benefits and other managerial variables that affect productivity.*
* * Describe nontraditional benefits that complement the wage/benefits package.*
* * Discuss possible legal changes on the horizon that may affect benefits planning.*

INTRODUCTION

The average American worker is now sophisticated enough to understand the various predictive models for the economy, the weather, or even the life of auto parts. Many of us do not need to be convinced that trends in benefits also fall into those categories. In this chapter, we would like to take a stab at making some predictions.

Overall, the deep concern for benefits administrators is the "runaway" aspects of health-care costs, and the nuances created by recent changes. Health-care costs are the front-runner because there are so many variables out of the control of the benefits specialist. Most disclose if they could see health care and other benefits as being directly linked to productivity, they could more easily justify the costs. The legal issues, such as Section 89 of the IRS code, deals with benefit discrimination, bringing about significant levels of paperwork, court decisions to clarify problems, and major concerns.

It appears from all the data that are surfacing that a group of variables must work together for benefits to have a significant impact. The impact is not of legal "do's and don'ts," but of a flexible proactive system to make the organization grow and thrive under any economic climate. This includes not only the interrelatedness of benefits with job analysis, and performance evaluations, but also with retirement planning, health care, employee assistance programs, and other benefits offered to employees.

BENEFITS: A KEY ELEMENT IN WORKER ATTITUDES

"My financial worries about retirement sometimes affect my job." Statements like this are muttered by 43 percent of workers under 45 years of age. In fact, almost one third of this group feel they may have to change jobs to meet their financial goals.[1] Workers regularly read that Social Security is experiencing problems. It is estimated that it will take two workers' contributions to the fund to support one retired worker. They see laws being changed to discourage individual savings through individual retirement accounts. They see companies trying to shift the burden of the cost of benefits to them. They see a lot of negative factors concerning benefits happening to them, and this is bound to influence how they react on the job.

The average pension plan is a hybrid of the constraints imposed by legislative bodies and those of the organizations themselves. If companies do not step in and push for legislation more suitable for retirement vehicles, the trends indicate that these legislative bodies will continue to dictate retirement policy. This will be reflected by more restrictive policies and burdensome reporting. If management wants the workers' "minds" on the job, they have to be open in their efforts. If the workers feel employers are the ones to mistrust and their actions are unreliable, then how can they mentally buy in to the philosophy of high-quality work? Patchwork solutions and fads must be replaced by systematic and comprehensive plans that do what they are originally intended to accomplish.

IS MANAGED HEALTH CARE THE ANSWER?

It is estimated that in 1990, the United States will spend $640 billion for health care alone. This breaks down to approximately $2,200 for every citizen.[2] The

---

[1] "Retirees Seeking Advice on Financial Planning," *Employee Benefit News* 2, no. 1 (January 1988): p. 12.

[2] "Mandated Care Growth Allows Employers to Pick Hybrid Options," *Employee Benefit News* 1, no. 7 (October 1987): 21.

bulk of this will undoubtedly be assumed by corporations. Proponents of managed health care believe costs can be reduced by preferred provider and health maintenance organizations. Experts cite that health-care facilities will take 30 percent to 55 percent of net income. With its present rate of growth, by 2010, Medicare expenditures will be larger than Social Security.[3] HMOs in their present form do cut cost by removing some free-market fee-for-service aspects of physician cost. However, health-care economists believe HMOs will not forestall inflation. Their cost, although starting from a lower base, are increasing as rapidly as conventional plans.[4] As the shake out in the HMO system progresses, the aftermath may not lower costs either. The outpatient system used by these organizations just shifts the locus of cost. Because of their pressure, conventional services, too, have shifted plans. For example, hospital costs have risen only 3 percent, while physician costs have increased 18 percent over the same period. To further argue the case, we see the outpatient side of Medicare has skyrocketed from $10 million to $27 million in just a few short years.[5] What all of this leads us to believe is that another frame of reference is needed.

An interesting view offered by several groups of economists is to accept the large percentage of gross national product that health care constitutes. Why? Because as an industry, its multiplier effect is so large that it supports approximately eight million jobs.[6] Although many jobs may be lost in one area, according to this supply-side economics belief those jobs will reappear elsewhere. That is, in actual numbers, there is neither a positive, nor a negative gain in the number of jobs. Whether or not this is the answer, the fact remains we must develop mechanisms to assist us in funding and managing health-care costs.

WHAT IS EXPECTED FROM CONGRESS?

Section 89 and the Beat Goes On

As eluded to in several parts of this book, the legislative bodies' initiative in benefits regulations has been numerous, and is unlikely to abate. Our only argument against legislation has been that it has the tendency to increase benefit costs. Yet, in a country where corporate executives earn six-figure incomes, the "costs too much" argument may fall on deaf ears. It nearly

---

[3] "Health Care Costs a Bundle," *Insight* 4, no. 32 (August 1988): 8.

[4] Ibid., p. 12.

[5] Ibid., p. 13.

[6] Ibid.

becomes an entitlement for workers to receive decent health-care and retirement benefits.

To illustrate, despite the furor, Section 89[7] took effect in January 1989.[8] Benefits managers have resigned themselves to have plans ready for the complex series of quantitative tests needed to prove their plans are not discriminatory. That is, they must show that the benefits offered do not favor the more highly compensated employees of the organization. Caution is being urged with Section 89. The real problem area of this law may well be in the qualification requirements. It states that "a plan must be written, legally enforceable, intended to be maintained indefinitely, and be for the benefit of workers; these requirements apply to *all* employee benefits, not just those subject to nondiscrimination rules."[9]

Not passing the qualifications test means, by government standards, that all benefits and services provided will be included in the employee's taxable income statement.

Should the Government Assume the Burden?

Whenever problems in society become overwhelming, we have grown accustomed to look for solutions from the government. Many argue that with the rapidly growing federal debt, it is unlikely that any help could be forthcoming regarding employee benefits. Added to that argument is the Tax Reform Act of 1986, and the unlikely nature of Congress to pass legislation favoring benefits like IRAs any time soon.

In 1987 a Task Force on Long Term Care was created by Congress. Its goal was to find private insurance alternatives for the health-care problem. On the catastrophic concern, there is a strong possibility that individuals will be able to purchase such insurance while the person is still healthy. However, the focus of this task force appeared to be heading in the direction of tax incentives. There are others investigating catastrophic care, equal access, and pension revision legislation.

The connection between long-term care and the changing demographics of the work force gives it a better chance to survive. More women are entering the work force now than at any time in our history. Many of these women fall into the category of having to care for children, elderly parents, and in-laws. It is safe to state that the current presidential administration will have to enact some type of child-care and elder-care legislation. We envision this being expanded to such areas as day-care centers for "sick" children, as well as day -

---

[7] Section 89 contains two parts—an eligibility test and a qualification test.

[8] Because of changes being imposed, companies were granted a grace period until fourth quarter 1989 to complete the plethora of paperwork.

[9] "Employers Resign to Section 89," *Employee Benefit News* 2, no. 7 (July 1988): 33.

care centers for adults. Child and elder care will probably be primarily financed in the private sector under pressure from the government. If businesses do not act first to prove they can operate these centers, then legislation will more than likely be passed mandating how it is to be done. This could only bring about more reporting paperwork and compliance audits.

More Changes to the 401(k)

A proposition now being considered by the Labor Department is a series of changes to 401(k)s. This proposition is directed at Section 404(c)—the Section providing the guidelines for 401(k) investment possibilities. The regulations include:

- A wide variety of investment objectives such as capital preservation, generation of income, capital appreciation, and liquidity.
- A provision to have the persons materially affect the potential return on their assets, and if desired, to minimize risks.
- One choice in the available options referred to as "safe." Safe can range from interest-bearing bank accounts, cash fund accounts, or government-backed securities.[10]

As expected, business has strongly opposed this legislation. However, this is a product the public desires, one that should have been among the options from the beginning. It is another case where organizations did not become flexible and responsive enough initially. As a result, legislation will replace their inactions.

Conclusion

Employers need to expand the boundaries of thought regarding benefits and anticipate benefits packages that workers value. Wherever possible and feasible, these must be incorporated into the benefits offered. Before any particular benefit is downgraded on the basis of cost, employers must recognize that some of the employee wants may be more nontraditional in nature. These wants, coupled with the more traditional benefits, may produce a proactive formula in dealing with benefits.

NONTRADITIONAL BENEFIT OPTIONS: LEARNING FROM THE SMALL BUSINESS

The work in the small-business environment offers individuals the challenge of doing a variety of tasks, and seeing with minimal dispatch what impact they

---

[10] Rich F. Stolz, "Options Provide Refreshing Look at 401ks," *Employee Benefit News* 2, no. 4 (April 1988): 19.

have on the success of the organization. Because of the typically small number of employees in the organization, receiving recognition either has not or need not be a problem. Responsibility and authority are present because the individuals are allowed the working latitude in directing the activities of a particular product, marketing effort, or the like. Almost as a by-product of these is a voice in decision making that directly affects their work. Additionally, the flexibility in handling personal matters, leave, and leisure-time activities are key elements provided in the small business.[11] To many workers these become valuable employee benefits.

The key components in smaller businesses are not the dollar units of benefits, but the feeling of having some control over one's own destiny. This is the same feeling people have when they are the "owners" of the business. The importance of these nontraditional factors is so strong that it is starting to move into such major corporations as Xerox in an effort to emulate the small-business organization. If we examine the high-tech organizations that are emerging in computer, research, and similar fields, the key components become the nontraditional factors such as liberal dress codes, feeling part of the team effort, goal sharing, the liberal use of titles, community esteem, and so on. These components are then combined with such low-cost perks as personal counseling, tax preparation, subsidized child care, and wellness programs.[12]

For example, many people would like to feel they are important members of their community. The small-business environment offers a degree of scheduling flexibility in this sense. That is, there is an excellent opportunity for one of the employees to act as a representative to service clubs in the town, and another on the board of directors of the local YMCA. In traditionally large organizations these activities are often restricted to one of the senior managers, restricted often for no apparent reason. With the liberalization of titles, more employees will be able to have both the community and personal esteem they desire. One cannot underestimate the importance of these nontraditional factors to the individual. The difficulty, unfortunately, is in translating the feeling of self-worth and identity in a community environment, to exact dollars for comparison. As long as traditional accounting approaches are employed, justifying such programs will be difficult at best.

---

[11] Adapted from Robert D. Swanson, "Compensation Options for Small Business Management," *Journal of Small Business Management* 22, no. 4 (October 1984): 31—38; Jerome M. Rosow, "Teamwork: Pros, Cons, and Prospects for the Future," in *Teamwork: Joint Labor Management Programs in America*, ed. Jerome Rosow (New York: Pergamon Press, 1986), p. 5; and Richard I. Henderson, *Compensation Management: Rewarding Performance*, 3d ed. (Virginia: Reston Publishing Co., 1982), pp. 334—37.

[12] Adapted from Joe B. Wyatt, "Science, Technology, and Employment," in *The American Work Force: Labor and Employment in the 1980s*, ed. Robert Ulrich and Rand Araskog (Auburn House, 1984): pp. 59—81; Rosow, "Teamwork," p. 5; and Stephen J. Holoviak and David A. De Cenzo, "Effective Employee Relations: An Aid on Small Business Struggle for Survival," *American Journal of Small Business* 6, no. 3 (Winter 1982): 49—52.

A FINAL NOTE

No one can predict the future. To assume we can is ludicrous. But as we review where we have been, we generate some support for where we are going. Looking back over the history of benefits, we saw that major changes in benefit offerings came about because of changes in worker needs and government legislation. These factors will continue to affect how benefits are offered. Recognizing this is a first step in the right direction.

The charge, however, becomes one of anticipating these changes, and seeking ways to deliver better products (benefits) to employees. But "better" cannot mean just more of them. Rather, we must look for ways to provide these benefits in such a manner that is cost-effective to the organization and beneficial to the employee. We cannot sweeten the pot while simultaneously bankrupting the organization.

Benefits serve a valuable purpose for workers, but unless employers take a more creative approach to manage their costs, continued growth could be in jeopardy. That result would benefit no one. A benefits specialist is responsible for effectively and efficiently managing benefits programs. This role does not manifest itself overnight. It evolves out of a lengthy process. Benefits administration has changed over the past few decades, and tomorrow's environment promises to be even more dynamic. How so? Again, predictions are just that — educated guesses. Yet we concur with the author of Table 12–1 that these benefits are the benefits of the future. This presents us with a future that is filled with exciting challenges and opportunities for managing an organization's benefits package.

TABLE 12–1   Benefits of 1995
(In Order of Growth)

BENEFIT	PERCENT
Flexible benefits	88
Medical spending accounts	87
Long-term care coverage	82
Elder-care benefits	77
Flextime	72
Employer-sponsored day care	66
Group universal life insurance	58
Mail order prescription drugs	54

Source: "Employee Benefits in 1995," Address delivered before the Council on Employee Benefits, October 9, 1987, by Thomas H. Paine, Partner with Hewitt Associates.

SUMMARY

After reading this chapter you will know that:

* *To achieve quality products with high output requires numerous variables acting in concert. The difficulty we have faced with benefits to date is they stand alone, often unknown by the workers. Their connection to productivity is rarely emphasized. Seldom do we read strategic plans that tie benefits for the achievement of corporate objectives. All the variables must have their focus beyond their own topic—in order to affect output and quality.*
* *Nontraditional benefits include a number of ideas that can compliment and personalize a benefits package. If we have three-hundred workers, there will be many sets of criteria that make up a good benefits package. Why then do we want just "one" for all. Nontraditional items can help bridge the gap to address this problem, and simultaneously, make benefits more proactive.*
* *The traditional benefits are at a crossroad. If we like our freedom of choice as a nation to select health-care providers, then we must accept the fact that it will cost more. If not, then national programs may be the solution. Which is the best? Neither option is optimum at the current level of known data. However, there is strong hope that cost management will work. And we know in thirty years the demographic shift will be upon us, and the baby-boomers will no longer be the problem. That is, by natural attrition at their advanced age, a more uniform age distribution across all groups will exist.*
* *Legal changes will never cease. We can always predict that with some sense of accuracy and confidence. There is speculation that the Tax Reform Act of 1986, which reduced the number of tax brackets, will be unworkable in the future. Currently the lack of lower retirement tax brackets have radically changed retirement planning. Achieving total equality for women and minorities and between managerial levels, is expected to continue—resulting in tighter pension controls.*

KEY TERMS

401(k)	Individual retirement account (IRA)
404(c)	Preferred provider
Health maintenance	organization
organization (HMO)	Section 89

QUESTIONS FOR REVIEW AND DISCUSSION

1. How is worker participation tied to higher output? How does it work with employee benefits?
2. How would you formulate a benefits package using nontraditional items to offer flexibility?
3. Provide arguments (a) for and (b) against a national health-care system.
4. What is the expected reaction of society to continued health-care use?
5. "Child-care and elder-care programs will be the benefits of the 1990s." Do you agree or disagree with the statement? Explain.
6. What benefits do you believe will be offered to employees in the year 2010?

ADDITIONAL READINGS

"The Future Look of Employee Benefits." *Wall Street Journal*, September 7, 1988, p. 29.

JOHNSON, TOM.   "Future of Employee Benefits Sets Conference Agenda." *Risk Management* 34, no. 1 (January 1987): pp. 54–5.

NELSON-HORCHLER, JOANI.   "Day Care: Benefit of the Future." *Industry Week* 233, no. 2 (April 20, 1987), p. 18–19.

SEIGEL, LAWRENCE, and IRVING M. LANE. *Personnel and Organizational Psychology*, 2d ed. (Homewood, IL.: Richard D. Irwin, 1987), pp. 498–512.

STAUTBERG, SUSAN S.   "Status Report: The Corporation and Trends in Family Issues." *Human Resource Management* 26, no. 2 (Summer 1987), p. 277-90.

GLOSSARY

Accept errors   Hiring job applicants who later prove to be poor performers.

Accidental death and dismemberment (AD & D)   A type of insurance that provides benefits for accidental death or loss of body parts.

Actuaries   Individuals who determine various payments based on the risk involved.

Add-on plans   A flexible benefits system whereby current benefit levels remain in effect and employees may purchase the benefits they desire, or extended coverage.

Administrative complexities   Problems associated with operating a flexible benefits program.

Administrative services only (ASO)   Claims processing function offered to employers who self-insure.

Adverse selection   A situation in flexible benefits administration where those in greatest need of a particular benefit choose that benefit more often than the average employee.

Age Discrimination   Making employment decisions about workers based on age. Workers age 40 and over are protected under Title VII of the Civil Rights Act.

Benefits   Payments in-kind made provided to employees to attract and retain their association in the organization, and that meet some need of each worker.

Benefits specialist   Individual in an organization, typically in the human resource management function, whose responsibility it is to administer the employee benefits program.

Biweekly pay systems   A pay system whereby employees receive their pay every two weeks. Under this system, there are normally twenty six pays in a year.

Birthday rule   Established in 1987, this rule stipulates that the dependent health-care coverage will be the primary responsibility of the parent whose birthday falls first in a calendar year.

Blue Cross   A health insurer that focuses its attention on the hospital end of health-care providers.

Blue Shield   A health insurer that focuses its attention on the physician end of health-care providers.

Bread-and-butter issues   Term used to describe the wages and benefits that union members seek to obtain in contract negotiations.

Break-even analysis   The point where total revenue equals total costs.

Cafeteria benefits   *See* Flexible benefits.

Cafeteria plans   *See* Flexible benefits.

Capital accumulation plans   Contributory retirement plans that permit employees to set aside monies, many on a tax-deferred basis.

Capital spending   Purchasing of major equipment in an effort to increase productivity.

Career counseling   An effort designed to assist employees in managing their careers.

Catastrophic insurance   Health insurance that provides coverage for major illness or injuries.

Civil Rights Act of 1964   This act, as well as its amendments and other similar legislation, prohibits discrimination on the basis of race, color, sex, national origin, age, religion, handicap status, and Vietnam War veterans status.

Classification method   Method of determining wage levels based on similar grouping of jobs.

Club memberships   An executive perk.

Commercial insurers   Companies like Connecticut General, Monumental Life, and so on, that offer health insurance coverage to employers.

Communication barriers   Used in this context, refers to any action that hinders information regarding benefits from reaching the employees.

Company automobiles   An executive perk.

Compensation administration   The determination of how much a job in the organization should be paid—focus is on the value or worth of each job.

Compensation program   The wage and salary programs of an organization, and their administration.

Consolidated benefits   *See* Coordination of benefits.

Consolidated Omnibus Budget Reconciliation Act of 1984 (COBRA)   Provides for the continuation of employee benefits for a period up to three years after an employee leaves the job.

Contributory plans   Retirement plans whereby employees make contributions on their own behalf.

Conventionally insured   Health insurance offered through traditional means, such as a Blue Cross\Blue Shield organization.

Coordination of benefits   Process whereby two insurers ensure that both do not pay for the same services.

Core coverage   Refers to basic benefits in medical coverage, life insurance, disability insurance, and standard time off from work with pay.

Core-plus option plans   A flexible benefits programs whereby employees are provided a core coverage, and then are permitted to "buy" additional benefits from a menu.

Corporate downsizing   The action taken by an organization in an effort to eliminate inefficient operations; or the reduction of the number of jobs in the organization.

Cost containment   A process whereby an organization attempts to effectively manage the costs of its benefits program.

Cost factors of flexible benefits   While flexible benefits may provide a system to assist an organization to contain benefits costs, the start-up costs are often great.

Costing benefits   The process of calculating how much any employee benefit costs the organization; also how much the entire benefits package costs.

Cost management   *See* Cost containment.

Death benefits   A term used in life insurance for a sum of money that will be/is provided to the survivor(s) should the policyholder die.

Deficit Reduction Act of 1984   Lessened company automobile benefits to executives by limiting the amount of depreciation that could be written off for expensive, luxury cars.

Defined benefit   A retirement program that specifies what the company will contribute and the amount of retirement the worker will receive.

Deferred contribution   Placing monies into a retirement account on a tax-deferred basis. Taxes are not paid until the money is withdrawn.

Development   Refers to the process of assisting employees in personal/career growth.

Demographics   The composition of the labor force.

Direct wage bill   The cost to an organization associated with paying employees either their salary or their hourly rate. The direct wage bill does not include the costs of benefits.

Disability insurance programs   Programs that provide for a continuation of income should an individual be no longer able to work because of injury or illness.

Discharge planning   Refers to an action reflecting early release from a hospital stay.

Double indemnity   A life insurance provision that provides for twice the policy amount should the death be accidental.

Downsizing   *See* Corporate downsizing.

Employee assistance program (EAP)   Program offered by employers to assist workers in dealing with personal problems they are encountering.

Employee Retirement Income Security Act of 1974   Established various rules for administering private pension plans.

Employee stock ownership plan (ESOP)   A retirement plan whereby money is borrowed from a financial institution using company stock as collateral for the loan. When the loan is repaid, the security for the loan is placed into an employee stock ownership trust.

ESOT   Employee stock ownership trust. *See* Employee stock ownership plan.

Exempt jobs   Those jobs in the organization that are exempt from the Fair Labor Standards Act—typically professional and managerial level jobs. Most exempt jobs are paid on a salary basis — not on an hourly basis.

401 (k)   A retirement program named after the IRS tax code that established its existence. The 401 (k) permits workers to set aside a certain amount of their income on a tax-deferred basis.

403 (b)   Similar to 401 (k) plans, the 403 (b) permits a 20 percent compensation contribution for educational and various nonprofit organizations.

404 (c)   Section of the IRS code that applies to 401 (k) investment possibilities.

Factor comparison method   A method of determining a wage level based on comparable job factors.

Fair Labor Standards Act of 1938   Established laws outlining minimum wage, overtime pay, and maximum hours requirements for most U.S. workers.

FICA   Social Security tax. (From Federal Insurance Contributions Act.)

Financial accounting standards board   Mentioned in this context reflecting its interest in handling unfunded pension liability problems and how to overcome them.

Fixed income   Income that does not vary over time.

Flexible benefits   A system whereby employees are presented with a menu of benefits and are permitted to pick and choose, within monetary limits, those benefits that best meet their needs.

Flexible compensation A system whereby employees choose a total compensation package, not just benefits, that best meets their needs.

Flexible credits Units used to purchase benefits under a flexible benefits program.

Flexible spending accounts A special flexible benefit that permits employees to set aside a specified amount of their gross income to pay for particular services, such as health-care premiums, medical expenses, dependent child care, and specific group legal services.

Full-cost multiplier A rule-of-thumb measure that a person's salary, times three, provides a basis for determining total employee costs.

Gate keepers Individuals often associated with HMOs, often a physician, who determine if services outside the HMO are warranted.

GNP Gross national product.

Golden parachute A protection plan for executives in the event a merger or hostile takeover occurs.

Gross margin The surplus of net revenue of sales.

Group performance bonuses Bonus monies awarded based on the total output of a group of employees.

Group practice An option of an HMO arrangement whereby doctors from various specialties combine their talents and offer their services in one location.

Group term life insurance A life insurance policy purchased by the company based on group rates.

Group universal life insurance plan (GULP) A life insurance policy that permits employees to invest a part of their insurance monies in competitive market portfolios, and have the monies accrue on a tax-deferred basis.

Health insurance A benefit offered to employees that provides some basic protection against the costs of medical treatment.

Health Maintenance Organization Act of 1973 Requires organizations offering tradition health insurance to also offer HMO coverage to their employees.

Health maintenance organization (HMO) A system designed to offer quality health-care coverage at a fixed cost to its members.

Holiday pay Paid time off for specified holidays.

Hours worked Standard hours worked in a year is 2,080 (52 weeks × 40 hours per week).

Human resource planning The process of ensuring the right number and kinds of employees, at the right time, capable of effectively and efficiently completing those tasks that will help the organization achieve its goals.

Hurdle rate A minimum standard rate of return for acceptability as an investment.

Impairment A form of disability whereby individuals are unable to work.

Incentive stock option (ISO) *See* Employee stock ownership plan.

Individual performance bonuses Bonus monies awarded for individual output over some set minimum level.

Individual practice An option of an HMO arrangement whereby a physician continues to operate his or her practice but contracts with an HMO to provide services for a fixed fee.

Individual retirement account (IRA) A self-funded retirement account that enables individuals that meet eligibility requirements to defer a portion of current income until retirement.

Integration plans Refers to a situation where monies paid to employees for retirement or disability, are consolidated with Social Security.

Job analysis   A process that provides information about jobs currently being done in the organization, and the knowledge, skills, and abilities needed by individuals to be successful performers.

Job description   A written statement of what the jobholder does, how it is done, and why it is done.

Job evaluation   A process of determining the relative worth/value of each job in the organization.

Job mobility   The willingness of one to move from one company to another.

Job specification   The minimum acceptable qualification that a job incumbent must possess to perform the job successfully.

Kaiser Steel plan   An organization-wide performance bonus plan.

Kelso plan   A successful variation of an ESOP at the Sears, Roebuck Company.

Labor force   Those individuals who are either working or actively seeking employment.

Labor shortage   A shortage of the supply of specific skills, knowledge, or abilities needed to fill vacant jobs.

Lean and mean organization   The outcome an organization achieves when it has eliminated inefficient jobs throughout the organization.

Legally required benefits   Employee benefits, such as Social Security, unemployment compensation, and workers' compensation, that almost all employers are mandated to provide to their employees.

Lincoln Electric plan   An organization-wide performance bonus plan.

Long-term disability (LTD) programs   Programs designed to provide replacement income for an employee who is no longer able to return to work, and where short-term coverage has expired.

Management by objective   A performance appraisal method that includes mutual objective setting and evaluation based on the attainment of specific objectives.

Mandatory bargaining issues   Items that must be negotiated in a labor-management negotiation. These include wages, hours, and terms and conditions of employment.

Matching contribution plans   A 401(k) feature whereby employers match the employees' contribution to this tax-deferred retirement plan.

Membership-based benefits   *See* Membership rewards.

Membership rewards   Rewards provided to employees simply from their association with the organization. Typically benefits are considered membership based. These rewards go to all employees regardless of performance.

Mission   A statement that identifies who a business is, and what business they are in.

Modular plans   A system of flexible benefits whereby employees choose among a fixed combination of benefit levels.

Mortgage assistance   A relocation incentive a company may offer to a job applicant that help that applicant with the activities of selling/purchasing a home.

Motivation   The willingness to do something, conditioned by the ability to satisfy some need.

National Association of Insurance Commissioners   Insurance regulators, who in this context cited or enacting the birthday rule.

National Labor Relations Act of 1938 (Wagner Act)   Federal Labor Legislation that legitimized unions right to exist and bargain with employers.

Noncontributory plans   Plans that are totally funded by the employer.

Nonexempt jobs   Those jobs in the organization that are not exempt from the Fair Labor Standards Act—typically lower-level jobs. Most nonexempt jobs are paid on an hourly basis.

Nonparticipating physician   A term used by Blue Shield organization to identify a physician who does not have an agreement with the organization to accept Blue Shield payments as payments in full for services rendered.

Old age, Survivors, and Disability Insurance (OASDI)   Part of Social Security designed to provide benefits for those who have retired, become disabled, or are survivors of those who died.

Open enrollment   That period of time, usually once a year, that permits employees to make benefit selection.

Operational plans   Specific plans detailing how the company's objectives will be achieved.

Organization-wide performance bonus   Bonus monies awarded based on the total output of the entire organization.

Outplacement services   Services an employer provides to dismissed employees to assist them in marketing their services and locating new positions outside the company.

Overtime pay   Pay for work over fourty hours a week, or more than eight hours a day.

Participating physician   A term used by Blue Shield organization to identify a physician who has an agreement with the organization to accept Blue Shield payments as payments in full for services rendered.

Patchwork programs   Refers to a situation where the latest management "fads" are incorporated into a company's operations.

Payroll-based stock ownership plan (PAYSOP)   Permits employers to give away stock with up to .5 percent of the company's payroll each year.

Pension   A retirement program.

Pension benefit guaranty corporation (PBGC)   The organization that lays claim to corporate assets to pay or fund inadequate pension programs.

Performance   The quantity and quality of products/services produced.

Performance agreement   A modification of a management-by-objectives system of performance evaluation.

Performance bonus system   Bonuses provided on the basis of employee performance.

Perks   Short for perquisites. Attractive benefits, over and above what is offered to all employees, typically offered to attract and retain executives.

Permanent partial disability   A permanent disability that does not result in an individual being unable to work in any occupation.

Permanent total disability   A permanent disability that results in an individual not being able to work in any occupation.

Piecerate plans   Payments made for actual work completed.

Plan year   The accounting cycle in a retirement program.

Plant Closing Bill of 1988   Requires employers who anticipate a major layoff to notify the affected workers sixty days in advance.

Point method   A method of determining wages through an analysis of points assigned to jobs based on such factors as skills, knowledge, working conditions, and so on.

Poor choice selection   A problem that occurs in flexible benefits administration when an employee fails to select appropriate benefits.

Pre-admission review   A process of ensuring elective surgery is necessary.

Preexisting condition   A medical condition that exists prior to enrolling for health insurance coverage.

Preferred provider organization (PPO)   A health-care arrangement where an employer or insurance company has agreements with doctors, hospitals, and other related medical service facilities to provide services for a fixed fee.

Pregnancy Disability Act of 1978   Recognized pregnancy as a disability and required that it be treated in the same manner that a company treats its other short-term disabilities.

Productivity   The quantity or volume of a major product or service that an organization provides.

Productivity Factors   Factors that influence productivity are capital, rate of interest, new technology, research and development, changes in the work ethic, government regulations, energy prices, and the influx of women and minorities into the work force.

Productivity programs   Programs/activities implemented in organizations in an effort to increase worker productivity.

Profit sharing   A retirement vehicle whereby employers contribute an optional percentage of each worker's pay to a trust fund.

Psychological assistance   *See* Employee assistance programs.

Purchasing power   The buying power of money.

Qualified plan   A retirement plan that meets IRS regulations.

Quality   A measure of how well a product/service is produced.

Quality improvements   Programs, such as worker training, corporate culture, quality circles, quality control, vendor/user relationships, and more capital expenditure, designed to enhance/improve the quality of the product/service produced.

Ranking method   A method of determining wage levels by comparing jobs against each other.

Rate of return   The return on investment a company earns.

Recognition programs   Programs designed to acknowledge employees for work well done.

Recruiting   The process of discovering potential applicants for actual and anticipated job vacancies.

Reject errors   Rejecting candidates who would later have performed successfully on the job.

Relocation expenses   Costs incurred in changing jobs that require moving to a new location.

Retrenchment   A mode of corporate downsizing an organization when the organization faces an environment of decline.

Scanlon plan   An organization-wide performance bonus plan.

Section 89   Benefit legislation in the IRS Code that requires employers to ensure that their benefit programs are not discriminatory in nature.

Selection   The process of determining which job applicants are hired.

Self-insured   A term for a company that underwrites, funds, and is liable for its own insurance program.

Self-funded insurance   *See* Self-insured.

Sex discrimination   Offering benefits in such a manner that discriminates against females.

Short-term disability   An injury or illness that prevents one working for a short period of time, typically, no more than six months.

Short-term disability (STD) Programs   Programs designed to provide replacement income in the event of injury or short-term illness. These include sick leave, short-term disability insurance, state disability laws, and workers' compensation.

Shortened work week   A work week consisting of four ten-hour days, for example.

Sick leave   Time off from work, with pay, for illness.

Simplified employee retirement account This type of retirement account is similar to 401(k) plans, except that contributions are permitted up to 15 percent of compensation, or $30,000. These plans, however, must be established by the employer.

Socialization A process of adaptation that takes place as individuals attempt to learn the values and norms of the work environment.

Social security Retirement, disability, and survivor benefits, paid by the government to aged, former members of the labor force, the disabled, or their survivors.

Social security disability insurance (SSDI) Provides for subsidized payments to eligible workers who are unable to continue working.

Social security survivor benefits Benefits paid to the survivors of an eligible Social Security worker. This benefit is a percentage of the employee's salary.

Spousal job search Assisting a new employee's spouse in finding gainful employment. Typically reserved for employees who are being relocated.

State disability laws State laws governing replacement income for individuals who did not become sick or were injured because of their job.

Straight-time pay Hours of work times normal hourly wage.

Strategic planning Process of establishing strategic plans.

Strategic plans Guiding directional plans that establish the goals and objectives of an organization.

Supermarket compensation *See* Flexible benefits.

Supplemental life insurance Life insurance coverage, purchased by the employee, to supplement the employer's coverage.

Survivor income benefit insurance A policy that typically provides for an annuity rather than a lump-sum payment to the survivors.

Temporary disability insurance (TDI) Income protection for disabilities resulting in individuals not being able to perform their jobs for up to twenty four months after injury or illness.

Third-party administrators (TPAs) An independent organization designed to assist employers in managing their health insurance.

Title VII That part of the 1964 Civil Rights Act that deals with employment discrimination.

Training A learning experience that seeks a relatively permanent change in individuals that will improve their ability to perform their current jobs.

Traditional health insurance Refers to the traditional membership program, whereby all an employee was required to do was enroll in the program.

Trasop Tax-credit based stock ownership plan.

Unemployment compensation Income provided to employees who are without a job and who lost the job through no fault of their own.

Usual, customary, and reasonable (UCR) Term used by health insurers, such as Blue Cross, to determine the amount a physician is reimbursed for services rendered.

Utilization review (UR) A process of determining if the proposed treatment of an employee's health condition by a physician and the hospital are medically necessary. This is a method of health benefit cost management.

Vacation benefits Time off from work granted to employees.

Vesting The permanent right to employer-contributed pension benefits.

Vesting rights The permanent right an employee has to employer-contributed pension benefits. Based on the Tax Reform Act of 1986, full vesting rights are obtained after five years of service, partial vesting after three years.

Voluntary benefits   Those benefits that an organization offers to its employees, over and above the legally required benefits.

Voluntary employees beneficiary association (VEBA)   Establishes rules for companies that self-insure.

Wage curve   The result of plotting of points of established pay grades against wage base rates to identify the general pattern of wages, and find individuals whose wages are out of line.

Wage structure   A pay scale showing ranges of pay within each grade.

Wage survey   A process of examining what pay levels exist in other organizations or professions for use in determining a company's wage structure.

Wage-hour act   *See* Fair Labor Standards Act of 1938.

Waiting periods   Time before a long-term disability takes effect.

Well care   A term used in reference to HMO coverage where members are encouraged to seek medical attention while they are healthy in an effort to diagnose potential problems early.

Workers' compensation   A legally required benefit designed to make payments to workers or their heirs for death or permanent or total disability that resulted from job-related activities.

SUBJECT
INDEX

NAME
INDEX

A

Abromowitz, Kenneth S., 76
Albertson, David, 64
Allen, Mary, 185, 188
Allen, Steven, 59

B

Beatty, Richard W., 45
Belcher, David W., 46
Bernardin, H. John, 45
Bogart, Stephen, 33
Bond, Robert L., 17
Bright, Henry, 84
Brittain, William P., 136, 144
Brown, Abby, 64, 111, 113
Brown, Thomas, 89
Bruzzese, Anita, 164

C

Cain, Carol M., 162
Cawsey, Thomas F., 42
Clark, Jeffrey, 33
Clark, Robert, 59
Cohen, A., 127
Curran, Peter F., 17
Cuthrell, Stephen, 136, 144

D

DeCenzo, David A., 40, 45, 137, 205
Densford, Lynn, 56, 168
Dessler, Gary, 140, 184
Diniro, John J., 100
Duffy, Elaine M., 136, 144
Durkin, Julie, 127

E

Elwood, David T., 59, 123, 124

F

Feibel, Laurence, 127
Feltman, Kenneth, 111
Ferguson, Karen, 111
Foulkes, Fred K., 24, 27, 30, 89

G

Gannes, Stuart, 66, 72, 84
Gottl, Ronald F.,II, 127
Granoff, Michael, 149